TWO
WORLDS

Books by William B. Ziff

THE RAPE OF PALESTINE
THE COMING BATTLE OF GERMANY
THE GENTLEMEN TALK OF PEACE

TWO WORLDS

A REALISTIC APPROACH TO
THE PROBLEM OF KEEPING
THE PEACE

BY

WILLIAM B. ZIFF

Harper & Brothers Publishers

NEW YORK *and* LONDON

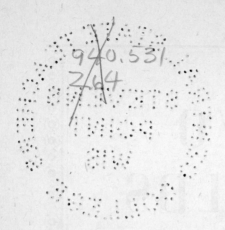

6-6

FIRST EDITION

E-V

CONTENTS

The author wishes to acknowledge indebtedness to the following publishers and authors for permission to reprint material on which they hold copyright:

Emerson Books, Inc.; *Conscience and Society* by Ranyard West

Harper & Brothers; *Private Monopoly* by David Lasser

Ginn and Company; *Political Science and Comparative Constitutional Law.*, Vol. I by John William Burgess.

Acknowledgement is also made to my friend Paul Richard for his advice and suggestions, and to my secretary, Miss Virginia Maves for her unfailing co-operation.

W.B.Z.

TWO WORLDS

"It has been frequently remarked that it has been reserved to the people of this country, by their conduct and example, to decide the important question, whether societies of men are really capable or not of establishing good government from reflection and choice, or whether they are forever destined to depend for their political constitutions on accident and force. If there be any truth in the remark, the crisis at which we are arrived may with propriety be regarded as the era in which that decision is to be made; and a wrong election of the part we shall act may, in this view, deserve to be considered as the general misfortune of mankind."

Alexander Hamilton, in *The Federalist*.

Preface

THE present volume is a sequel to my previous book, *The Gentlemen Talk of Peace*. Its purpose is to restate the basic conceptions of that earlier work in terms of the present international crisis.

The terrible fears which have shaken the world along with the invention of atomic explosives, have led to the assumption that the estimates which applied to the world of 1944, when *The Gentlemen Talk of Peace* was issued, are no longer valid.

As we shall see, however, this judgment is only partially the correct one. In large measure it represents a disabling corruption of logical reasoning.

Though it is self-evident that a climactic situation exists, capable of overturning all human affairs, it is not the result of some new and unexpected agency such as the atomic bomb. Rather, it is the product of a maturing crisis which was quite as evident in the restless years preceding the birth of the bomb as it is today.

From the date the first visitation of atomic horror burst upon the unfortunate living creatures who a moment before had been the inhabitants of the little Japanese city of Hiroshima, all historic conceptions of security were suddenly shattered. Problems of human relationship to which men had been long inured, became terrifying and acute, touched with the monstrous overtones of the unknown.

1

Etched in a fantasy of giant shadows in the glare of this fantastic explosion, stood a host of grim questions which in the pre-atomic twilight mankind had half ignored. These derived from all of the unsolved problems of the industrial era, its social and political failures, the shortcomings of its statesmen, the self-centered egoisms of its peoples, and the economic derangements which marked the age.

To thoughtful men, the picture which lay revealed was grave, and full of evil portent. It was a picture of human ineffectuality, of the incapacity of man to master his environment, of violence, self-seeking, fear, suspicion and almost churlish shortsightedness. Seen all together in a common tableau, it gave an impression of impending unhingement, of a world careening crazily to its own destruction.

Paced by the nuclear physicists, the scientific and scholastic world has laid down the dictum that only world government can save mankind from utter annihilation at the hands of the new incubus it has let loose. We are told that the already fantastic military potentials of this weapon will increase in geometric progression with time; and that delivery of the bombs to their targets cannot be halted by any conceivable means envisionable by man; that all nations will ultimately discover the secret of the bomb's manufacture; that all previously known military advantages have become useless; and that the next war will be a push-button affair in which the contenders will dissolve each other into gases by long distance.

II

Though we undoubtedly are moving away from the present political order and toward a world state, we must face a quite practical situation: (1) we also are moving toward war; (2) the sense of urgency and of panic which has been promoted by the declarations of the scientists tends to place a false value on events and on the nature of the current situation.

The threatening disequilibrium which we must remedy is not the product of the A-bomb, but the result of old causes which must themselves be remedied if any permanent cure of the problem is to be brought about. It is the reasons for war which must be corrected, rather than new force introduced by which man will be further harassed and enchained.

In any event, as we shall see in a further discussion of this subject, an authority capable of enforcing world legislation cannot be set up without suppressing vital world forces now balanced in intense rivalry against each other. Whether in the guise of such outbreaks as those visible in the Spanish civil war, the American Civil War before it, or in the present unsettled condition of China, the creation of world government will not fail to bring about the very wars its existence was intended to prevent.

The present schemes will not halt the conflicts of material goals and social ideals which agitate the great brackets of mankind. It will not forestall the dramatic climax in the relationship of the U.S.S.R., the enslaved Orient and the embattled free-enterprise states of the West, when the balance of world power will appear to be in danger of crumbling. That will be the moment when the world will find itself shaken by the third phase of the great World War which already has had two earthshaking convulsions.

None of the major issues involved are less powerful and resistant than those which divided the American North and South during the middle of the nineteenth century, or those which lashed at the terrified body of Europe during the Thirty Years' War, or those which resulted in Russia's Red October Revolution.

In the writhing efforts of Asia to throw off its shackles and the increasing determination of imperial Europe to forge them tighter, as well as in the struggle going forward between Russia and the West for possession of men's souls, may be

glimpsed those terrifying problems whose nature must be
taken into account if there is to be peace.

If man is to have the right to create a world free of criminal
enterprise, he must be able to envisage such a world rationally.
His vision cannot be obscured by the delusion that he can buy
this result cheaply by the introduction of blueprints on the
legal level, and backed by the cold steel of military force.
This is a continuation of the dangerous jugglery with which
the nations currently extort concessions from each other by
the alternative threat of power action. The compromises are
not compromises of principle, but of position. They do not
spring from inalienable causes but from conceptions of national self-interest in which pure expediency dominates.

Despite the lofty premises to which the statesmen are attached in their quest for world order, it is universally recognized that an undeclared state of hostilities already exists
between the U.S.S.R. on the one hand, and the Anglo-
Americans on the other; and that the first blows of World War
III already may have been struck in China and Iran.

This practical situation and the formula for a universal
order functioning under a system of organic law, cannot be
reconciled except by a frank acceptance of the premise that
men the world over can be frightened by the new weapons
into a rational scheme of conduct.

In support of this view it has been said that the moral nature
of man has not progressed as fast as his achievements in
science, manufacture, invention, and discovery, and that he
must be protected against himself. This implies that man is
wicked by nature and must "advance" along some pathway
of ethical rehabilitation.

This is a false and unscientific approach to the problem.
Man is no more or no less moral than he has been, and cannot
be made more moral than he is. While the actions of man are
bound to reflect the influences which act upon the civic bodies

of which he is a part, man cannot be rescued from his own nature, nor can he be removed totally from the historic processes which have molded the complex social patterns under which he exists.

It is true that mankind as a mass longs above all for order and security. But it is also true that man is a complex being, the result of the cumulative impressions of his long heredity, as well as of those immediate circumstances which beat upon his senses.

Man has been formed by nature to exist under many and varied conditions. Although his sense of accommodation to environmental situation is great, his sense of obstinacy and tradition is even greater. He possesses profound social loyalties, a myriad of emotions, fixed conceptions, beliefs, and persuasions which incline him to resist radical innovation of idea. He cannot be got to abandon all of his historic interests, convictions and fixed principles of conduct by any swift means at the disposal of a normal free society. He must proceed to new environmental thresholds by degrees, laboriously dragging along with him the clanking chains of ancient prejudices, myopias, fears and images.

The alternative to progressive action is the revolutionary formula devised by Marx, Lenin and Hitler, and the stream of other cyclone-borne figures before them. Here old values, old institutions, old figures and old respectabilities are demolished at a blow. The old order is dissolved by an almost maniacal force to which opposition is hopeless. In this tremendous blood bath which pursues its goals with unrelenting purpose, new legitimacies are established, new gods are shaped, and what was formerly illegitimate and criminal becomes respectable and sacrosanct.

Above all, no progress can be made unless the function of law as a living expression of historical utility, is clearly understood. It cannot be introduced as a wraithlike apparition unanchored in the sanctions of the great human mass which adheres to it. It cannot be all piety and no force, unless it is to be a sanctimonious face for wickedness, bad faith, duplicity and fraud, as has been the case with all so-called "international law" which has preceded. It cannot proceed from totally false premises, such as those to which the nations are committed in the U.N.O., that all states large and small are equal to each other and possess equal rights and duties in the community of the world.[1]

This absurdity is matched by the even more dangerous one that nations possess a moral conscience which must be policed, and that for this purpose there must be invoked a world police authority with sufficient power to enforce the decisions of the world government.

This is a question which later will be examined in detail. In brief, however, it may be observed that such a police authority inevitably must find itself in ultimate control of all weapons and confronted with the temptations such control could not fail to bring about.

What would be the influences on the small coterie of men who inevitably must control this body? Race hate? Class or social fear? The need to suppress Spartacide revolts? A new intervention against Stalinism, or some new Trotskyism perhaps? Or the implementation of the Marxist theme of world revolution?

Who would keep these things in equilibrium without the introduction of a classless, raceless world where the major competitive factors between organized groups of men no longer could exist? To those who possess a knowledge either of history or the nature of men, the dangers are evident

---

[1] This premise, from which our nation never has departed, originally was laid down by John Marshall, then Chief Justice of the United States Supreme Court in 1814, in a matter arising from a dispute involving Russia and the tiny republic of Geneva. Here Marshall repeated the dictum of "the perfect equality of nations. Russia and Geneva have equal rights."

enough, as are the inconsistencies which would be sure to make such a scheme insupportable.

World order cannot be approached down a single legal avenue, which allows all other aspects of human existence to remain untouched. By necessity, it compels an approach which takes into account all of the conditions of the age: the structural affinities of the existing societies, the forces agitating them, the pressures which give them shape and cohesion, and the magnetic attractions which act upon them.

The problem of social organization is rooted deeply in the historical drama of the past. No matter how turbulent the times, the problem is always one of organic causes, and of growth processes which may be speeded up but cannot be skipped.

If a rational order is to rise from the anarchy which now threatens international society, it in turn must be based on rational suppositions. This is the light under which we must examine the great atomic discovery which for the moment has so desperately frightened thinking humanity. Despite its staggering power, the importance of this phenomenon can be exaggerated, taking on a mystic significance as destructive to rational concepts as the explosive action of the bomb itself.

When a great scientist tells us that we must create a world state to control atomic energy or face "the horrible prospect of man's total annihilation," we must believe that this reflection is at least partially the product of strongly stimulated human emotions arising from the general social crisis.

Though one of the major triumphs of human achievement, the discovery of atomic energy will not supplant the historic influences acting to mold the political destinies of the peoples.

What has been brought to the fore through the medium of the bomb is that the political organization of men is woefully inadequate for the business of the machine age. In the presence of this most terrible and potent of modern weapons, man himself appears to be far from a nice creature. He appears, moreover, to have become the puppet of his inventions, and may be literally on the way to destroying himself through the medium of his own machines.

This thought, while horrifying, is not new. It was advanced by Douhet after World War I, in relation to the airplane. The Douhet school of theory supposed the bombing plane to be an irresistible agency of terror, which might put an end to wars in a matter of hours, or might bring about the mutual extermination of all contenders.

III

As apart from the natural expansiveness, exaggeration, and vaulting opinion which is sure to spring from a subject as bizarre, obscure and terrifying as this, the sober conclusions which must be gained are approximately as follows:

1. If the bomb and the military apparatus it invokes is to render obsolete the present machinery of war, it presages also the total bankruptcy of the diplomatic approach, and the utter impossibility of implementing any international program anchored in the conventional treaties, alliances, pacts and arrangements.

2. Based on the tremendous costs, engineering and scientific know-how, and the physical resources required to manufacture it, the bomb increases rather than waters out the power of the large state as compared to its smaller neighbors.

3. The advantage granted to America by its possession of the bomb is a temporary one. Any large nation possessing a sound scientific tradition, and capable of exerting the physical effort required, eventually will discover the means of manufacturing it.

4. No counteraction exists to nullify the effects of the bomb or to neutralize its power; nor is there in sight any

effective agency capable of serving this purpose. There are, moreover, other weapons in existence or in prospect, which may be fully as deadly as the bomb itself. This means, for the present at least, the ascendancy of pure, crushing, brute power over the traditionally decisive elements of generalship, strategy and tactics.

5. Despite the almost hysterical tendency to make it the sole point of reference in this respect, the critical nature of the age does not derive from the bomb alone, but has merely been accented by it. Neither the political nor economic problems of our time can be controlled by outlawing the bomb, or by placing it in the custody of some international agency, even if the latter course were feasible.

6. We may assume that the essential power relationship of the United States to the world, or of the various countries to each other, has not been destroyed but simply revised and placed on a new level in which the element of time has become for a little while the determining factor. In particular, the power balance of the United States and the Soviet Union may have changed very little, since we do not know whether the Soviets do or do not possess the bomb, and may merely conclude by inferential logic that they do not.

7. It is unsound to consider that the terrors of the atomic bomb are such as automatically to make for world peace. This is a view which events of the past fifty years have proved to be inaccurate. The bomb constitutes a restatement in terms of the increased frightfulness of weapons, of a proposition stated many times before—that the nature and power of modern arms themselves would be an effective deterrent to war, since the suicidal nature of an impending conflict would be obvious to all the peoples involved.

Far from stopping wars, it may be believed that the atomic bomb only will make them more deadly and more destructive. Alfred Nobel thought the invention of dynamite would stop war by making it too terrible to endure. As we have noted, this also was said of the raiding plane with its tremendous loads of incendiaries and demolition charges, and, in particular, of the robot bomb, by which means the entire civilian economy of nations became a legitimate target.

Wherever great stresses and strong tensions exist between organized societies of men, these either must be dissipated by a correction of their organic causes or result in war. No matter how horrid the weapon, the state or ruler which means to be the aggressor will act when some circumstance occurs which appears to have turned the scale in favor of its own enterprise.

IV

It is evident that whatever the gains of men in the fields of science, technology and the arts, on the social and international political level the world still is in the horse-and-buggy stage, and that in their emotional relationships with each other, men are scarcely out of the Stone and Bronze ages.

The statesmen and diplomats of today continue in the spirit of Talleyrand, Disraeli, Gladstone and Mark Hanna, functioning in an atmosphere of international privilege, deceit, piracy and intrigue. They see statecraft surrounded by a glow of strategical considerations no more affected by morality than the great power movements of some military commander, and committed to relatively similar goals. They view their nations as privileged corporations operating in the general jungle of international life, which reserve to themselves under the name of national sovereignty, rights of competitive power action whose ultimate outcome can be nothing else than war.

As the A-bomb has brought sharply home to us, under these conditions it is the very achievements of science, invention and discovery, around which the ultimate hopes of mankind are centered, which are providing the greatest possible menace to civilization.

In the atomic age, the industrial base of combat efficiency becomes of greater, rather than lesser, significance. The atomic bomb is not a lone phenomenon but the culmination of a grand military sequence. Both in its complicated and costly processes of manufacture, and the precision apparatus required to deliver it to its target, the bomb is the very symbol of the power conditions of this century.

The capacity to fight a modern war is intimately related to the capacity to produce wealth, with the possession of raw materials, and the ability to decentralize industry over a wide area. The whole sequence of organization, reaching from the laboratories to the mines, and through the network of channels for manufacturing and distributing the finished product, is required for sound military function.

This includes possession of every manner of heavy and light machinery, mastery of a maze of chemical processes, and a competent network of sea, land and air communications. It poses, above all, the existence of an intelligent, loyal and numerous population, since the ultimate denominator in human warfare cannot be machines, but only men themselves.

As long as man himself is the trigger mechanism of his machines, which do not possess an independent volition of their own, he cannot be completely wiped out in a war of the new weapons as has been feared, though human civilization may be badly crippled as it has been numerous times before in the course of history. The question of destruction is one of degree, unless some unforeseen and inadvertent catastrophe occurs as a result of chain hydrogen or nitrogen experiments, so as literally to set the atmosphere on fire and obliterate all life on this planet.

V

It cannot be doubted that the future belongs to great federal unions or empires, operating under centralized political control and capable of a supreme exploitation of the properties of the machine era. They must possess a long catalogue of minerals, ores, farm and forest products and other raw materials, ranging from the ferroalloys and palm oils to that androgynous mother of cataclysmic energy, uranium. A sovereign area conforming to these dimensions must have access to the major world highways by air, sea and land; and be able to provide a continuous and balanced market for its industrial and agricultural output without reference to the activities of foreign states.

If this estimate is accurate, the small nation-state must find itself at an increasing and appalling disadvantage, fatally handicapped in whatever direction it turns, and compelled to organize its material economy along the most constricted lines. Far from being a force in the contemporary universe, the small nation is merely a potential victim of aggression, and a focal point of trouble. It is grotesque to think of such states as Estonia, Greece, or even Italy, in the role of sovereign political corporations defending their right to separatism by the use of armies, navies, tariff walls, currency systems and batteries of diplomats.

Today, markets, manufactures, and military operations themselves, all are on a hemispheric scale. They cannot successfully be conducted otherwise. The existence of a great many minor nationalisms operating at counterpurpose to this pattern throws a sabot into the entire machinery of international operation and is an invitation to anarchy and world disunion.

A state like Bulgaria, for example, cannot mass produce. She cannot build automobiles, airplanes or even agricultural machinery on a basis competitive to the big industrial countries. She is dependent on the good will of her larger neighbors even to find a market for her agricultural products, which under the new industrial dispensation must become more and more dangerously specialized.

From the military side, the almost complete helplessness of the small nation is an expected offset to its growing inadequacy as an economic or social unit. In the end it must become a lackey to some nearby great power, or the object of conflicting spheres of aggression.

The great federal state, on the other hand, cannot fail to respond to the benefits of science and invention by progressive increases in its physical power. These gains, in turn, must force it to move toward a completion of the organic base on which that power rests. If the state lacks markets, it must reach for them. If it requires an outlet to the sea, it must make it essential to its policy that such outlets be secured. If it needs coal, iron, oil or any of the other materials necessary to industry, it must act to acquire them. If any one of its military flanks are exposed to attack, it must move to seize or neutralize the territories adjoining.

These are the unmistakable terms in which the real world moves, and in which the stream of dynamic existence is organized. The combination of appetite, need and opportunity on the part of the big state, and the increasing incapacity of the small nation to meet the terms of competitive existence, is compelled to have untoward results. As long as there is an independent Iran, an Austria, a Turkey, or a rich but helplessly suffocated India, there will be peripheral clashes, uncertainties, wars and the threats of wars. There is no possible way

to adjust the inconsistencies, rivalries and contradictions provoked by the mere existence of this myriad of weak and
unprotectable states. They are like the unarmed wild beasts
of the field: no other provocation to aggression is needed than
that provided by their own succulent flesh.

The major fact which emerges from these estimates and
which cannot be overstressed, is that *decisive power no longer
is the result of various ententes and combinations of states
whose shifting alliances determine the existing balance of
power*. Today there are only two states which answer the
definitions by which power can be measured. These are the
United States of America and the Union of Soviet Socialist
Republics. These two great states hold between them the
greater part of the world's military and war-making potential
and have become giant magnets which are acting to draw all
others within their own orbits.

The mere existence of two such power systems within a
disorganized universe is certain to lead to a clash of interests
on a dozen levels and a hundred peripheries, none of which
can be contained by any peace machinery or mediation apparatus which may be placed into existence.

VI

Whatever may be uncertain about this prospect, one element, at least, is positive: despite his vast gains of material
knowledge, man has not yet learned to live with man on this
planet.

The uneven nature of the growth of peoples and the mark-
edly different influences which have acted upon them historically, have given us a world of many powerful and resistant
crosscurrents.

In addition to the conventional state and dynastic structures, there is the great cross section of the world's industrial
proletariat, the followers of Marx and Lenin. There are the

revolutionary syndicalists and anarchists, who, though small, possess a potency which cannot be fully assessed until the current crisis has been liquidated.

There is the world of classic imperialism, offset by a world of solidifying racial bitterness which sees the universe as a single competition between Nordic and non-Nordic man, or increasingly in the Orient, a contest for supremacy between the dark and Caucasian races. There are the theocratic world systems, and in particular that of Moslem intransigence, whose enthusiasms for the suppression of the wicked and unbelieving are only restrained by a consciousness of its own weakness. There remains the feudal world of Franco and Perón with its strong medieval cast of mind; and the failing world of free-capital enterprise, with its almost fierce sense of personal adventure, privilege and responsibility.

All of these universes do not exist in altogether clear definition. They merge, clash and abut on each other, sometimes in a series of dimensions which merge like darkness and light, and sometimes take the rigid and definitive shape by which state power is measured.

Behind the obscuring haze where this all-important tableau is being acted out, we may be sure that not only material change but psychological revision as well is being generated and suckled. These presage an existence whose tempo and form will be radically different from any we have yet known.

The alterations in the spiritual and ethical outlook of man will be as great as those which are bound to affect his physical environment. The ruin and havoc which have ravished his cities and destroyed the accumulated wealth of his labor will find its counterpart in the ruin and demoralization of his inner being. This world-wide soul sickness and universal neurosis will remain for a generation at least, as one of the constituent factors of the new society. It cannot be ignored and will show itself in many directions, not only in national chauvinisms, but in sharply accentuated class, race and religious contests. Irritability, doubt, skepticism, fear, and morbid disrespect for old obligations and values, mark the spiritual unhingement of vast agglomerations of men.

The problems affecting the internal economy of nations, therefore, will be fully as complex, and pose even more pressing difficulties than those affecting their external affairs. New social concepts and extreme philosophies are certain to exercise an overwhelming fascination over the minds of great and widely separated human masses, unless some early correction can be made of the causes generating them.

As sane and solvent as its economy may be, even the United States will find itself faced with difficulties the extent of which has yet to be plumbed. For our country as well as others, the touchstone to these problems would appear to be the activities of the U.S.S.R., both as a competitive state and as the hub of a universal and militant social philosophy.

It is useless to discount the nature, gravity, or extent of these questions. They must be faced, examined and dealt with if we are to weather the storm of approaching crisis.

It is clear to the blindest of men that the usual diplomatic juggling will not see the world through this dilemma. The situation is one of great immediacy, in which we no longer can dawdle, or, like Micawber, "wait for something to turn up."

If we are to trust to anything but blind luck, we now must operate according to plan.

If our decisions are the correct ones, our nation and with us the world will have an opportunity to enter an era of unprecedented prosperity, and perhaps peace. If they are wrong, the automatic drive of events themselves will shape our course; we will lose essential control of our destiny, and will find ourselves pitched bodily into a period of desperate military struggle.

This time, perhaps it will be our cities which will be rav-

ished by the gutting teeth of atomic explosives, and by those
terrible visitations of mechanical terror which new improve-
ments in the military art are daily bringing into existence.
What we have known and loved as Western civilization will
come to a dramatic end, and some new phase of organized
human existence will take its place.

There is no need to enter into a discussion in further detail
of these possibilities. That they will be the result of a failure
on our part to answer the insistent problems posed by this
century, must be conceded.

William B. Ziff

Washington, November 15, 1945

Chapter One

YET ANOTHER LEAGUE

THE question of a collaborative universe, of a world run by law rather than by force and appetite, assumes a peculiar importance, as the very central question of our times.

This is the more insistently true since the invention of the atom bomb, but a deep and uneasy sense of urgency already hung over the early discussions on this subject at the first Moscow Conference. It was understood then by the participant powers that the League of Nations was dead beyond all possible awakening; and that mankind shortly would be compelled to come to a great and new decision on the question of world order.

It was under this hammer-drive of events that President Roosevelt, Prime Minister Churchill, Marshal Stalin, and a virtually unknown Chinese gentleman named Foo Ping-sheung measured each other in person for the first time at their historic meeting in the late fall of 1943.

The alliance between these powers had been one of grim necessity, not of natural choice. Behind the virtuous phraseology of the statesmen, and the assurances of mutual esteem exchanged between them, there existed an air of uncertain armistice.

The U.S.S.R. had been virtually an outcast nation, only grudgingly accepted in the councils of the world. Even at this late date it still was ostracized by a considerable portion of the nations. Russian Communism had openly proclaimed its hate of the pluto-democracy represented by the powerful United States. Time after time, Communist doctrine had named British world imperialism as the appointed enemy with whom it was destined to lock horns in relentless struggle.

On a score of fronts, the Russian and British juggernauts had massed power machinery and probed each other's defenses. The rulers of the Kremlin with the rankling memory of Denikin, Semenov, and Wrangel, whose counterrevolutionary terror had been openly subsidized from London and Washington, retained an irradicable suspicion of the purposes of Anglo-American statecraft. The Kremlin astutely believed that the British Foreign Office had conspired to bring about the resurrection of a strong military Germany in the expectation that it would turn the edge of its sword against the hated Bolsheviki. Moscow was persuaded that it was with these same objectives in mind that the leaders of Whitehall had consented to Japanese military aggression on the continent of Asia.

In this tangle of events, Stalin shrewdly had lent himself to a maneuver which to the Russians completely reversed the situation. He had signed a nonaggression pact with the Nazis which for all intents and purposes amounted to a military alliance.

He had ended the long smoldering animosity with Japan by a similar pact, at the conclusion of which he had thrown his arms around the Japanese representative and exuberantly embraced him.

As a result it appeared that it would be the Nazi sword-rattler and the free capitalist states of the West who would wear each other out in a deadly conflict in which the Soviet Union ultimately might be the total beneficiary. Thus, the tables had been neatly turned until Stalin himself suddenly was victimized by a violent and unprovoked assault which came within an ace of finishing him and his regime forever.

The Chinese delegate to the conference was present largely as window dressing, and as a concession to the euphemism that the meeting was one of four great powers, in which the interests of Asia were engaged. Both Russia and Britain looked on China as a legitimate field for their future operations; both were determined that she must never grow strong.

The weight of the existing crisis had caused the powers to pool their assets after a fashion. The British who had been menaced as never before since the days of William the Norman, were for the moment willing to make any reasonable concession which would weld the fighting forces of the U.S.A., the U.S.S.R. and the Empire into a solid phalanx of controlled military action. Churchill had managed to work out a more or less intimate association with the United States on this basis, with control fixed in the upper echelons through the board known as the Combined Chiefs of Staff.

A more cautious view was taken in reference to the Chinese, the position being guided by the perpetual fear of revolutionary uprisings among the armed masses of Britain's oriental possessions. It was for this reason that London had prevented Stilwell's Chinese from entering the Burma theater until it was too late, and the campaign already lost.

The representatives of the United States sat with the solid assurance of a nation whose principal evils had resulted from an era of surpluses of everything, and which was now proving its unmatched resources of competence on the battlefield. Washington had constituted itself banker, economic storehouse and tutelary authority for all who cared to join the common cause.

The Russians who were fighting the bulk of the battle and had already shed an ocean of blood contributing to the benefit of states which Communist doctrine had sworn to destroy, viewed their associates at the conference table with suave distrust. The Kremlin doubted the integrity of the position taken by the Anglo-American partners. It doubted the efficiency and logic of the air war against the Germans, and demanded a second front of great mass armies. It suspected that the Anglo-Americans were seeking to fight a cheap war of relative inactivity while the Germans and Russians bled each other white on the prairies of eastern Europe.

The proof of these suspicions lay in the fact that no Anglo-American airman was permitted to fly over Soviet territory even for the purpose of delivering Lend-Lease airplanes. These were taken over by Russian fliers at the border. The exchange of military information despite the *de facto* alliance between the Kremlin and the Anglo-American combine, was so slight as to be described as "sketchy."

Though seeking to create a world authority armed with sufficient power to prevent the disaster of continued war, each of the states at the conference attended as the jealous guardian of its own sovereignty, privilege and position. Its individual welfare and the power methods by which this might be insured were the basic goal of each of the statesmen, despite the high-flown rhetoric and lofty principles with which they enveloped their intentions.

Each was conscious of an intense dissembling on the part of the others, and suspected even more.

This was the atmosphere in which the eminent statesmen met with each other at Moscow during the first conference. They were men from totally different worlds.

Strongly counterbalancing their mistrust and perhaps distaste for each other was an even more overmastering fear of what the future might bring, and of the postwar role to be played by each of the powers in its quest for security in an age of scientific weapons. It was felt more particularly by the Anglo-Americans, and perhaps specifically by the British, that some sort of world organization was now mandatory. London was conscious that its power position was badly de-

teriorating due to the revised relationship of battleship and
airplane, and the upsurge of national ideologies everywhere.
Her statesmen frantically were seeking some formula which
would prevent another and perhaps ruinous test of strength
after the existing hostilities had ceased.

It was the Chinese alone who favored real world unity
backed by the unequivocal force of universal law. They considered that they had nothing to lose but their poverty, and
the servitude in which their nation had lost itself.

It was under these influences, with all their collective weak-
nesses, faults, impulses and promptings that the seed which
matured into the present United Nations Charter was created
and fertilized. In the midst of the sonorous platitudes which
committed the conferees to the vague political generalities of
the times, was the single, hopeful assertion which possessed in
its wording almost the aspect of a query: "that they [the
conferees] recognize the necessity of establishing at the
earliest practicable date a general international organization,
based on the principle of the sovereign equality of all peace-
loving states, and open to membership by all such states, large
and small, for the maintenance of international peace and
security."

While realizing the imperative need for some type of physical machinery which would keep the nations from each other's
throats in the unfolding future, they approached the details
of the subject with the usual caution. As the discussions
developed later, and as they were pared, mulled over and
worked on at Dumbarton Oaks and San Francisco, the choice
of the public leaders of the world was seen to come down to a
new league of nations, where the many independent states
could continue their existence, and where the existing prerogatives, interests and power positions would remain virtually
intact.

II

This revived league of nations, now known as the United Nations Organization, though possessed of significant innovations, was in principle identical with its discredited predecessor. It was brought to the sympathetic attention of the American public with the full weight of official approval. All the genius of the publicists' art was turned on in a whirlwind campaign in which not the slightest pretense was made at exculpating the basic contradictions which made the Charter unworkable.

This appears to have been the mood under which the Charter was ratified. No measure in American history has been approved by anything comparable to the overwhelming show of hands by which this document received its official endorsement by the Senate of the United States.

In this parade of almost unanimous consent, the Charter was eulogized as one of the great historical developments of all time. It was compared to the Magna Carta and the American Constitution, and even to the supreme words of religious authority, for its effect on the future conduct of the nations.

On the date this document was ratified by the United States Senate, the newspapers were carrying an account of fierce tensions which had arisen between the very group of states which under the Charter had made themselves responsible for the peace. British troops were in Syria where they were providing arms and assistance to Syrian irregulars engaged in a savage struggle with the French. The head of the French Republic, General Charles de Gaulle, was bitterly assailing Premier Churchill, accusing him of conspiring to remove the French from the Levant in order to take their place there. Russian power maneuvers in Poland and elsewhere in Europe were going full blast. In Greece an equally ironical event was taking place, where British arms were engaged in reducing another causal ally of the war to a semicolonial status.

The mutual anxieties and fears found further expression in plans for improved armaments on the part of all the nations which could create them. In the United States, officials warned of the need for a far-flung network of military bases, and for an air force of crushing proportions to protect the nation from the deadly perils with which it was sure to be confronted in the postwar years.

The United Nations Organization is certain to go down in history as one of the unexplainable phenomena of an age of blind spots in which the most plainly observable relevancies were studiously ignored in favor of illusions whose insubstantiality must have been more or less patent to everyone. The new league was universally accepted despite the fact that everyone was aware of its incompetency. In our highest legislative assembly men voted to ratify this document though they made not the slightest pretense to faith in it, regarding it simply as an innocuous concession to international pietism.

In view of the massive difficulties whose gross outlines even then were visible, it must have been apparent that the new league had no independent power potential whatsoever; and that instead of setting the world on the road to security, it had placed it on a detour full of easy and facile expedients which could end only in the mire of world disillusion. It thus automatically operated to defeat any true solution of major problems, and proffered the elongated shadow of security rather than an effective reality.

Reduced to its simplest terms, when the spokesmen for the new United Nations Organization spoke of international law, they did not mean law; they meant some disguised extension of the old isolationist position which for practical purposes left each of the nations as it was before, a law unto itself. This was what they meant when they said that the sovereignty of even the smallest state must be unimpaired.

The machinery they proposed had a sacrosanct ring when designated under the flattering title of law. Actually, it consisted only of a series of arrangements and pledges among the various nations and came down to a pattern of world alliances and agreements of collaboration.

The new system was based in theory on the comparison with the equal rights and duties exercised by individuals in their relations to the commonwealth. In the explanation offered by Mr. Stettinius, "Every peace-loving state, however small, has the same supreme authority over its own territory as any other state, however large. Each such state, irrespective of size, is an international individuality. Each, therefore, has both a right to a voice in the affairs of the family of nations and a responsibility to share in the task of creating a peaceful world order."

Having offered this absurdity which presupposes that Russia is only an enlarged Monaco, and the United States a greater Luxembourg or Iraq, the Charter sententiously advises "all members to refrain in their international relations from the threat or use of force against the territorial integrity or political independence of any member or state, or in any other matter inconsistent with the purposes of the United Nations."

In this dictum is implied a comparison of the role of nations to that of private citizens under municipal law, an unsound analogy which will be examined later at length. For the moment it is sufficient to point out that citizens are not allowed to run in gangs; nor do they carry with them an arsenal of weapons superior to that at the disposal of the police.

The contradictions which affected the purposes of the Charter unavoidably were carried over into the superstructure of the new league.

A General Assembly is provided for in which all of the United Nations are to be represented equally.[1] The Assembly, however, possesses no power and is to be little more than a

[1] The sole exception is that of the Soviet Union, which is to have three votes, or one for each of its principal constituent republics.

debating society. The theory advanced is that belligerent nations will be able to talk themselves out of their hot tempers here, and that disputes somehow will manage to adjudicate themselves amicably by these means.

In an age when the first law of military strategy is the surprise transition from peace to war, this reliance on elaborate tournament tactics is little less than astonishing. It is a continuation of the feudal ideals which dominated the two Hague Conventions, where it was correctly conceded that the warrant to make wars is an essential part of the right of nations, vested in them by reason of this sovereignty. The fact of the legitimacy of war is amply acknowledged by the introduction of certain "rules" for the waging of it, together with the concept of mediation by outsiders before any declaration of hostilities rightfully or morally can be issued.

Under the Hague Convention, for example, the nations are enjoined "to conduct their operations in accordance with the laws and customs of war," and agree that "the laws, rights, [*sic!*] and duties of war apply not only to armies, but also to militia and volunteer corps," which as far as the fine art of mass assassination is concerned must fit themselves into the restricted conditions laid down.

At the core of the General Assembly is an exclusively-held corporation called the Security Council. The Security Council alone possesses the authority to invoke economic or military sanctions. It alone can mediate, arbitrate or crack the skulls of quarreling states.

On this all-powerful body sit permanently the so-called Big Five: the United States of America, the U.S.S.R., the kingdom of Great Britain, and the republics of China and France. Six others are elected from the balance of the nations on a rotating basis.

Under examination, as we have noted, the Big Five are seen in reality to be the Big Two. Of the others, China is a potential great state; Britain and France, inevitable third-raters in the final definitions by which power is to be measured.

Each of the Big Five possesses interests which place it in essential conflict with at least several of the others. One, Great Britain, is devoted to a failing and antiquated politico-economic system which its statesmen are desperately attempting to shore up by freezing the status quo permanently in great parts of the world. Another, the Soviet Union, is in the dynamic expansion stage and is devoted to revolutionary goals inimical to the interests of almost every other member of the league. Still another, China, threatens in the course of time to upset the entire balance of power in every direction by the industrial organization of its countless millions, and by its insistence on fracturing the ardently held fetishes and privileges of the white man.

This assorted group of states not only possesses absolute veto power as a unit, but the same power individually, so that at any time a state may cancel the application of sanctions to itself, or veto any proposed action by the league. Indeed, it may go further, and cause a satellite state to take an aggressive action useful to the interests of its master, and then act to prevent the matter from coming to a hearing.

Thus if any of the Big Five elects to make war, or assist the activities of some bellicose puppet, the United Nations Organization is powerless to halt it. All the guilty state need do is say that it objects to an investigation. Thereupon, no trial can be held and no investigation conducted.

The same ubiquitous rule applies in reference to a future amendment to the Charter itself. Such an amendment *requires the unanimous consent of all the powers.*

What this amounts to is that each of the big powers is given the right to police itself, and to be the sole judge of its own acts. The actual language used is as follows: "Decisions of the Security Council on procedural matters shall be made by an affirmative vote of seven members. Decisions of the Security Council *on all other matters shall be made by an affirmative vote of seven members including the concurring vote of the permanent members.*"

Reduced to its own simple logic, it would appear that under the Charter there is no authority to discipline any one of the states actually capable of making war; nor is it likely that any of these would vote contrary to the long-range goals it has set for itself, or against what it deems to be its essential interests.

Though the language used is involved and circumlocutory, the large states also possess the exclusive power to keep order in their special regions, thus assuming the position of the medieval lord toward his villeins.

What this is certain to lead to may be judged by the activities of Nazi Germany in the so-called sphere of influence it arrogated to itself in central Europe; or by the actions of the Soviet Union when the temporary *rapprochement* with the Nazi Reich granted Moscow a free hand in Finland and the Baltic.

If despite these safeguards an aggressor state finds its position within the U.N.O. compromised, it may withdraw. This right is without restriction, except that the withdrawee would be expected to publish its reasons for so acting.

III

The great question is not whether the United Nations Organization is deficient in one character or another, but rather whether any league, no matter how organized, is capable of performing the functions assigned to it. It is entirely misleading to conceive of the problem as solely between some isolationist philosophy and the present pattern offered by the United Nations Organization. The question actually is quite a different one: it is whether the world can be organized along those modern lines dictated by the presence of mass production, distribution, science, invention and the means of swift communication. It is a question of trade, of economics, of manufacture, of military defense, and of those social adjustments which are compelled to follow in the train of the machine age. Thus, it becomes, in principle, a question of whether the present archaic political structures which act like so many watertight compartments to keep men separated from each other can be broken down and consolidated along rational lines to meet the needs of this era.

The theoretical background by which the definition of league organization may be measured is simple: any relationship which depends upon a system of pacts or alliances between sovereign states is, no matter how disguised, a relationship which rests on eternally shifting balances in which power is the foremost element.

Power relationships have little to do with the authority of law. They are concerned only with force, with appetite and the capacity to gratify it. Might invariably breeds a smug acceptance of its own legitimacy. Those who command the weapons capable of assuring their domination are apt to see in their possession of power a sign of their own superiority.

Once the game of power is begun, there is no end to the need for continuing it. Power always runs parallel to privilege which is its single excuse for being in existence. Thus it involves the automatic erection of protective devices which by their essential nature are non co-operative. Any attempt to mend such a relationship by charter is in effect an effort to exorcise devils, and bears no conceivable relevancy to sound enterprise.

The sovereign unit cannot be controlled from the outside, but must behave according to its own nature. The state, like the individual human being, tends to emphasize its own good social qualities and to disregard or underrate its bad ones. "The result is the varying misjudgment of our relationship with others from which all human units suffer . . ."[2]

To the sovereign state, its own needs and conscience are the final criteria of virtue and hence of law. It cannot fail to rationalize any condition relating to the rights of others or to its own moral obligations, by transforming the situation to suit its own requirements.

It must be considered as axiomatic that the ambitions and hungers of the nation-state come first, and will be mirrored faithfully in its policy. This is not because the people of these countries are necessarily unmoral, but because the principle of sovereignty bears no possible relation to morality. The sovereign state must be concerned primarily with the immediate well-being of its citizens, and not with some long-range world plan by which that welfare might at some point be jeopardized. Opportunities for advantage, the demand for security, the need of markets, raw materials, seaports, river routes, or new settlement areas, will determine the course of the nation-state without relation to any pacts, treaties, or guarantees which might exist. This is even more true of the democracies than it is of the dictatorships, due to the force of pressure which can be exerted on authority by the citizen mass.

Nations which are strong or whose actions are dictated by some emergency, invariably grow impatient with textual restrictions. Their course of action tends to be based on the assumption that the emergency justifies the act and the end the means.

The self-conceived need of the Soviet Union for protection on its European flank could not be modified by the individual rights guaranteed to Estonia, Latvia and Lithuania by the League of Nations. The "rights" of Colombia did not prevent us from abetting a revolution on the Isthmus; or those of the Iranian Shah from removing him bodily in order to provide a

[2] Ranyard West, *Conscience and Society*, p. 187.

secure wartime pathway to Russia. Under the conditions which apply in contemporary international life, the policy of the sovereign nation is under a dual pressure from:

1. The spontaneously generated appetites rising from within its own body. The impact of labor groups seeking to sustain a high standard of living for their members, or of manufacturers anxious to obtain a disproportionate share of world markets, is superior in its effect on the ultimate attitude of the state to any possible set of obligations which might refer to the welfare of others beyond its borders; and
2. Competing states seeking to attain identical goals. This may be seen in the struggle between the U.S.S.R. and England over the Dardanelles and Iran.

It is useless to castigate these actions, or to denounce them as disreputable and blameworthy. That they are shabby enough is true, but their lack of virtue is not one of moral deliberation, but rather is inherent in the nature of the present political order.

IV

All of this can be seen in detail in the pathetic record left by the old League of Nations. The sorry decrepitude which befell that body is commented on somewhat ruefully in the report of the Pan-American Union Conference of 1942. "The defect in the organization of the League of Nations might perhaps have been overcome," it reads, "if its actual members had upheld its principles more effectively. But instead the policies of the great powers influenced the decisions at Geneva, and, in some cases, prevailed over the spirit of the Covenant.

"The Locarno Agreements, for example, instead of gravitating to the League and adding to its authority were, in a sense, inspired by contrary sentiments. . . . The same great powers conceive the purpose of the League more in terms of maintaining the *status quo*, than in terms of promoting the welfare of the international community."[3]

The members of the League agreed to the violation of China by Japan in 1931 when Manchukuo was invaded. They failed to restrain Italy from invading Ethiopia in 1935. They did not reject the unilateral British violation of the Versailles Treaty which made it possible for the Hitlerite Reich to have an air force. When in March 1939, Germany repudiated the Munich agreement, it was apparent that collective security, as meaning security through the composite actions of many governments, was a delusion.

In making the comparison between the old League of Nations and the new United Nations Organization, it is somewhat illogical to conclude that the former failed because it had no power with which to enforce its decisions. In the League Covenant, the nations set up safeguards which in certain respects were superior to those embodied in the U.N.O. These failed to function because the League could not reconcile two utterly antagonistic ideas: the sovereign independence of the individual state and the authority of international law; the identical impasse in which the U.N.O. finds itself.

When in 1918, Woodrow Wilson and David Lloyd George made provision for an economic blockade against any aggressor nation, they thought they were putting teeth into the League. They had it worked out that if a nation were quarantined economically, its life would be throttled, and it thus would be prevented from making war.

That argument in those days sounded just as plausible as the new argument that the League must have sharper teeth and that we must organize an international police force.

Though the League provided for unified action to confine

[3] Pan-American Union, *Preliminary Recommendations on Post-War Problems* (1942), pp. 6 and 7.

an aggressor, when aggression came there was no unified action. When it came down to the question of punitive measures against Japan for her aggressions in Asia, against Germany for her aggressions in Europe, against the Soviet Union for her aggressions against Finland and the Baltic countries, or against Italy for her assaults on Ethiopia and Albania, the powers refused to accept the responsibility.

They knew what that responsibility meant: it was war.

Whether within the cover of a league charter, or without benefit of such stipulations, war is always the same. The nations which wish it will have it, and those who do not wish it or are not ready for it will shrink from it.

This is observed in the biting charges hurled at the League Assembly by the South African delegate, Mr. Te Water, on the historic jettisoning of Ethiopia in favor of the Italian conqueror. "Fifty nations," he asserted, "led by the three most powerful in the world, are about to declare their powerlessness to protect the weakest in their midst from destruction. I desire to say here that this renunciation by the most powerful members of the League of the collective decision most solemnly taken by us all under the obligations in which we declared ourselves bound, can only be interpreted as a surrender by them of the authority of the League. . . . I am to declare that this surrender cannot be interpreted as impotence in safeguarding that trust, *but as a simple denial of their ability to bear the sacrifices for its fulfillment.*"

This recognition was echoed by Maxim Litvinov, the great Soviet Commissar for Foreign Affairs. "I assert," he cried, "that Article XVI equipped the League with such powerful weapons that in the event either is applied every aggression can be broken. The melancholy experience of the Italo-Ethiopian conflict does not contradict this assertion. Not only was the terrible mechanism of Article XVI not brought into play but at the very outset there was a manifest striving to confine the action taken to the barest minimum. Even economic sanctions were limited in their scope and function, and even in this limited scope, sanctions were not applied by all members of the League."

It was not in the imperfections of the Covenant, averred Mr. Litvinov, where the causes of this collapse must be sought, nor in the absence of America from the deliberations. Rather it was in the tendency to adapt the Covenant to the existing state of mind.

Thus the practical Litvinov conceded that the failure of the League could not be fairly attributable to a lack of participation on the part of the United States, as has been familiarly charged. It is unlikely that the United States would have resorted to force against members who transgressed against the Covenant. Although the United States maintained an official position of nonmembership, it did co-operate in practice with important affiliates of the League. M. Litvinov himself was to point out: "We see from the example of the United States that the League may reckon on nonmembers in obeying Article XVI, and reckon on them all the more the more energetically its members act themselves."

It seems fair to ask: are we not faced with identically the same problem today? How if the relatively easy method of economic quarantine failed because the member nations themselves would not adhere to the pledge for unified action, can we expect nations to permit the use of their *armed forces* against some power deemed to be threatening the peace? In the old League, the nations would not even act to throw an economic blockade against Japan and Italy, much less Germany. How then, when the far more hazardous and costly method of armed force is to be used, can we expect such a unified action? When it was suggested to President Roosevelt that the principles of the Atlantic Charter and of Dumbarton

Oaks be invoked on Poland's behalf, he asked bluntly: "Would you want us to go to war with the Soviet Union?"

The fundamental weakness of all leagues is shown in the ease by which even the most sacred obligations assumed by their members can be evaded if the will exists to do so. It is to be noted that whenever it suited the convenience of the great powers, they did not hesitate to conclude the most important agreements outside the League's framework, presenting these as in the case of the pacts of Stresa and Locarno, as *faits accomplis*; or to abandon all confining pretense and revert to the simple clarity of power politics.

It is also not without meaning that the interhemispheric conference which gave rise to the Act of Chapultepec was called outside the jurisdiction of the Pan-American Union. In theory, at least, the Pan-American Union is an American league of nations in miniature, and is the source of applying inter-American law. Nevertheless, for the purpose of short-circuiting our political opponent, the Argentine, and to keep that country from having a voice in the deliberations, we considered it expedient to hold this rump session, from which the Argentine and the equally suspect state of San Salvador were excluded.

An example of the amoral character of pledges is the document known as the Atlantic Charter. The sacred assurances it once proclaimed to the peoples of the world as expressing the inalienable purposes of the United Nations have in the minds of most people taken on the aspects of an international hoax. On their face, the stipulations of this almost forgotten document, as compared to the power actions of the nations signatory to it, offer a complete example in opposed principles. Under the Charter the countries were (1) "to seek no aggrandizement, territorial or other; (2) they desire to see no territorial changes that do not accord with the freely expressed wishes of the peoples concerned; (3) they respect the right of all peoples to choose the form of government under which they will live; and they wish to see sovereign rights and self-government restored to those who have been forcibly deprived of them; (4) they will endeavor . . . to further the enjoyment by all states, great or small, victor or vanquished, of access, without discrimination and on equal terms, to the markets and to the raw materials of the world which are needed for their economic prosperity; . . . (8) they believe that all of the nations of the world, for realistic as well as spiritual reasons must come to the abandonment of the use of force."

Without exception, wherever the power interests of any strong state have been concerned, the Charter has been as totally disregarded as if it never existed. This we shall observe later in detail in our examination of today's events.

V

Another and even more discouraging circumstance is that connected with the investigation and punishment of war crimes.

At the first Moscow Conference, the U.S.S.R., the U.S.A., and the United Kingdom issued a warning to the accused Nazi criminals in the form of a manifesto, so stern in the icy clarity of its language as to be almost ferocious. "At the time of the granting of any armistice," it read, "to any government which may be set up in Germany, those German officers and men and members of the Nazi Party who had been responsible for, or had taken a consenting part in the above atrocities, massacres and executions . . . will know that they will be brought back to the scene of their crimes and judged on the spot by the people whom they have outraged. Let those who have hitherto not imbrued their hands with innocent blood beware lest they join the ranks of the guilty, for most assuredly the three allied powers will pursue them to the uttermost ends of the earth and will deliver them to their accusers in order that justice may be done."[4]

The edict which referred specifically to the terrible butcheries of the Jews was equally inflexible and uncompromising. "All who knowingly take part in the deportation of Jews to their death in Poland, or Norwegians and French to their death in Germany," it stated, "are equally guilty with the executioner. All who share the guilt shall share the punishment."

Such an indictment as this obviously involves the summary punishment of many hundreds of thousands of individuals, and the immediate establishment of adequate tribunals participated in by all of the allies.

When the time came to place these declarations into operation, the almost total reluctance of the Anglo-American governments to act was highly publicized by the spectacular resignations of Sir Cecil Hurst, chairman of the London War Crimes Commission, and of Herbert Pell, the distinguished American representative. Indeed, instead of acting against Fascists as they had promised, in many cases the representatives of Anglo-American power were consorting with them. In Bavaria, the Americans appointed as police superintendent of Munich a Colonel von Seisser, who had been one of the early associates of Hitler in the Munich beerhall episode. In the interests of its Mohammedan policy, the British facilitated the escape to Paris of the notorious Haj Amin el Husseini, a sanguinary scoundrel who had been devoted hand and foot to the interests of the Hitler regime.

Up until the special set of political conditions ushered in by the atomic bomb, the Russians steadfastly refused to participate in a general scheme of collaborative punishment. They

[4] This pronouncement was declared to be "without prejudice in the case of the major criminals, whose offenses have no particular geographical localization and who will be punished by the joint decision of the governments of the Allies."

offered no evidence to the United Nations War Crimes Commission, except in the case of the major war criminals. Neither did they submit lists of names of those accused, or of the actual or intended fate of those who might be in their hands. Instead they went ahead unilaterally in a political circus of their own, liquidating those persons whose removal served their own particular set of interests, independent of their political antecedents, and without public notice.

Those accused of a scattering of crimes against British and American military personnel were swiftly tried and dispatched by Anglo-American military courts. In the case of General Anton Dostler, indicted for ordering the execution of fifteen American soldiers without trial, the hearings began at 4 P.M. on one day and sentence issued at 9 A.M. the next. In Czechoslovakia, the deputy mayor of Prague, accused of high treason, was tried, sentenced and executed within three days.

The attitude toward the dead European intellectuals and liberals, and toward the six million Jews who had been slaughtered, was quite a different one. Only the most paltry and casual effort was made to exact retribution.

Even the bloody perverts and functionaries who were caught red-handed in the notorious murder factories at Belsen, Oswiecim and elsewhere merely were taken into custody. Later, a number of these people were made the subjects of elaborate trials in the British and American zones, in which the legalities were dragged out at exaggerated lengths over many long weeks. As a result, a mere handful were declared guilty, and some of these received limited sentences.

At Lueneberg, a British court placed on trial the notorious S.S. Leader Josef Kramer. Known as the Beast of Belsen, the defendant and his associates were guilty of the most heinous offenses known in the annals of criminality. Under their jurisdiction were the gas chambers of Auschwitz and the terrible abattoirs of Belsen. Here more than two million people

were degraded and murdered, including some of the first
scientists, scholars and writers of Europe. They had been made
the victims of sadistic experiments, and subjected to the most
monstrous tortures. The practical German mind which thus
had gotten rid of its potential competitors by mass murder
did not neglect to use their cremated remains for fertilizer and
the rendered fats from their bodies for soap, as they first used
the bodies of the doomed women in their military brothels.

The steps taken to insure a fair trial were almost weirdly
exaggerated, and involved with every possible technicality.
The defendants were represented by a Major Winwood, appointed by the British administration for this purpose. He
opened the defense with the declaration: "I have the honor to
represent four of the accused"; and mitigated the actions of
his clients on the score that their victims after all had been
"only the dregs of the ghetto."

With the exception of isolated individuals, most of whom
will be judged by military courts for specific acts against
Anglo-American military personnel, the effort to punish war
criminals bears a suspicious resemblance to the war crimes
fiasco which followed World War I.

As this is written, twenty top-ranking Nazis have been
arraigned for violations of international law. Included among
them are a number of professional soldiers, much to the dis-
concertion of military men the world over.

To create the necessary basis for this action, a new body of
applying law has been supplied by the Inter-American Juridical Committee. It establishes a revolutionary set of regulatory
principles to govern the actions of nations, and to fix the personal responsibility of their officers, who no longer are to
enjoy the immunity formerly granted them. Moreover crimes
antecedent to the inception of the law itself are to be made
responsible to it.

In the introduction of this new and synthetically created

body of doctrine, we observe again the singular fantasy which has gripped the minds of men in these times. Since this so-called international law exists on no stable political order, its jurisdiction is only as good as that of the individual tribunal which handles it; hence its ultimate uses are literally unpredictable. Under the newly devised regulations, crimes against the peace are to consist of "planning, preparation, initiation or waging of a war of aggression, or a war in violation of international treaties, agreements or assurances, or participation in a common plan or conspiracy for the accomplishment of any of the foregoing."

This definition obviously would apply to any nation unfortunate enough to lose a war, and is not necessarily restricted to the brutalities of the Germans and Japanese. The possibilities of interpretation may be seen in the facility with which Mr. Rankin, the representative in Congress from Alabama, contumaciously refers to all opponents as "Communists," or the ease with which Communists themselves discredit all honest opposition as "Fascist."

It is obvious that since this alleged law is responsible only to organized and competing power forms, its interpretation will depend entirely on who it is that calls the tune. The judge will be also the plaintiff, and, *ex necessitati rei*, the party with the greatest armaments.

The prescription sets up the category of war crimes as consisting of "murder, extermination, enslavement, deportation and other inhumane acts committed against any civilian population, before or during the war; or persecutions on political, racial or religious grounds in execution of or in connection with any crime within the jurisdiction of the tribunal, whether or not in violation of the domestic law of the country where perpetrated." As criminals on this score, are included all who participated in the formulation or execution of these acts, whether leaders, organizers or accomplices, as well as the heads

of the state and responsible officials in governmental depart-
ments.

By definition, this certainly would warrant the Poles to
demand the trial of Marshal Stalin, Molotov and General
Voroshilov; or the Indians and Greeks, the apprehension of
King George VI, together with Messrs. Bevin, Eden and
Churchill. It as easily could include the military, civilian and
scientific leaders of the United States for their manufacture
and use of the atomic bomb, which the Japanese have vehe-
mently protested. Without stretching the matter too much, it
certainly would warrant the seizure of such worthies as Gerald
Smith, Father Coughlin and other American preachers of discrimination and violence.

By a modest stretch of logic, it could be considered that the
racial sanctions operated by the white man against Negroes,
Orientals and others, come well within the purview of this
clause. If present Soviet propaganda among these people is
any criterion, Moscow certainly would take this position.

This effort at substituting catechetical doctrine for the
processes of organic authority means merely that force,
whether devoted to moral ends or not, has been clothed with
the dignity of law.

VI

A tendency exists to believe that if the U.N.O. were
"strengthened" by increasing the composite authority of the
organization itself against the individual member-states none
of these difficulties of contradiction would be experienced.
Each of the powers would be constrained to accept the general
decision of the collective body on issues coming before it, and
to adjust its policies to this fact.

The key to the troubles of the infant security league is
adjudged to be the veto power reserved by each of the great
states over the collective actions of the others.

This is a utopian conception which in itself provides ample reason why the veto provision cannot be relinquished by either America or Russia without a guarantee of a majority on the Security Council.

In any kind of league made up of equal members, regardless of the assurances exchanged between them, the world is compelled to be divided into camps. This is due to substantially the same reasons which would apply if the league superstructure were not there. As long as Russia is suspected of harboring a scheme to Communize the world, or suspects the capitalist states of maneuvering to crush her; or as long as there is a British Empire which cuts across the vital interests of many nations, the actions of the great powers will be galvanized by what appears to them to be the nature of their individual interests.

This is not alone due to the cynicism of the politicians and diplomats, but is inherent in the organizational defects of the entire league system. As such it is a mirror of the actual conditions under which social and political structures on this earth are compelled to operate.

As long as nations are divided by the quest for material advantage or by sharply differing social beliefs and objectives, their actions must be a reflection of these facts. The claim that the delegates to the U.N.O. will sit as free agents voting on the issues according to the worth of submitted arguments is altogether illusory. As appointed nominees, they will arrive under instruction; and in no event will make decisions contrary to the wishes of their governments.

If the veto safeguard were eliminated, the power of the U.N.O. in many respects would be superior to that of the American Congress, or in Russia to the Supreme Council of Soviets. The Communist party, all but deified as the guardian of the Revolution, would become just another political organization.

Even if such an abdication were thinkable, if the Communists were in the minority in the coagulating world government they would be in trouble. Their situation would be entirely comparable on a global scale to that of the Red sectors of China, whose clashing disagreements with nationalist China are irremediable under the roof of a common equity and must one day be liquidated by force.

If the shoe were on the other foot and the weight of coercive authority was possessed by a Bolshevik combination, the Western world would feel its institutions menaced and its very life in danger.

There is no possible community of interests existing between the two systems so overmastering as to allow either to submit its fate to the hands of a potentially hostile central body possessed of crushing power, for this is what relinquishment of the veto means.

If the U.N.O. were to be a truly democratic body, the entire problem of authoritative action would have to be removed from the Security Council and brought to the Assembly, where the collective decision would be made by a majority vote. Considering the pattern of military and economic power as it now exists, this is so obviously a piece of nonsense that it scarcely merits discussion.

The league principle was not born with the Wilsonian League of Nations. It has been tried on many occasions before in history and in every case has been found wanting.

Perhaps the earliest of these historic associations to be of consequence was the Amphictyonic Council, made up of a confederation of Greek republics, all of whom had equal votes in the central executive.

Despite the independence of the member states, the latter body possessed considerable authority. It could discipline its members, decide controversies between them, and employ the full force of the confederacy against the disobedient.

The outcome, as we are told by Madison and Hamilton in their classic *Federalist* papers, was that the more powerful members kept the others "in awe and subordination" tyrannizing successively over them. "The smaller members, though entitled by the theory of their system to revolve in equal pride and majesty around the common center," were reduced to satellites of the two big member states, Athens and Sparta, which "became first rivals and then enemies." In the end, the liberties of Greece crashed as a result of their mutual struggles.

In Europe itself, previous to the League of Nations, there existed another league, startlingly similar in power principles to the structure which has emerged from the San Francisco Conference. This was the old Concert of Europe, created in 1815 at the Congress of Vienna.

When one compares the machinery and background of the Concert of Europe with that of the United Nations Organization, it is amazing to notice the similarities. The leading powers of the time were genuinely determined to effect a condition of permanent balance among themselves. Assurances were exchanged and an article written into the compact binding the great states to meet at fixed intervals and to arrive at a peaceful settlement of all problems.

This arrangement looked forward to the final disarmament of the warring nations of Europe, which then contained the central power apparatus of the world. It proposed the establishment of a permanent international court built on the authority of a code of law which all the countries would be obliged to respect.

The Concert of Europe ended in the expected clash of interests. It became an instrument of extreme reaction, in which the conservative and monarchial elements sought to prevent the spread of democratic revolutionary movements. England, which then sympathized with these new dynamic forces, was compelled to withdraw from the Concert, just as it may be expected that Russia will be compelled to withdraw from the United Nations Organization if her activities are not protected by the veto device.

VII

A prime example of the unrealistic quality of the league principle, even where it extends into the actual realm of confederation, is contained in the experiences of the American states prior to the founding of the present Federal Republic in 1787.

Until that time, the states composing the union consisted of thirteen separate and individual sovereignties conjoined with each other in a so-called League of Friendship. As in the case of the League of Nations, and the U.N.O., they were linked to the common union by a group of multilateral security agreements, for the purposes of their "common defense, the security of their liberties, and their mutual and general welfare."

The theoretical authority of the "union" on paper far exceeded any powers which might conceivably be relinquished by the member states of the United Nations Security Council to the world union. The American union possessed many of the trappings of government. It could send and receive ambassadors, was empowered to establish a uniform system of weights and measures, regulate Indian affairs and settle disputes between the states. It possessed, however, in common with the United Nations Organization this fatal defect: it was a union of nations, rather than of people. It could not levy taxes, or in other ways deal directly with the individuals it essayed to govern.

Armed forces were raised by the states individually, who appointed all officers of or under the rank of colonel. The expenses of war, though defrayed from a common treasury, were "supplied by the several states in proportion to the value of all land within each state," by taxation levied directly by themselves.

The Congress met on the first Monday in November in every year. Each of the states was entitled to one vote.

On every important act it was necessary to secure the assent of a majority of the assembled states, which meant that these votes had to be ratified by their respective legislatures.

It was soon apparent that the states had a charter, but no unity. The Congress found itself weak and ineffectual. Matters of the most critical importance became the subject of interminable debate. The net result was any number of pious resolutions, but "Washington's armies were left to perish of cold and hunger."[5]

The system resulted, wrote Hamilton, in "slow and scanty levies of men in the most critical emergencies of our affairs; short enlistments at an unparalleled expense, [and] continual fluctuations in the troops, ruinous to their discipline and subjecting the public safety frequently to the perilous crisis of a disbanded army."[6] "The States near the seat of war, influenced by motives of self-preservation, made efforts to furnish their quotas which even exceeded their abilities; while those at a distance from danger were, for the most part, as remiss as the others were diligent. . . ."[7]

Under the league system, Hamilton continued, it would "rarely happen that the delinquency to be redressed would be confined to a single member; and if there were more than one who had neglected their duty, a similarity of situation would induce them to unite for common defense. . . ." In the end, this "would amount to a war between parts of the Confederacy concerning the infractions of a League, in which the strongest combination would be most likely to prevail, whether it con-

[5] John F. Hoyland, *Federate or Perish*, p. 45.
[6] *The Federalist*, pp. 127-128.
[7] *Ibid*, p. 92.

sisted of those who supported or of those who resisted the general authority."[8]

Rivalry grew rapidly among the states; and soon it became difficult to secure a quorum to the Congress altogether. "After the first of March, 1781, so irregular were the states in attendance and so swiftly grew the spirit of apathy toward the Confederation, it was practically impossible to obtain the consent of nine states to any proposition."[9]

In June, 1783, a mutiny of Pennsylvania troops besieged the State house in Philadelphia where the Continental Congress met. The Congress was forced to flee, and convened in Princeton, New Jersey. Its unpopularity was such that from Princeton it went to Annapolis and then to Trenton, New York, and Lancaster. It became, says Thorpe, "a wandering council without the protection of a strong national sentiment."[10] Indeed, the Congress was often called "a foreign government" and violently castigated in the debates of the various state assemblies.

By 1785, General Knox wrote to Washington that the rivalry and even hostility among the states was so intense that "the different States not only have different views on the same subjects, but some of them have views that sooner or later must involve the country in all the horrors of civil war."[11]

The states began to make laws against one another for the promotion of their trade, and high tariffs were laid between them. Massachusetts and New Hampshire adopted mutually reciprocal sanctions prohibiting the export of such commodities as rum, textiles and leather. New Jersey insisted that her commerce should not be subject to tax when entering the port

[8] *Ibid*, pp. 94-95.
[9] Francis Newton Thorpe, *The Constitutional History of the United States*, Vol. I, p. 246.
[10] Francis Newton Thorpe, *The Constitutional History of the United States*, Vol. I, p. 252.
[11] Allan Nevins, *The American States during and after the Revolution, 1775-1789*, p. 546.

of New York, and finally sent an ultimatum to the Congress insisting that it would pay no part of its quota to the revenue of the Confederation unless interstate commerce were regulated to its own advantage.

When in an effort to settle the terrible quarrels over the question of the navigation of the Mississippi, Congress attempted a solution, the southern states threatened immediately to secede and to return to the British Empire; "whereupon the Northern States threatened secession unless the proposals were accepted!"[12]

Connecticut was quarreling with every one of her neighbors over territorial questions. An invasion by the militia of Pennsylvania over the frontiers of that state resulted in a massacre. Pennsylvania also was on the verge of war with Virginia over whether the better route to Fort Duquesne (now Pittsburgh) was through Pennsylvania or through the latter state. One American brigadier wrote that "the Pennsylvania and New England troops would as soon fight each other as the British." Sectional feeling was so high that even George Washington was enabled to write of the New Englanders that "they are an exceedingly dirty and nasty people."

Debtors wandered from state to state, taxes were prohibitive; money issued by the Congress dropped to less than two cents on the dollar. The whole internal situation degenerated into one of upheaval and disorder. The unrest, mutinies, and disregard for central authority finally culminated in the abortive movement known as Shays's Rebellion. Shays, a former captain in the Continental Army, had organized the farmers of Massachusetts for revolt. Governor Bowdoin collected a body of militia, chiefly from the wealthy and college students, to meet the outbreak.

This was the last straw. When the Constitutional Conven-

[12] John F. Hoyland, *Federate or Perish*, p. 48.

tion of 1787 finally met, the fortunes of the united colonies had fallen to their lowest ebb.

The contempt of the states for the national administrative machinery was so great, wrote Alexander Hamilton, that "Congress at this time scarcely possesses the means of keeping up the forms of administration. . . . Each State, yielding to the persuasive voice of immediate interest or convenience, has successively withdrawn its support, till the frail and tottering edifice seems ready to fall upon our heads, and to crush us beneath its ruins."

VIII

The cause of these failures is not hard to find. It involves, in each case, a confusion in the meaning of terms, and the nature of the sovereign state itself.

The illogic of its approach lies in the contention that a confederation of states functioning under limited articles of agreement is comparable to an actual government in its capacity to lay down law and execute its decisions. This is as much as to say that an eagle is a bird; a sparrow is a bird; therefore they are both birds: therefore a sparrow is an eagle.

This line of reasoning is based on an attempted comparison of the authority and duties of the league members to the authority and powers of the courts existing domestically in the various countries.

It is assumed that there can be placed into operation an international police body, springing from the co-operative will of the nations to enforce an enduring peace. This police body immediately would act against any aggressor who dared to challenge the orderly processes of law. Thus, the right to take the law into its own hands by any nation would no longer be an attribute of sovereignty, but only of the community of nations.

Even if one were to grant all the intervening questions

which on the table appear to be completely unanswerable, the problem of reducing national sovereignty to workable proportions, without at the same time substituting an international authority which would rule by virtue of its own control of the instruments of power, is an impossible one to solve.

The central principle of any type of law enforcement which is designed to work is that the federal law must be superior to any competitive law which can be provided by the member states themselves. There can be no limitation in the nature of the power of law, but only in the character of its extent. The whole mechanism of authority compels it to have jurisdiction wherever lawful government legitimately can apply.

A society which cannot regulate trade between state and state, control levies on imports and exports, tax its subjects, or in other ways maintain its own supreme jurisdiction, has no government and hence can have no law.

This was sensed by the brilliant Hamilton when he bluntly informed the American Constitutional Convention that "the great and radical vice in the construction of the existing Confederation is in the principle of *legislation for states or governments, in their corporate or collective capacities*, as contradistinguished from the *individuals* of which they consist . . . . the consequence of this is, that though in theory their resolutions concerning those objects [to be attained] are laws, constitutionally binding on the members of the Union, *yet in practice they are mere recommendations which the states observe or disregard at their option*."

Both by reason of equity and logic, it is necessary to reject the idea of the collective conscience and responsibility of nations. The federal law, wherever it is to exist, must reach for its authority directly to the consent of the individual subjects.

Nothing could be more erroneous than to make a compari-

son of the processes of municipal law with those of so-called
international law. Only the individual possesses a social conscience or the moral sense which makes him susceptible to
control by law, and it is only the individual who can be made
the object of police power. His relationship to the central
authority is based on a complex set of conditioning factors.
At bottom is the fact that the individual easily can be controlled. He does not possess interests antagonistic to those of
the commonwealth itself, nor does he have at his disposal the
means of successfully resisting the decisions of the central
authority by force.

Quite contrary to the influences acting upon nations, the
innumerable social constraints which press upon the individual
from all sides compel him to subordinate his acts to the common welfare. The authority of the state stems from this type
of social conditioning, and from the fact that appellants know
decisions will be enforced. Lawbreakers have no choice but
to accept the determination of a judicial or punitive authority,
even though its findings may be bitterly resented.

A nation is in an entirely different category. Far from being
the subject of law, it only can be dealt with by that mutual
consent embodied in a treaty between equal members.

Treaties as often as not are the result of the exercise of force
or the threat of it on states which have no alternative but to
yield. A certain amount of fraud in negotiating compacts
between states also is considered legitimate. It is a recognized
principle that "a nation need not disclose the weak spots in
its own armor."[13]

By their nature treaties are subject to alteration from time to
time as the interests and leadership of the affected states
change. Intrinsically no treaty is capable of enduring beyond
the immediate self-interests of the nations which made it. Its
effect on the peoples of these states is indirect, and is in no

[13] Lord Birkenhead, *International Law*, 5th ed., p. 141.

way comparable to that of domestic law by which the limit tolerances of antisocial attitude are fixed.

Since a sovereign state is a power form, it and no one else can rule the conditions of life which apply to its citizens. This logic is implicit in the use of the term "sovereign." As long as a state remains sovereign, it is compelled to be guided solely by its own self-interests or by the pressures of internal groups acting upon its policies.

The conception of sovereignty not only involves the idea of equality but that of independent action as well. By maintaining armies, navies and batteries of diplomats, and by control over its own currency, trade and immigration laws, each nation-state serves notice that, in the last analysis, it will seek to gain its ends either by the use or continued threat of force. It will make and break the rules to suit itself, and wherever its vital interests are challenged will have recourse to subterfuge, conspiratorial action or, if necessary, brute force.

As long as each nation is able to determine by its own measurements, without subordination to any superior authority, the policies it is to pursue in connection with tariff, trade, immigration, commerce and labor, its statesmen will endeavor to exact the utmost from whatever bargaining position they happen to find themselves in. If in the course of economic or mercantile rivalry, conditions arise which lead to the use of force, this will be considered legitimate, since the nations utilizing force will feel that they have been driven to it, and that their vital interests are at stake.

Irrespective of treaty commitments, other nations will be guided by similar considerations, wherever a state of hostilities exists among their neighbors. If their welfare is to be served by participation in the struggle, a reason will be found to enter it. If because of weakness or the prospect of profit, the state elects to remain neutral, it may do so without lack of moral tone, even though one of the belligerents is the victim and the other obviously the aggressor.

The shifting fate of treaty arrangements is pictured in the history of all alliances which ever have been made between so-called equal states. No one has ever been fulfilled beyond the self-interests of the stronger party to the arrangement. The attitude is accurately given by Lenin, a charmingly direct and forthright man, on the occasion of the return of the Russian delegation from Brest Litovsk at the end of World War I, after having been forced to agree to a ruinous treaty with Germany. When the document was laid before him, Lenin did not even bother about reading it. He remarked: "I don't intend to fulfill it anyway, except insofar as I am forced."

The professional diplomat who may be a most moral and decent individual in his personal relationships, must by the character of his task adopt the same impersonal view toward the struggle of mass hordes as is assumed by a military commander in battle. In their essence these attitudes are given squarely in a comment by Thucydides in his classic, *The Peloponnesian War*. Answering a contention of ethical right raised by the people of Melos following an invasion of their country by Athens, the Melians were coolly informed: "Right, as the world goes, is only a question between equals in power. The strong do what they are able, and the weak suffer what they must."

In the United States in the very midst of the Dumbarton Oaks discussions, we find the House Foreign Affairs Committee calling on the government to use military force and to ride roughshod over treaties if required, to secure any Nazi war criminal who managed to find safety in a neutral country. This remarkable resolution called on the United States to join with the other allies "in the use of such means as may be necessary—irrespective of the limitations of any treaties of extradition—to secure the person or property of those persons determined to be war criminals, who have already fled or who may hereafter flee to any neutral nation, or any other nation that may harbor them or afford them a place of asylum."

This cold demand, of course, is simply another exposition of that most ancient of dogmas, that a good end justifies a bad means; but it does not express the faith or reliance in the processes of law which must be expected if such an instrument as the San Francisco Charter is to survive.

A review of the current world situation provides ample proof of the transient nature of the assurances given by the nation-states to each other, and of the progressive deterioration which ultimately must overtake the covenants and pledges in which they are contained.

We need look no further than our agreements with the wartime government of Yugoslavia; and the facility with which the statesmen of the United States and Britain supported first the Minister of War in that government, Draga Mikhailovich; and then under pressure from Moscow, outlawed Mikhailovich and recognized the Soviet-sponsored Marshal Tito Broz.

By these means we acquiesced in the progressive destruction of the legal government of Yugoslavia, which had fought on our side from the beginning, and acknowledged the prior interests of the Soviet Union in the Yugoslav territories.

Diplomacy, also, saw nothing unusual to fighting first for the territorial integrity of Poland[14] against the German invader, and then forsaking that principle in favor of the alleged security needs of the Russians, who reduced this causal ally of the war to the status of a satrapy of their empire.

It is interesting to observe that the compacts which guar-

[14] Poland had been offered the alternative of "honorable vassalage" by Berlin; and resisted the German war machine under the same urgent promptings from London which later were given to the government of King Peter of Yugoslavia.

anteed the independent existence of Poland had been recorded under the collective authority of the League of Nations. One of these was a nonaggression pact between Poland and Russia, signed in 1932. Another was a similar engagement between Poland and its neighbor, Germany, in 1934.

In August of 1939, the Soviets unexpectedly exploded one of history's great bombshells in the shape of their accord with Germany. This constituted a limited Russo-German partnership, in which each of the parties agreed to refrain from the use of force against the other for a period of ten years, and to give neither aid nor support to other powers whose acts might threaten the interests of either.

This agreement was followed almost immediately by a Russo-German invasion of Poland. Despite the treaties which bound both countries to the Polish Republic, the two partners in this new enterprise announced that Poland had ceased forever to exist, and proceeded to divide the territories of that unhappy country between them. This partition was solemnly ratified by still another agreement between the victors marking out each other's gains.

When despite the assurances of eternal friendship exchanged between them, Germany invaded the Soviet Union in turn, the compact partitioning the Polish Republic was repudiated. A series of new treaties were signed by which Russia recognized the Polish government-in-exile as the legal government of Poland, and agreed to the restoration of all territories seized from the prostrate Polish state. By these documents, which made a great deal of to-do about "respect for international law," the two countries bound themselves in indissoluble concord, and became military allies.

Soon after, the Russians repudiated their engagements to the Polish government-in-exile and installed their own puppet regime at Warsaw.

After the meetings at Teheran and Yalta, we find a *de facto* arrangement entered into whereby the Anglo-Americans concede the eastern third of Poland to be the property of the Soviet Union, together with the three Baltic republics; all of this without discussion with the existing governments of these states, with whom we officially were allied.

In return Moscow agreed to release its hold over the balance of Poland, and to allow the creation of a democratic regime in which the Polish government-in-exile would participate.

Not more than two weeks after, Madame Tomasz Arciszewski, wife of the Premier of the Polish government-in-exile, was arrested by the Russian police in Poland and held as a political undesirable. When the British government raised a vigorous protest, the lady was released. But a few hours later, the principal resident supporter of the Polish government-in-exile, Prince Janusz Radziwill, leader of the Polish conservative party, was arrested by Russian police and deported. The Polish underground was ruthlessly exterminated as a competitive and dangerous force, though from British standards these were the prime patriots of Poland. A great part of the remaining Polish intelligentsia which had managed to survive the German occupation was now systematically liquidated and deported to unknown destinations in the East.

As the Russian teeth began to grind down on the torn body of Poland, the statesmen of Great Britain and the United States, having weighed carefully the Russian intention as well as the will to carry it out, saw no further choice open to them but to agree. They now jettisoned their ally, the Polish government-in-exile, and accepted the new puppet regime as unavoidable.

In his classic speech to Commons covering the situation, Mr. Churchill exculpated the Russian action on the basis of Russia's legitimate need for a security zone. He did not explain the fact that security was supposed to have been provided for by the new United Nations Organization.

Great Britain itself has followed a somewhat similar course in making sure of its own security needs. We find our small ally, Greece, treated as if it were a conquered country, its freedom crushed and an unwanted form of government imposed on it. Here the patriots who fought the war through on our side have been disarmed, and ex-collaborationists and known reactionary elements armed. All real decisions are made by British officials or their appointees, just as is the case in India, Iraq, or Palestine.

Indeed, wherever their material welfare seemed to be involved, no one of the great powers has hesitated to abandon its pledges, sometimes when the ink had hardly dried on the paper. We observe in Rumania, Bulgaria, Italy, Yugoslavia, Germany, Austria and elsewhere, the identical phenomenon of power action.

Though the powers had mutually promised each other that there would be no interference by them in the internal life of any of the countries, they continued to operate with all of the furtive secrecy and unilateral surprise action which always has characterized the jungle of international diplomacy.

This situation has proceeded despite the agreements which emerged from the historic meetings at Yalta, Teheran, Moscow and Potsdam. It is also despite a formal contract of mutual assistance entered into between Britain and Russia on May 26, 1942. Under this treaty of alliance, which is to run for twenty years, the high contracting parties agree to be bound by the twin principles of "not seeking territorial aggrandizement for themselves, and of noninterference in the internal affairs of other States." "Each High Contracting Party undertakes not to conclude any alliance and not to take part in any coalition directed against the other High Contracting Party"; and to render each other all possible assistance, economic, political or otherwise which would enable them to take "common action to preserve peace and resist aggression in the post-war period."

Yet it cannot be doubted that the great rivals in this period are none other than the high contracting parties themselves, who are moving with vicious though carefully concealed intent to mousetrap each other, as against the ultimate showdown encounter each feels to be inevitable.

An excellent example is contained in the insistent Russian pressure on Turkey, as well as in the equally firm counter-pressures exerted by Britain to thwart it.

In the late summer of 1945, the Kremlin instituted against Turkey the familiar pattern of action undertaken wherever an authoritarian state has cast its designs upon a small neighbor. A bitter and vituperous campaign of accusation was started in the Soviet press, characterizing the Turkish government as being composed of Fascists and banditti. Soon after, and despite the pyramid of agreements which had resulted in the San Francisco Charter, the Soviets demanded of Istanbul that it relinquish to them the Transcaucasian districts of Kars, Artvin and Ardahan, the great Turkish naval base at Iznik, as well as bases in Smyrna and on the strategic Mediterranean islands which patrol the entrance to the Straits. The Kremlin also sought a revision of the Montreaux Convention in favor of the U.S.S.R., and a corridor through Turkish Thrace to the Aegean for the new Russian satellite, Bulgaria.

In undertaking this action against the Turks, the Kremlin not only had to ignore the terms of its treaty with Great Britain,[15] whose interests were vitally involved, but also to vacate still another nonaggression agreement existing between itself and the Turkish state.

[15] Had these exactions been agreed to by the Turks, the British immediately would have faced the unpalatable fact that the Mediterranean lifeline to Asia and the Middle East was imperiled, with Iran, Iraq and the entire Levant placed under irresistible Russian pressure.

Another such denunciation of a sacred obligation, though this time more to our liking, occurred when Moscow renounced its neutrality pact with Japan in the spring of 1945.

From the date of its inception on April 13, 1941, until its denunciation on April 13, 1945, this pact had been scrupulously observed. As late as March 30, 1944, an additional convention had been signed between the two nations involving important commercial exchanges which were to continue for a period of five years. Nevertheless, when it was seen that Japan was on the point of collapse, the Soviet Union to enforce its own historic interests in this section of the globe, declared war and invaded. The explanation offered by Moscow was that "the pact of neutrality between Japan and the U.S.S.R. has lost its meaning." The Kremlin saw its justification in the neat discovery that Japan "was fighting Russia's allies and had aided Germany in the war against the U.S.S.R."

IX

The cynical quality of these power actions has been thrown into glaring perspective by the advent of the new weirdly devastating agencies of destruction at which the world now stands aghast. Power procedures of this type and the atom bomb simply do not fit together into the same kind of universe. They represent an antagonism in logic which nowhere can be reconciled.

Where once they were merely reprehensible, these actions now are sinister in the extreme, and make for a world in which anything can happen, without warning and with explosive force.

It is possible that had the Russians been first to discover the bomb, all the world might now be well on its way to Communism. However reasonable this assumption might appear as an interpretation of preceding events, it still is a matter of conjecture and perhaps of prejudice. The hard fact remains that it is the Anglo-Americans who hold the bomb, and who by their possession of it have placed the world on notice that collective security is a delusion.

The existing condition amounts to an almost complete abandonment of the principles of the San Francisco Charter in favor of the power of unlimited force in the hands of two of its signatories. The fact that these two states conceive of themselves as impressively moral and judicial in their outlook, in no sense alters the situation or ameliorates its unpleasant qualities.

The new situation is assessed frankly by the British Foreign Secretary, Mr. Ernest Bevin, in the candid observation that "a great many of the assumptions on which we worked in San Francisco will have to be radically revised."

Winston Churchill, one of the principal architects of the Charter, now coolly informs Russia and the world that "the bomb brought peace." He speaks in open castigation of "Communist forces which have obtained or are in the process of obtaining dictatorial powers" in Europe. He asks of the United States that they "act up to the level of their power and responsibility, not for themselves but for all men in all lands."

Both the meaning and intent of the great English statesman's language are no longer burdened with the customary diplomatic obliqueness, but are crystal clear: the time is short; the situation is grave; the mutual enemy as incorrigible as ever. In the tight little period allowed to Anglo-American military predominance, "we must remold the relationships of all men and all nations in such a way that these men do not wish, or dare, to fall upon each other for the sake of vulgar, out-dated ambition, or for passionate differences in ideology, and that international bodies by supreme authority may give peace on earth and justice among men."

Behind this curtain of doubletalk, the Russians will see a determination to utilize the current advantage conferred by the bomb for the purpose of securing an impregnable British position on the entire Eurasian scene. The Russian fears that the new United Nations Organization would be used as an adjunct to Anglo-American policy and for the purposes of policing the U.S.S.R. thus are given some substance.

Though they themselves have set the prime example in power maneuvering, the Russians are entitled to state on the ethical premises of the San Francisco meeting: "It was understood between us that we all were to share in the responsibilities for a free world, and that the use of force was to be the collective obligation of the nations. If you do not now give us the secret of the bomb, it will mean that our worst suspicions are justified and that your intentions toward us are bad. Therefore, our actions in perfecting our own security sphere for which we have been so much criticized, are not censurable at all but totally vindicated by events."

In the presence of such absolute instruments of power as the atomic bomb, the whole system of pretense on which the United Nations Organization is founded splits to pieces. When Mr. Truman announced that the bomb was such a terrifying and devastating instrument that it must be kept as a secret of the Anglo-American powers lest it fall into the hands of those who would wreak measureless havoc on the world, he was in effect making a declaration of old-time isolationist philosophy. He was announcing an Anglo-American determination to keep the peace against the interests and purposes of the balance of mankind, if necessary. By unmistakable logic he was expressing the disbelief of Americans in the world security system they had helped to create.

As far as other peoples are concerned, Anglo-American possession of the bomb deprives the world security system of any suggestion of security it might ever have contained. It is unrealistic to assume that nations competitive to us can bear the same easy confidence in our ability to requite this awful responsibility, as we ourselves.

As moral as our nation undoubtedly is, no one who ever has felt the weight of our mass production competition can delude himself about our determination to maintain our own security and living standards at all costs. These will come first no matter who else is affected. As for our British partner, it hardly would be possible to convince France, Greece or Egypt that she was incapable of aggression; or Africa and the Orient that aggression was not implicit in the very imperial system of which Britain is the chief exponent.

The other side of the problem is even more difficult and obscure. The suggestion that we can make the situation good by giving away the secret of the bomb's manufacture, has little to recommend it. If no reliable world authority exists to take it into custody, we will have succeeded only in equipping potential rivals with the results of our military research and experience. If such a course is sensible at all, it should apply not only to the bomb, but to *all military secrets as well as armaments*, which on the face of it would have to be discontinued as a burden to the American people and a menace to the world.

In principle, if it is possible to ban the use or manufacture of atomic weapons, it is possible to ban the use and manufacture of all lethal machinery which might be used for the purpose of mass murder.

Examination of this prospect shows it to involve a strict international control of armaments; as well as a rigid inspection system over the manufacturing plants of all nations. There would have to be a careful check on all fissionable raw materials capable of being converted into atomic energy, and, presumably, a program of licensing for productive use.

It may be assumed that neither complaint nor indictment of the guilty can usefully be made to the domestic courts of the impeached country, but only to some authorized international tribunal, capable of enforcing its decisions.

The system of regulation required to control the bomb

would be tighter than that now maintained by the government of the United States over the activities of any of its forty-eight members. An international apparatus capable of performing this function obviously must possess an authority over the nations at least equal to that of the American Federal government in its relation to the several states.

This brings us back directly to our three basic judgments:

1. Sovereignty and the proposed controls are mutually self-annulling. They cannot both exist. Just as a woman cannot be slightly pregnant or a living creature slightly dead, a nation cannot be partly sovereign. It either is sovereign or it is not sovereign.

2. If a world order emanating from the jurisdiction of a central world authority is to be brought about, it can proceed only from a community of world interests. This community actually does not yet exist except through the negative instrumentality of the bomb.

3. A genuine solution of the fundamental world impasse can come solely through removal of the fundamental imbalances which now give weight to the business of power politics. These imbalances cannot be corrected by charters, by pledges or by declarations of common solidarity. They rest on:-

   (a) the glaring and increasingly unequal distribution of opportunity, power and natural wealth among the nations, the disrelation of the forces acting to shape their national existence, and the consequent incongruity of their aims, interests and goals.

   (b) the massive prejudices and irreconcilable social concepts which sharply mark off great sectors of the world's peoples from each other.

The conditions of mutual self-interest which operated to unite the American provinces plainly do not exist on a world scale, whereas certain opposing conditions of mutual repugnancy do exist. As long as Caucasian imperialism continues, or the dynamic and historic sense actuating the Russians differs radically from our own, the establishment of an autonomous world authority is a practical impossibility.

This does not mean that these peoples are possessed of some evil genius or are necessarily antisocial. It may be accepted that most of them are like ourselves, affected by the circumstances around them, and are neither demons nor angels.

X

The attempt to outlaw weapons and engines of war has been made a number of times before in history. At no time has it ever succeeded. The Hague Tribunal forbade the dropping of missiles from balloons and aircraft. The Second Lateran Council in 1139 attempted to ban the then most deadly of weapons, the crossbow, as an instrument "hateful to God and unfit for Christian use."

The single triumph of international compact in this direction is that covering the use of poison gas. The reluctance to utilize this lethal medium, one may believe, was a matter more of expediency than of humanity, for its efficient use would require absolute control of the air, enabling it to be laid down in great air barrages. This neither the Nazis nor the Japanese possessed; while our own armies could not be the first to use this weapon out of deference to a conditioned public opinion at home. Though they did not risk its use on the battlefield for fear of a merciless retaliation in kind, the Nazis did murder several million Jews by this means back of the lines.

The proposal to outlaw the bomb is based on a false impression of the problem, which ascribes to law and justice powers independent of the material pattern by which human existence is organizable. It represents a confusion of the goals of morality with the circumstances of government and bears little real relation to those fundamental issues which must be determined if the world is to be at peace.

This tendency to confound law with force and to consider it as independent of government and politics, has resulted in the fantastic conclusion that the so-called "rule of law" is capable of resting on a disembodied ethical base independent of the immediate or real interests of the participant states themselves.

The assumption is made that by an integration of common purposes with so-called international law, "we shall transfer our differences from the turbulent political atmosphere of self-interest to the purer, serener air of impartial justice."[16]

While it is true that law may be imposed by the sword, in a normal self-governing society it can exist only by the consent of the individual to whom it is applied and whose interests it purports to regulate. The formula is simple: law can only proceed from government and government implies supremacy.

What we choose to term international law is based on treaties which, in turn, form the contract law of states. It follows that international law by its own terms is an imposture. Indeed the celebrated legal authority, Lord Birkenhead, states that due to the intrinsic unenforceability of international law, "all rules are of the nature of suggestions for the guidance of conduct." [17] The authority of these regulations evidently rests on little more than an appeal to the better nature of men.

XI

Despite the serious and apparently unbridgeable inconsistencies involved, the important fundamental in which the present league is expected to differ from its predecessor is in the use of armed force against aggressors.

Here we come to a most disconcerting question: a regula-

[16] Professor Carr, *The Twenty Years Crisis*, p. 219.
[17] *International Law*, p. 141.

tion which applies to sovereignties does not possess the same values as that which affects the individual citizen under domestic law. Its coercive power is far less, and it is subject to such interpretation as organized social units habitually have given concerns which affected their own interests.

It will be seen that aggression itself becomes a matter of definition. Hitler accused Poland of being the aggressor in the recent war, asserting that Germany has acted only in its own defense after extreme provocation. The Nazi Fuehrer fulminated against Beneš of Czechoslovakia, and described that gentleman in his speeches as a dangerous plotter and war criminal. Japan stentoriously nominated the Chinese resistance forces both as aggressors and Quislings devoted to the wicked interests of European exploiter-states. Tokyo represented itself as being the heroic cutting edge in the great flaming sword of Asiatic freedom, and referred to its military forces as armies of liberation.

The British speak of the dispossessed Greek patriots as aggressors, and of the desperate and virtually outlawed Palestine Jews as "terrorists." When the sixteen leaders of the Polish democratic, agrarian and socialist parties were taken by the Russian authorities by a ruse similar to that employed by the United States against the unlucky Seminole chief, Osceola, they were termed the leaders of an aggressive plot against the Soviet Union. It is a simple and understandable piece of logic that according to the findings of a Moscow court, the effort of these Polish leaders to prevent their native land from falling under foreign domination constituted an actual act of aggression.

Is it not plain that wherever the rule of force applies, the aggressor officially never can be the fellow with the biggest armaments and the will to use them? It is not likely that he will allow himself to be proved in the wrong in any case.

Once the capacity to enforce law is identified with a specific set of national interests, the law itself ceases to have any more validity than did the Weimar Constitution under the Nazis.

The rule of force can at no point be reconciled with the rudiments of law. There is a total disrelation between the two in principle, involving two mutually exclusive ideas. Professor Borchard observes that to try to make force legal by internationalizing it is to attempt the conversion of politics into law. This invokes the unworkable theory of a "just war," subjecting every disfavored nation to the threat of punitive regulation.[18]

As we have observed, as long as a state is sovereign, its requirements are decided by its own geographic, military, social and economic position. By virtue of its sovereignty, it is compelled to be its own judge as to the needs of its citizens and their relationship to the world. Large collections of individuals such as compose the nation-state develop group loyalties which are capable of being invoked. Since they are able to offer organized resistance to any action contrary to that dictated by their own will, and also have the spirit to do so, what is required for their control is not police, but military power.

A strong nation cannot be managed by law. It only can be coerced by superior military power in the hands of other states. For this reason, no useful analogy can be drawn with the type of restraint imposed on individual persons under domestic statutes. None of this can apply to the mass machinery of war involved in the military actions of states against each other.

When it comes down to the question of actual coercion or policing, wherever a large state is concerned the job cannot be accomplished short of a global war. The big state and its allies, in or out of a league, will resist.

[18] Professor Edwin Borchard, *American Journal of International Law,* January, 1943.

If, for example, it were the United States which had to be policed, a matter which for the sake of nicety must be considered, it would require the total resources and combined industrial establishments of all the other states even to attempt the job as long as our air power retained its present superiority.

As the potential blueprint is outlined under the Charter, all member nations are obliged to "hold immediately available national air force contingents for combined international enforcement action." Plans for the application of armed force are to be made by the Security Council, with the assistance of a Military Staff Committee appointed for this purpose.

It seems reasonable to believe that no one of the states is going to consent to the use of its armed forces against itself, or for the purpose of bashing in the heads of its friends. It is also clear that until an actual world government is established and the prior authority of the states abolished, the basic loyalty of the legions at the disposal of the United Nations Supreme Command would not be that command but the governments of the participant states.

It must follow, too, that war against any powerful enemy means total mobilization; hence, a punitive expedition automatically would involve control over the internal affairs of each of the loyal states. There would have to be restrictions on raw material, changes in the taxation systems, and a wartime conversion of factories to the use of the military.

Such a situation would appear to make mandatory the free consent of the peoples concerned and their enthusiastic regard for the war. If one is to judge the antecedents of the spirit of sacrifice from the historical record, there would have to be a mass transfer of loyalties from the present nation-states to the central world command.

What is latent in all these assumptions is the implication that the fellow with the big stick also possesses moral authority to make the decisions which are to pass under the term of "effective collective measures for the prevention and removal of threats to the peace." It is inferred that those states which are deemed to have broken the covenant are to have their skulls cracked by the use of force in the control of the more righteous states.

The nations in whose hands these vast responsibilities are laid are not the more ethical or even the most populous ones. They are simply the wielders of the most effective military power, on which they place an almost complete reliance. Thus the real areas of authority remain where they were before, in the hands of the countries with the biggest air fleets, armies and munitions industries.

There is no way to get around the fact that the issue involved in the handling of police power by a league is not the introduction of law, but the settlement of political questions by force.

No solution which comprehends the regular prospect of armed intervention by one set of states in the affairs of others is worth its salt to humanity. It represents a frank reliance on the old creed of the mailed fist, which has been responsible for much of the present crisis. Such a state of affairs is a continuous implementation of the doctrine that might makes right. All that can be proved by these means is that the victor possesses the heaviest artillery, the best airplanes or the most scientific type of bomb.

XII

To those possessed of a dynamic and historic sense it is apparent that when there is too much talk of peace it is already the beginning of war. It reflects the uneasiness of humanity, which feels war coming but does not wish to admit it.

Even in the early flush of enthusiasm for the Charter its

disrelation to the real situation made necessary a dual interpretation of identical circumstances, the one supplying a rational offset to the other. The existence of this strange duality in respect to the U.N.O. is indicated by a host of pronouncements. One of these is contained in a magazine article by Harry Hopkins, at the time an outstanding American advocate of the United Nations Organization. Written in the midst of the deliberations which gave birth to the Charter, Hopkins asserted that our nation must "accept a new and tough concept of world affairs. . . . The earth is not civilized enough to make world-wide disarmament practical for peace-loving nations."

In a similar vein, and during the same period, General of the Army H. H. Arnold described the United States as constituting the "first target" of the next world aggressor, and asserted that for this reason our nation must remain "the world's first power in military aviation."

Even the Charter's official engineer, the then Secretary of State, Edward Stettinius, did not consider it awry to state on the eve of its completion that the success or failure of the new security organization *would depend on the ability of the U.S.A. and the U.S.S.R. to get along together.* If their interests clashed, there would be war and the U.N.O. would fall apart. If, on the other hand, they managed to agree, it was clear that either or both could be guilty of the worst crimes in the human calendar, and that the United Nations Organization would continue to go through the motions of preserving the peace.

The Soviet journal *Izvestia*[19] expresses a similar view, warning that just as "victory in the war against Hitler Germany *depended on the unity of the three leading world powers, the U.S.S.R., Great Britain and the United States, on their close cooperation depends the fate of the peace.*"

It will be noted that there is no reference to international

[19] Issue of July 11, 1945; reprinted in the Information Bulletin of the Embassy of the U.S.S.R. in Washington, July, 1945.

law, despite the great to-do which had preceded at the San Francisco Conference. Here is a frank recognition of a three-power world, unequivocally rooted in old-fashioned power diplomacy.

Whatever construction may be placed on all this, at least it does not represent an acknowledgment of the supremacy of law. It is an admission on the part of the world's most authoritative men that the security question is far from solved and that the best we may be able to hope for may be a new armaments race and a contest for power within the U.N.O. itself.

It is reasonable to expect under these circumstances that neither the Americans nor Russians will let down their guard, and that Chinese, British, Indian, and Argentine reasoning follows in kind, limited only by the difficulties of implementation.

It may even be suspected that the world is on the verge of a new armaments race of heartbreaking proportions and on that total scale peculiar to the demands of a scientific age.

Though the United States is in the throes of ostentatious disarmament it is accompanied by the disquietude and alarm of its most competent thinkers. We have retained a meaningful control of such superdestructive agencies as the atomic bomb, jet-propelled robot planes and great mass-produced super bombers; and seek to anchor our security position in a series of far-flung bases whose primary assumptions must involve offensive operations.

The Russians, in turn, are working feverishly to re-equip their industry and to make good the promise of their superior position in Central Asia. Military training is universal. In the case of the naval schools of Ushakov and Nakhimov, and the famous Suvarov Military Academy, it starts with boys of seven. Army officers have become a favored caste. They receive extra food rations and are exempted from the payment of taxes.

Russia also considers herself a potentially great naval power, and is in the process of building both the necessary bases and a powerful fleet.

The U.S.S.R. is endeavoring particularly to flank its territories with a *cordon sanitaire* of satellite nations, operating this time in reverse. The Yugoslav Army has become in everything but name an extension of the Red Army and is kept on a total war footing. "The reborn Polish Army," declared the Polish Premier (July 21, 1945), "is one of our most tremendous assets. . . . We have started to build a Polish Navy. For the magnificent equipment of our armed forces, and for the expert training they have received we are indebted to the great Soviet Union." Hungary is to have a heavily mechanized conscript army under Soviet tutelage. In Prague, General Bohumil Bocek announced (May 20, 1945) that the organization, armament and training of the new Czechoslovakian armies would be identical with those of the Red Army.

Even China and the Latin countries are attempting to build competent military establishments. It is with an eye to these objectives that all of the states now measure their industrial programs.

Chapter Two

ADMINISTRATION WITHOUT POLITICS

To THE political and military aspects of the United Nations Organization there is appended a skeleton apparatus for international economic and social regulation. This paraphernalia includes the Economic and Social Council, the International Court of Justice, the Trusteeship Council and still other organs.

It may be assumed that these new agencies will suffer from the identical deficiencies which afflict the parent structure, and will not be able to perform the functions assigned to them; for if they are able to do so, it can mean nothing else than an end to the sovereign independence of all the nations, and a war of muscle for control of the new apparatus between the top powers.

The International Court of Justice may be dismissed as a sententious ornament incapable of assuming any of the jurisdictions it would require in order to operate. It is in no essential different from the Permanent Court of International Justice created in 1920. Its authority can proceed only from the patronage of its most powerful clients, who would be at the same time the only possible defendants whose actions would require serious control.

This affiliate of the League was formed to dispense equity between nations in the matter of contract law contained in treaties, as well as on the general international practices which pass under the name of international law.

73

Where the powerful were concerned, it either made no decisions at all or its mandates were ignored. "In the whole history of this Court, there is not recorded a single decision which coerced a government against its will in a matter in which it could have resisted in the event of the non-existence of the Court."[1]

The Trusteeship Council is not likely to amount to more than the Mandates Commission of the League of Nations, to whose findings no one of the states gave more than polite notice. When on one occasion the commission accused Great Britain of defaulting on its instructions under the Palestine Mandate, and of "having turned the Mandate upside down," London did not even bother to reply.

These contradictions of purpose and powers unavoidably affected all of the technical organs of the League. Though it is usual to ascribe some moderate success to these affiliate agencies as contrasted to the almost total failure of the League on the political side, the true "measure of success attained by the League's technical organs was very small . . . as compared with the magnitude of the tasks to be performed."[2]

At no time was there dealt with any of the fundamental issues which affected the real welfare of the nations.

The techniques elaborated for the present Economic and Social Council of the U.N.O. are simply a rehash of these old approaches and present nothing new in essential concept. At best the powers of the existing body are of an indifferent order. It may "make or initiate studies and reports with respect to international, economic, social, cultural, educational, health and related matters, and may make recommendations with respect to any such matters to the General Assembly, to the members of the United Nations, and to the specialized

[1] Ranyard West, *Conscience and Society*, p. 190.
[2] A. G. B. Fisher, "International Economic Collaboration and the Economic and Social Council," *International Affairs*, October, 1945.

agencies concerned. It may make recommendations for the purpose of promoting respect for, and observance of, human rights and fundamental freedom for all."

Though this provision is weak, the train of thought it inevitably gives rise to is contained in the proposal of Congresswoman Helen Gahagan Douglas that the United Nations War Crimes Commission be empowered to punish those responsible for economic as well as military crimes.

At the Philadelphia Labor Conference, it was urged by the United States representative that "the United Nations should agree in principle that the maintenance within each nation of high levels of employment and national income is a matter of international concern." Carrying this logic a step further, the Australian government called for an international agreement which would compel all nations to carry out domestic policies designed to maintain high levels of employment.

Such possibilities however would appear to be somewhat on the Utopian side. Any attempted seneschalship over living standards, competitive costs, currency and economic schemes, social and racial freedoms, cuts directly across the authority and vital interests of whole governments and their supporters among entire classes and groups. If a government no longer retains absolute control over its currency, its social, political or economic measures, or even over the prejudices and antipathies it inherits from its supporting electorate, it no longer is sovereign but a satrapy of some mightier power.

It is a misnomer to consider politics distinct from economics and the circumstances of commerce, industry, finance and labor. These cannot be disassociated from the sovereign quality of the state, and lend themselves even less to outside jurisdiction than political and military concerns.

The dilemma is hardly one based altogether on delusion; for any acquaintance with the problem offers ample proof that modern industrial trade no longer can continue efficiently in the limited confines of the existing nation-states. The restrictive regulations devised by each nation in the furtherance of its trade position unquestionably constitutes an evil which cries to heaven for correction.

There is obvious merit to the conception that conditions of labor, the value of money, the means of transportation, the freedom of markets and the accessibility of raw materials, involves not only a national interest, but an international one as well. The very right to regulate these conditions provides the sovereign state with an arsenal of weapons for use against others and is contrary to any sensible scheme of international order.

The assumption is not so much that the state has a larger obligation to international society than to its own citizens, but that its citizens are at least partially subject to the powers of economic laws which may be supreme over the laws of the state itself.

These recognitions, however, do not harmonize the independent role of the state with the abdication of its powers such an international consent would involve. States by their nature cannot be restrained from using a favorable bargaining position to the utmost, or from protecting the commerce of their nationals by whatever legislation is required; nor could any government which neglected these measures remain in power.

This riddle is the heart of any security plan which seeks to enable the better nature of man to take hold, and at the same time retain the forms of political independence; for it is here that the immediate welfare of the sensitive citizen mass is most notably affected.

Examination does not lend assurance to such a prospect. Even the agreement at Chapultepec by which trade preference was assured the Latin American republics, fractured the spirit of the projected free world society. Our bargain with Latin America means the creation of bilateral types of agreement to the disadvantage of other countries. Such an arrangement in one way or another is bound to affect the competitive position of those consuming and producing states which are excluded from it.

All of the nations obviously act in their own interests. Whether on the military, ideological or economic plane, the whole plan of sovereignty involves the utilization of all available resources to the national benefit irrespective of its consequences to others. Hence, the more effective the planning, the greater the international friction which must result. A planned economy on the part of any state means an attempt at elaborating a self-sufficient economy. This in itself involves a discriminatory assault on those nations which continue to maintain an undirected free economy, and whose own domestic markets are subject to outside exploitation.

Even more fatal than the usual manipulations, currency and tariff walls by which nations endeavor to squeeze each other for profit, is the complete withdrawal from the free trade area of a virtual universe such as the U.S.S.R. Russia's capacity to maintain a totally closed economy and at the same time compete in the world's free trade markets, is bound to be an increasingly serious problem.

The great trading bureaus of the authoritarian state have behind them the full political power of their nation. They not only are overwhelmingly large, but also overwhelmingly powerful, compared to the largest corporations America conceivably could place in competition against them.

The key to normal enterprise as it is understood by our own producers is profit. This is not necessarily true of the authoritarian state, where ideological, military and political considerations may take priority. Under the controlled economy, the entire cost-price chain from the raw material to the ultimate consumer is determined in all its aspects by the state itself. Since this is the case, the item of profit is a ledger transaction, which need not be the prime consideration where important strategic gains are in the offing. In outlining the advantages enjoyed by the large grain farms of Russia, Stalin conceded that as state enterprises they did not need to be disturbed by the question of profit. "Under capitalism," he said, "large grain farms do not enjoy special credit and taxation privileges, whereas under the Soviet system, which is designed to support the socialist sector, such privileges exist. . . ."

So far, the Russians have concentrated on the manufacture of capital goods, and have had difficulty in filling the enormous needs of their own people in the still scarce consumers' commodities. A day must come, however, when a surplus will exist. The Russians then will find themselves on the export market in a competition replete with political as well as trade implications. With the best will in the world their monopoly methods both in buying and selling cannot fail to offer them overwhelming opportunities for advantage, which must lead to dumping and a thinly disguised trade war.

This effort to make the most of a strong bargaining position, which any large exclusive buyer possesses, cannot be curbed by any machinery open to a league of nations. Within five years Russia expects to be the world's biggest cotton producer, tripling her present crop; and at the same time plans to enter the profitable export market in cotton textiles, thus directly threatening all of Britain's prime sources of income. She also is making preparation to compete with the United States in the production of trucks and other vehicles, which will be sold throughout Asia and perhaps Europe and South America.

The inherent antagonisms which exist between the two systems are observable in what is now taking place in eastern Europe. The irreconcilable nature of this competition was seen when the three planetary Baltic states of Lithuania,

Latvia and Estonia were suddenly wrenched away from the free enterprise system by force, to gravitate around the central Soviet sun at Moscow. Today in the case of Poland, Hungary, Rumania and other east European countries, the same course is being followed, and these areas are being incorporated into the tightly closed trading system of the U.S.S.R.

The machinery by which this has been accomplished has been a set of treaties by which the habit of free trade is being efficiently demolished. The raw materials and finished goods required by the U.S.S.R. are accepted in a mass exchange for industrial and raw material products furnished by Russia. Poland, for example, exchanges her coal, copper, cement, zinc, woolen and cotton piece goods, for telephone equipment, wood pulp and various staples. Under a five-year agreement with Hungary, the U.S.S.R. is to take over ownership of 50 per cent of the little country's factories and plants in exchange for needed goods. In Rumania, the agreement calls for the creation of Russian-Rumanian syndicates for the administration and development of the nation's natural resources, to the exclusion of other foreign trade. If Rumania requires manufactured materials not securable in the U.S.S.R., the necessary purchases are to be made through a Moscow-controlled banking syndicate.

II

The fulcrum of our foreign policy is the belief that world peace is securable through collaborative economic action; and that we can manage to mold the inner policies of the nations to productive ends by a show of good will on our side. This has involved us in a stream of loans, gifts, disbursements and economic favors to other countries.

Unfortunately, these have at best a short-term significance.

They represent not the spirit of collective security but the largesse of a wealthy benefactor to those petitioning his favor.

As long as economic nationalisms continue and political walls separate the true productive forces of society, these methods must be regarded only as handouts seriously draining our own economy and only temporarily helpful to the beneficiaries. As we are discovering, such a program will not bind the Latins to our side; nor will it rescue the British from their dilemma, or modify the program which the U.S.S.R. conceives for itself.

A foreign policy based on gifts and economic pressures creates a relationship which is essentially unsound. It assumes that the nations are willing to forego long-range objectives for interim financial advantages, and that the power *status quo* can be more or less retained as it is.

All of this is implied in the Bretton Woods arrangement, and the new series of disbursements planned to begin with a loan to Great Britain of $4,400,000,000. The total proposed outlay is to be approximately $15,000,000,000, going to Russia, France and other countries. Since practically all of the bonds and loans made by the United States to foreign countries are in default, these disbursements must be regarded as grants-in-aid rather than as normal banking transactions.

Despite the juggling by which these amounts are made to disappear in the ledger balances, they are the symbol of very real resources and expended work-hours. A loan of $4,400,-000,000, which subsequently is taken out in American goods, must by any kind of logic involve the sweat, labor and raw materials which goes into the mining, processing, manufacture and shipping of the commodities concerned.

What each of the great power systems seeks is not some hypothetical recession into a regulated world economy, but to make itself as independent as possible of all others, with the obvious purpose of freeing itself from a fatal reliance on outside producers.

Unless there is a healthy settlement in advance of all world issues, such a loan to Great Britain will make not for less, but for further autarchy within the Empire. This is connoted by the very depth of the struggle in which Britain is engaged to retain and expand it.

In the case of the Russians, similar considerations apply. They are not seeking credit for the purchase of consumer commodities, but capital goods and heavy machinery which would increase the self-sufficiency of the Soviet state.

The policy of the Russias must frankly be conceived as one aimed at outbuilding the capitalist countries so as to make Russia independent of the balance of the world. The policy, in effect, is autarchic and isolationist, not collaborative. The Russians are not anxious to build up an international trade and for the sake of the current comfort of their citizens sacrifice the essentials of their long-range policy; nor can they be expected to give over their fundamental goals for the sake of temporary economic gains.

This may be seen in the nature of the assistance sought by Moscow under its tentative request for a six-billion-dollar loan. It is not for shoes, food, pharmaceutical and other products of light industry, but for plant equipment, telephone, telegraph and power lines, for machine tools, locomotives and railroad cars. What the Russians are after is not the products of heavy industry, but the heavy industry itself.

This is a situation which no amount of rhetorical observation can remedy. It exists contrary to the assumptions of the Bretton Woods agreement which was rushed through the United States Senate on the plea that the very economic life of the world depended on it.

The then Secretary of the Treasury, Mr. Morgenthau, told the Senate that "what we have done here in Bretton Woods

is to devise machinery by which men and women everywhere can exchange freely, on a fair and stable basis, the
goods which they produce through their labor." The International Bank, and Monetary Fund, were to resolve "the
planless, senseless rivalry that divided [the nations] in the
past." This measure was presented as "the alternative to the
desperate tactics of the past—competitive currency deprecia-
tion, excessive tariff barriers, uneconomic barter deals, [and]
multiple currency practices."

In the place of such bilateral deals, the bank was to give
orderly expression to the construction and developmental
needs of all the subscribing nations and to perform for world
commerce the role intended for the U.N.O. in the realm of
international security. The bank was to make available "long-
term financial aid . . . at reasonable rates" for those countries
impoverished by the war, or whose economies were in other
ways imbalanced.

The theory was that such a condition was to the peril of
mankind generally and required collaborative correction by
an agency of the world community itself.

Yet almost a year later, we find that only minor states or
those closely dependent on our financial favor have ratified
the plan. Russia allowed the deadline date to go past without
doing so. Great Britain used the question of her membership
as a basis for further bargaining; and made her ratification
conditional on a favorable loan direct from the United States
Treasury.

In return, in what amounts to a new bilateral deal, Great
Britain promises to remove the trade barriers which efficiently
wall off the so-called Sterling Bloc, of which more anon.

The question was presented to the Congress as a quite
practical one of opening up to American goods world markets
now closed. With equal practicality, the British made it
known that the reduction of tariff barriers or even the making

of loans is not sufficient; a way must be found by which Great Britain's present imbalance of imports over exports can be corrected.

This involves greatly increased British export sales, and can have no other meaning than special preference in favor of British goods, since Britain, as we shall see, does not dare be thrown on the world's free trade market without risk of ruin to the special position she now occupies in world commerce.

Our examination of that position will show that in its present situation, London is compelled to make the most of the purchasing and trading advantages she possesses in the shape of her Empire.

If Britain's conditions cannot be met, it is declared that an all-out trade war will have to be instituted removing the sterling system completely from the world trade economy so that it will function, like the Russias, as a self-contained universe.

These assertions are accompanied by the same covert threat of ultimate chaos once offered by Weimar Germany. "If no adequate help is forthcoming," warns a semiofficial spokesman, Sir Norman Angell, "Britain will be forced, by sheer physical need, into a Socialism or Communism of a very severe and ruthless type."[3]

These high pressure demands, in view of Britain's unquestionably serious situation, may be reasonable enough. They do not, however, serve to lend assurance to the Bretton Woods plan, which is seen to consist of a rehash of old notions, dealing largely with the removal of symptoms instead of causes.

The Bretton Woods proposals are far from a panacea for the cure of the world's present economic ills. They do not solve the disequilibriums proceeding from the reigning politi-

[3] *The American Mercury*, December, 1945.

cal crisis. They are incapable of balancing the national trade ledgers of profit and loss of any of the countries. They cannot remedy mistakes of public policy, or substitute for an essential weakness of trade and geographic position. In order to succeed, these concepts involve the isolation of the finance economy of the state from its military and political position in the world, and hence, to separate it from the conditions of sovereignty itself.

Such a result obviously is an impossible one.

III

All of these subventions are a poor risk. If they are to be justified at all, it is only by virtue of the continuing emergency, by which they are to be considered as political rather than ordinary banking transactions. It was in this light, for example, that we regarded the great sums expended under the American Lend-Lease Act.

Beyond these overriding considerations which we could hardly ignore in the interests of our own welfare, America cannot continue to support an eternally bankrupt Europe and Asia, and to export its wealth to a demoralized universe, of whose political insolvency World Wars I and II give ample evidence. We may in fact find some difficulty in adjusting our own economy to the new problems of existence, and to recover from the exhaustion brought about by our recent outlay of loans, gifts and military expenditures. It is only the misinformed who can ignore the fact that we now are living off our fat, and that our supposedly inexhaustible riches are rapidly disappearing in the shape of a permanently mined soil and greatly depleted mineral wealth.

The terms of the British loan provide in effect for an economic alliance between the United States and the group of countries dominated by the Sterling mechanism; but be-

yond tiding her over for a period of several years, this transaction cannot settle any of Britain's basic problems.

Great Britain finds itself entering the postwar period in
desperate economic straits. She has lost a large share of her
markets; her economy is insolvent; it will be a struggle for
her to produce enough goods for home consumption alone,
let alone for export.

There would appear to be no remedy for these troubles
short of a mitigated type of international Fascism centering
in London and backed physically by interlocking interests
in the United States. If the present imperial economy is to
survive, it must be in possession of monopoly advantages
greatly disadvantageous to the position of many other states.
This requires the intervention of British politics in the
country's export dealings, which are compelled to subsist on
favored trade agreements, bilateral arrangements, restrictive
currency devices, trade blockades and government-subsidized
cartels. World trade, based on a full interpretation of the free
enterprise system, in which would be eliminated discrimina-
tions, restrictions, quotas, embargoes and preferential trade
barriers, automatically would eliminate the benefits of imperial control, leaving only its bitter residue of costs.

The very founding principles of the British as well as the
Russian systems are antagonistic to the expressed ideals of the
United Nations Organization to which these states have for-
mally subscribed.

The power scheme under which England exists is a relic
of the day of sailing vessels, when control of the great sea
routes meant control of the world. Possession of coal and oil
and a redoubtable seafaring population made Britain for a
time the great manufacturing center of the world, and gave
her possession of the transoceanic shipping trade.

In the early days of industrial capital, England became a
rich country through the head start she obtained as a mercan-

tile power. She served as banker and manufacturer to the world. Raw materials were imported, and sent back to the points of origin at a profit in the shape of finished goods. They were carried in British bottoms, financed by British capital, and protected by British political and naval pre-eminence.

In the heyday of her success, England was incomparably the world's greatest producer and purveyor of manufactured goods. The skill, energy, audacity and ingenuity of her people, their political stability, plus her possession of coal and iron, and the physical position of the Island itself, helped to create a unique position of world leadership.

Britain was the first to discover the secret of low production costs through the application of invention to the industrial arts. She became master of the science of transportation, and learned to combine these skills with a prudent yet bold and far-sighted scheme of finance.

This was the secret of British commerce, which was the spearhead and precursor to British imperial penetration. British mercantile superiority was necessary to British imperial rule as much as was British control of the seas.

By the middle of the nineteenth century, the manufacturing position of Britain visibly became affected by the entrance into competition of the nations of northern Europe. These were followed in turn by the mass production methods and superb facilities of the United States; and soon, it may be expected, by the Soviet Union, China, Brazil and others.

In 1913, the year before World War I, English exports, combined with income from investments abroad and banking and shipping services, showed a favorable trade balance of approximately $900,000,000; providing a surplus available "for increasing or replenishing her foreign investment account."[4]

[4] Dr. William F. Hauhart, *England's Decadent International Economy*, p. 7.

By 1931, this favorable balance had turned to a substantial deficit. For the first time, the island kingdom began to be forced to live off its accumulated capital.

By 1945, under a rationing system more rigid than during the worst part of the war, it is estimated that Britain was spending abroad at the rate of eight billion dollars a year, and was receiving in income from abroad about three billion a year.

The seriousness of this situation must be judged from the fact that Britain is an exporting nation which has over-developed its manufacturing economy at the expense of its agriculture, and is hence highly sensitive to every change in world condition. Only 6½ per cent of the population of England, Scotland and Wales are occupied on the land. More than 60 per cent of Britain's food requirements must be imported, as well as the greatest proportion of the raw materials she requires in her industries.

She is thus in a position exactly opposite to that of the U.S.S.R., and is the least self-sufficient of states.

It is conceded that even with a 50-per-cent increase in exports, Britain's annual deficit still would run to almost $850,000,000. To survive, the British must more than double their exports.

This brings us to the nice question—*at whose expense?* Great Britain already possesses a heavy disproportion of foreign trade. Her situation is less likely to excite the sympathy of potential rivals than their cupidity.

World-wide industrialization is under way everywhere, making even the current exports of the Island disproportionately large. This may be seen from the fact that, in 1936, the British market still absorbed 19 per cent of the total imports of the world, compared with 11 per cent for the United States, 6.9 per cent for France and 1.3 per cent for China. China possessed only 1 per cent of the world's export trade, and the Soviet Union an amount similarly negligible.

The feudal era cannot be continued in a partial vacuum. Whatever the wealth, power, prestige and know-how conferred on any state through the instrumentation of the machine age, the results are not rigid, absolute and static, but tend rather to be universal and all-pervasive. Granting the presence of natural intelligence, human energy, and physical resources, the benefits of industrial achievement cannot be restricted to single nations or groups of nations, but must overflow like a huge tidal run, into every areaway and available cranny.

Russia already has expressed its intention to sell the expected surplus of its manufactured goods in world markets. Chinese competition, especially in textiles, is certain to make great inroads in England's highly profitable oriental trade, and perhaps cause it to disappear altogether.

Even the British Dominions have shown a tendency to look out strictly for themselves in the matter of industrial competition and to seek foreign trade in active rivalry with the mother country.

Brazil and other Latin American states are attempting to industrialize and are certain to protect their infant industries by the usual bilateral arrangements, tariffs and trade walls. Latin America will not only supply its own cotton textile needs, but seek export markets. In this field Brazil would possess a towering advantage over Britain in the shape of low labor costs, new mass production machinery, and a balanced economy. Brazil also can locate its factories and spindles right at the raw material source. Great Britain would have to import all of its cotton as well as most of the other raw materials required in the manufacture of cloth, paying for these and their transportation in cash.

It is safe to say that wherever British portfolio holdings abroad represent mere capital-finance imperialism, as in the case of her ownership of Argentine railroads and public utilities, they ultimately will be confiscated; and that this also will prove true of British investments in her densely populated Asiatic possessions. These countries already are in various stages of revolt against the conditions of colonial life, which no longer fit the circumstances of this century.

The British also must deal with the fact that their industrial plant is antiquated, and that their capacity for mercantile initiative has been hamstrung by the system of imperial privilege. How deadly the effect of privilege can be in a competitive sense is shown in the extremely low productivity which affects many British industries, and especially in the low output per man-hour as compared to similar industries in the United States.

In such commodities as rubber and tin, which once were British monopolies, intense competition may be expected. The United States, which consumed about 60 per cent of the world's rubber supply, now possesses a plant capable of producing synthetic rubber at practically the price it can be profitably sold in Malaya. Ordinary prudence must force this country to turn to South America for much of its additional natural supplies, rather than run the risk of being cut off from them as occurred during the past war.

The same situation applies to the industrial services, such as oceanic shipping. Before the war, British vessels carried more than 40 per cent of all sea-borne trade. Today the United States possesses 56,500,000 dead-weight tons of merchant shipping tonnage compared to about 13,000,000 gross tons owned by Great Britain.

Even if America is willing to share the position with Britain and make her a gift of excess tonnage in our possession, it is certain that Russia, China and other states will be unwilling to act on the island kingdom's behalf at the expense of their own welfare. As these countries continue to industrialize, they will tend to rely more and more on their own merchant marine, and in other ways offer competition to British manufactures and carrying trade.

Thus British trade finds itself in a vice from which it cannot be rescued by any type of financial legerdemain or international regulation.

The British possess only three possible ways out of this impasse:

1. To merge their interests in a world or large-scale regional federation;
2. For the balance of the world to increase its consumption of British goods, irrespective of competitive prices, quality or national interests;
3. The organization of world trade in a web of imperial cartels, in which the United States would join as a partner.

The latter is the program favored by British business and the present government.

Britain's international behavior bespeaks the recognition that an uncontrolled international free market would be disastrous to her economy. Here the interrelationship of modern economics and power politics clearly can be seen. Though in a milder guise, the British power action in its simple postulates bears a considerable resemblance to the economic motivations which actuated the German Nazis. If Britain is unable to compete with the mass-production methods of the United States and the Soviet Union, she is still less able to withstand the cheap labor of India, or the efficiency and superb geographic position of the Jews in Palestine. From the British view, it is necessary for these countries to remain as sources of cheap industrial materials, as well as great consuming markets for textiles and other simple types of mass-produced British goods, if England is to survive. Therefore the rapidly marching forces of evolution must be stayed in these countries, which must at all costs be kept from industrializing.

It is these premises which furnish the reasons why the soldiers of a state rich in democratic tradition are fighting the world over to subdue the inhabitants of Java, Indo-China, Burma and Siam. It is why the British must maintain armed garrisons in Egypt, Palestine and India.

For these reasons, we see Great Britain, though a foremost exponent of democracy at home, obstinately supporting dying imperialisms and decaying dynasties abroad. This is the cause for British commitment to reactionary Moslemism, its support of the Greek royalists, and of the Portuguese Fascist, Salazar. It is one of the reasons it is impossible for the United States to place an embargo on the Perón regime in the Argentine. Such a blockade would not be successful without British support, which London cannot risk giving lest its huge investments in Argentine utilities and services be adversely affected.

From the commercial as well as on the military side, the advantage of supervisory control even over little Greece is considerable. American ships, for example, must secure advance British consent for all freight rates charged, and furnish detailed lists of all cargo carried, before they may dock and unload at any Greek port.

Distraught, overextended, and hard-pressed, the British have found themselves forced more and more into isolationist and authoritarian measures. These are concentrated chiefly in the trading unit known as the Sterling Bloc, which serves to conserve the dwindling assets of the Empire and to protect British industry against competition it is not prepared to meet.

Though Washington demands the abandonment of these devices as a condition of the new loan, it is difficult to see how this can be accomplished without the ultimate ruin of

British industry, or by a new imperium in the form of an Anglo-American cartel agreement to divide the world between them. Short of the latter result, it may be assumed that any modification in the working terms of the sterling area will be of a transitory nature.

The mechanism of the Sterling Bloc is based on a familiar pattern whose workings could be seen in the prewar activities of the German trade machine in the Balkans. It rests on the vulnerability of world free trade operations to any point of totalitarian control or monopoly administration.

The sterling-area agreements derive their efficiency from the very practices and exchange controls which were denounced at Bretton Woods and San Francisco. The bloc includes the United Kingdom, the territories mandated to Great Britain, British protectorates, Saudi Arabia, Egypt, Iraq, Iran, Ethopia, and all of the Dominions with the exception of Canada and Newfoundland. It also includes a number of European countries which are bound to the bloc by an accumulation of sizable sterling balances which are permanently frozen unless utilized by continued transactions within the sterling area.

The British pound is artificially pegged at a considerable overvalue in terms of real exchange, and the exchange controls are linked with licences to do business, import goods, or to make payment in dollars. Individual American business men seeking to trade in these areas can do so only by specific permission from the government; a condition which applies as much to Jamaica and the other islands lying off our shores, as it does to India, Palestine, or Africa.

This restriction of competition and free enterprise automatically takes on certain aspects of a closed economy, and tends to create all of the conditions of economic warfare and bilateral trade which British statesmen themselves decry. India, for example, has about one million pounds sterling in the London bank to her credit and wants to deal with the United States, but cannot do so.

The economic nationalism which has resulted has not failed to have its expected counterpart in Britain itself in various internal price controls and subsidy schemes aimed at curtailing the free market. By the planned production and controlled exchange of saleable commodities it is hoped to effect a healthier balance of export and import trade.

This tendency proceeds from two directions. On one threshold there exists a planned socialization process which already has been carried a considerable distance. In power is the Labour party, with a program of gradual nationalization of the great interests and monopolies. This party though starting out honestly enough as a true party of the Left devoted to the goal of international socialism, finds itself caught in a tangle of contradictions between its own doctrines and the realities of Britain's imperial position. Under the circumstances it has little choice but to continue the Tory policy in Britain's foreign relationships if it is to keep the ship of state from bankruptcy, and itself remain in office.

The second of these trends proceeds from the great industrial combines, who favor an international cartel arrangement, which lends itself perfectly to synchronization with Labour's blueprint for nationalization.

All these plans involve the general spirit of the planned economy, and a compromise of private ownership and free enterprise with government control and regulation.

At the same time that such basic operations as the iron, steel, transport and communications industries are being taken over as government monopolies, a concurrent move is on foot to organize British business in compulsory trade associations by which output and prices can be controlled and new competitors kept out of the market. By both means, England's economy is intermeshed into the politics of the state, the whole system funneling through subsidies, quotas and other governmental aids into the omnipotent Bank of England, which rapidly is becoming the central control point by which the nation's mercantile economy is to be directed by the state.

As early as June 1935, the Federation of British Industries was calling for the "elimination of excess plant capacity, . . . a coordination between supply and demand; limitation of new entrants into industry; [and] expulsion from the conduct of business of firms 'which can never hope to become profitable.' "[5] In 1939, the Cotton Board demanded that the government grant it powers to fix prices, and sought the elimination of small and "inefficient" operators, in order to secure the frank benefits of monopolistic action described under the title of "unified and united commercial policies."

Both English business and government circles have been heavily impressed with the profitable efficiency with which British cartels have operated in Africa and Asia, in rubber, cocoa, tin and other commodities. Their prime object now is a partnership with the United States. They propose to divide up world trade, eliminate competition for free markets, and freeze out new industrial competitors.

The direction of these policies was shown at the big Chicago Aviation Conference following the Dumbarton Oaks meeting. Here the British came with a plan which in effect represented the cartelization of the aviation business, hardening it in a rigid mold against the competition of new world industrial rivals. These proposals the American delegation rejected.

The over-all British design is an ambitious and comprehensive one. "The national framework would be capped by a world trade alliance, a supernational cartel—to control trade, allocate world production quotas, determine world

[5] Lasser, *Private Monopoly, The Enemy at Home*, p. 79.

prices, and handle the problems of raw material sources."[6] This gigantic project involves, in the words of one of its sponsors, Sir Edward Jones, head of International Tinplate cartel, "the regulation of domestic production and distribution internationally in each individual country."[7]

IV

In many of its aspects the British cartel plan is brilliantly attractive, though its undesirable features more than offset any benefits which may derive from it.

The cartels unmistakably are expressive of a primary form of power. They are a form of answer by big business in the free trade states to the monopoly advantages enjoyed by the trading bureaus of the authoritarian countries. Cartels themselves, however, are fundamentally antagonistic to public regulation, and as they develop must lead unfailingly to domestic Fascism.

The cartel is a tacit acknowledgement of the international nature of both industrial production and marketing, and is a true reflection of the fact that the nation-state no longer encompasses the full community of human interests.

Here, too, the cartel creates the usual contradictions which enter into all efforts to rationalize the predicament of the nation-state. Instead of solving the questions of adjustment which plague the parochial state, the cartels produce new and perplexing conflicts of interest and loyalty leading to a situation which can imperil the life of the state itself.

In its arrangements for the division of international trade, the cartel operates on dangerous horizontal levels limiting the development of industries essential to the welfare of the nation for the sake of short-sighted profit objectives. In the

[6] Lasser, *Private Monopoly*, p. 90.
[7] *Ibid.*, p. 91.

deal between Standard Oil of New Jersey and I. G. Farben, for example, the latter agreed to stay out of the oil business if Standard Oil would stay out of chemicals. These allotments involved not only the suppression of patents and critically important processes, but the cessation of investigation along certain technological lines.

As a result of such trading agreements, the United States suddenly discovered at the beginning of World War II that American firms had not been allowed to make synthetic rubber, or quinine substitutes. The development of manganese, zinc and other ores had been curtailed; and industrial processes involving important savings and great efficiencies, put under wraps.

The French munitions trust, Schneider-Creusot, is said to have maintained dealings with the Germans throughout the war. This firm is reported to have owned the big Skoda munitions works in Bohemia, and to have made liberal contributions to the Nazis' rise to power. So it is said, did the Anglo-Dutch oil king, Henri Deterding, and others.

During the midst of the Munich crisis, the Federation of British Industries met secretly with the official Nazi industrial trust, the *Reichsgruppe Industrie*, "to complete an agreement for interlocking British and Nazi enterprises, and for the promotion of vast international cartels." The Düsseldorf Conference was concluded to the satisfaction of both parties on March 15, 1939. This was *one day after Hitler entered Prague*.[8]

V

Though unsubsidized American business men must suffer severely as a result of the economic nationalism which grips

[8] Report by Wendell Berge of the Anti-Trust Division, U. S. Department of Justice, to the United States Senate Committee on Military Affairs, October 15, 1943; cf. David Lasser, *Private Monopoly*, pp. 39-40.

so large a portion of the world, the logic of oppressive competition can apply equally to our own methods. It exists in every case where a rich and strongly mechanized nation possesses extensive dealings with its poorer and nonindustrial neighbors.

It easily may be suspected by the smaller countries that the United States argument for a general removal of trade barriers is not as altruistic as it appears, and springs rather from a desire to appropriate world markets and to prevent the growth of local industry elsewhere.

From the viewpoint of a state such as Brazil or China which is just beginning the industrial cycle, this formula would forever consign it to the agrarian and small handicraft stage. Such a state would have little possibility of industrializing itself unless its young manufactories could be protected by the usual wall of tariffs, currency manipulations and trading restrictions. Along this line, a Chinese writer, Dr. T. S. Chien, declares that free and unrestricted trade may be a blessing to other nations, but would "work great hardships to China. . . . Many Chinese believe that for ten years following the war China should levy protective duties and take other steps to give her infant industries a chance to prosper."[9]

To the existing industrial countries with their fixed overhead costs and high living standards, there is an unacceptable side to this contention. To them it means that Chinese merchandise should have the right to precipitate disastrous competition in the free markets of the world based on low Chinese scales of pay, and a debased currency.

Whether the operation makes economic sense or not, all nations henceforth will attempt to create a balanced industrial development in competition with all rivals, thus bringing into existence all of the more insupportable aspects of economic warfare. If it does not do so, the agricultural state

[9] "New China's Demands," *Foreign Affairs*, July, 1943.

realizes that large industrial neighbors, by occupying a monopoly position in reference either to the purchase of raw materials or the supply of machinery and processed goods, hold over it powers of life and death.

By the sudden application of tariff restrictions or monetary controls, the big manufacturing state can coerce its non-industrial partners in a wide variety of ways, ranging from getting deeply into debt to them, to smashing the markets of the victimized country by purchasing and re-exporting its products at lower prices. This maneuver actually was under-taken by the Germans prior to World War II, in order to spoil the markets for the countries of origin and make them dependent upon her.

Even such a country as the Argentine, without coal or iron, and otherwise prosperous, is making desperate efforts to create a balanced industrial base for its economy. Each of the states feels that both its prestige and its political future make economic diversity and some degree of self-sufficiency necessary.

In all the Latin American nations protectionism now is the order of the day, even though it means that a good white shirt which can be purchased in the United States at $1.95 is available in inferior quality of local manufacture at $5.00. Despite the Good Neighbor policy, strict regulations now cover the needs of favored industries. The fear of North American commercial penetration is associated with the even greater fear of financial and political servitude.

Just as the small nation cannot give up its attempts at self-sufficiency, it is hardly possible for any of the great states to abandon their traditional economic objectives. The privileged position of the United States, which we are certain never to relinquish voluntarily, is indicated from the following facts: with about 6.1 per cent of the world's population, the United States has produced almost 80 per cent of the world's automobiles. It possesses more than 57 per cent of the world's telephones and 53 per cent of its railroads. It has 70 per cent of the world's motion pictures, and about 42 per cent of the total number of radios. It consumes 53 per cent of the world's sugar, 48 per cent of its coffee and 72 per cent of its milk.

It must be accepted as axiomatic that each nation has no alternative but to preserve the scale of living of its workers, protect its commerce, and accelerate the efficiencies and competitive power of its industrial establishment, irrespective of the effect which might be had on others.

Any effort at international regulation of commerce would have to be an effort at equalization of advantage. Here the problem of equalizing the cost of production alone in the various countries would be impossible to solve, whether due to relative efficiencies, low-scale wages, wealth, resources or mass production methods.

Even in such activities as those embraced in the United Nations Food and Agriculture Organization, the quest for preferment dominates the deliberations. The Russians absented themselves from the meeting of the International Labor Organization, and refused to join the deliberations of the Far Eastern Advisory Commission, when they thought it was to their advantage to do so. They did not attend the Chicago Aviation Conference. As owners of a great part of the short North Circle route, which they have managed to keep closed to foreign aerial navigation, the Kremlin undoubtedly considered itself as having little to gain and much to lose by such a discussion.

It is also not without logical significance that Moscow stayed away from the meetings of the United Nations Educational Organization, where it was proposed that "biased teaching of history" be outlawed. The realistic Russians must have wondered how there could be a meeting of the minds on this subject. Did the gentlemen of the United Nations

Organization propose, for instance, to have Russian text books recognize Trotsky's special services to the Revolution? And how did they expect to merge the extreme differences of outlook between Whitehall, Washington and Moscow in the realm of pure historical interpretation?

Chapter Three

"THE QUEEN OF SPAIN
HAS NO LEGS"

THE logical development of the policies at present pursued by the United States and Russia is war.

The approach of this tragic contest already has been heralded by a series of preliminary affrays in many border spheres. This tormenting rivalry extends in a great variety of directions, and occupies many levels. These range from contrasting concepts of military security to immovable differences in social ideals. They involve opposing prejudices, ambitions and viewpoints, and a conflicting reading of the very meaning of human purpose and destiny.

Each is fortified by a conviction of inviolable rectitude as contrasted with the fundamental diabolism of the other. Each is being propelled by great historical undercurrents of whose force they are scarcely conscious.

At some future juncture there must be either a reconciliation of these clashing aims, or a final all-out struggle for supremacy.

As soon as the collapse of the Axis appeared to be a mathematical certainty, the two master powers began to take stock of their revolutionary situation and to estimate its implications for the future. They were in the midst of this cautious appraisal when the sudden volcanic upheaval of the atomic age junked these computations and threw them into the ash heap.

The situation which remains is one of uncertainty in which all measurements are extremely problematical. This however may be judged: irrespective of the euphemistic authority of the U.N.O., it is of extreme importance that Americans secure a true estimate of the intentions, attitudes, objectives and problems of the U.S.S.R. We must analyze the potentials of organized physical power existing between ourselves and that most enigmatic of states; the quality and nature of our comparative geography, resources, military organization, demographic balance, aspirations, goals and institutional forms.

These will possess a decisive effect on our own security problem, since in any estimate of the future, it must be our relationship to the Soviet Union which will determine principally the nature of the foreign policy our nation must pursue.

It does not require an undue stretch of the imagination to visualize the power world as consisting of these two great states, with all other nations existing as buffer areas between them. To hush these self-apparent facts which are the very substance of today's reality, and to assert instead a principle of parity applying to some eighty nations, is to descend into inconceivable absurdity. It is a piece of pure dissimulation, which may be likened to the classic observation: "The Queen of Spain has no legs," made by the court chamberlain of Spain when he returned to an Aragonian manufacturing town a gift of silk stockings its citizens had offered the Queen Mother, Isabel de Portugal.

As far as this generation is concerned the future will not be determined by pious international humbug, but by the relative power and strength of the two great federated behemoths who now are measuring each other off in the international lists.

To ignore this factual situation is a dangerous piece of hypocrisy. The Queen *does* have legs. Moreover, this set of concealed attributes must be discussed frankly and without pretension.

The importance of this conclusion scarcely can be minimized; for if there is a single mandate which is laid upon the American people in this century, it is to make certain that the divergencies which distinguish our view on life from that of the Soviet Union, nowhere and at no time lead to violence, and to that clash of irreconcilable wills which results in war. No matter how such a conflict might be justified or where the moral equities might reside, it would be a disaster of unparalleled dimensions from which humanity might never recover.

II

While it may be assumed that the Russians possess a fairly accurate knowledge of the United States together with its political and economic conditions, American understanding of similar conditions in the U.S.S.R. practically does not exist. What takes place behind the grim curtains of Soviet isolationism is largely a matter of conjecture. The position and power of Stalin, the status of those who are likely to succeed him, the economic situation of the country, the amount of popular support given the existing regime, and the purposes which galvanize Russian conduct, are curtained in mystery.

The enigma is deepened by the swift growth of Russophobia in the United States, which, with its opposite phantasm of ardent pro-Sovietism, effectively obscures what little exists to be seen.

Rumor alleges Stalin to be dying; that the discipline of the Red Army is rapidly disappearing; that Russia already has cracked the secret of the bomb; that Europe itself is about to disappear in a monstrous cataclysm of Red revolution. It is variously argued that the Russian Revolution has entered a period of consolidation, that the U.S.S.R. has changed from a revolutionary to a world power and that the old flaming program of its insurrectionary puppet, the Comintern, has been abandoned.

It is conjectured that Russia may now be in the hands of the generals; that it has become a military state, and that it is on the point of the same reckless adventures which marked the course of the young Napoleon when his armies fell like a leaden hail over Europe.

What is clear is that the opportunities for vigorous Russian expansion on every part of the Eurasian continent are so great that they may become a source of irresistible temptation. The fear exists in the Western democracies that future Russian moves will be a matter of timing, and that the world balance of power may already have been shattered, remaining in equilibrium only temporarily through the grace of the atomic bomb.

The West sees Asia no longer passive, but in the throes of challenging the old legitimacies. If its peoples are not being spurred on by Russian arms and agents, they have at least been aroused by Russian equalitarian doctrine. Asia is blindly on the march. A growing resentment, truculence and sense of world power dominates her people, a situation from which Russian policy could not disentangle itself if it would.

As a result of the German assault on Europe, the classical social structure of that continent has all but disappeared. Great groups of men have learned to take the law into their own hands. They have been taught violence and a disrespect for the old authorities. After five years of murder, trickery, arson and brutality, Europe is in an almost hopeless state of flux, a prey for any strong master who sees in its grisly situation a sign that the hour of his own destiny is approaching.

There is little faith left in Europe. Catch phrases and slogans no longer interest men whose concepts have been brutalized by a breakdown of the old social values. The claims of parliamentarism leave them cold. They have learned to associate that system with their sufferings and regard it with suspicion and doubt.

These people long above all for discipline, for security and for peace. It is easy to inform them that the capitalist and parliamentary system has failed; that the new Europe cannot be organized successfully by these methods, and that authoritarian regulation is an urgent necessity if life is to go on and civilization survive.

The impression is left in the beaten minds of Europeans that behind the sanctimonious professions of the Anglo-Americans is the simple objective of securing their own welfare. They are looked on as representing an obstinate, exploiting plutocracy, which everywhere seeks to reintroduce into the life of Europe, hated feudal regimes. Behind the pretense of benevolence, they are suspected of being incredibly selfish, and of cynically supporting the most reactionary elements on the Continent.

Even worse, in the eyes of the Europeans, the Anglo-Americans appear to have no program. To many of these distraught and harassed people, it appears that it is Russia alone which offers anything new, or some promise of a practical solution to their problem. The net result has been the extensive natural growth of Soviet sentiment on the Continent, of which we are aware. In some countries, Communists have become the leading party. In every European state their strength must be reckoned with.

Together with the rigidly closed economy imposed by the Russians on the territories they control, these circumstances have served to create in the West an almost unreasoning terror of social revolution, of Communist conspiracy, and of the overreaching Soviet Cyclops.

Watching this tableau which it is disposed to overestimate, the West unquestionably is nervous and tends to have an itchy trigger finger. Beneath the dissembling and the correct phrases in which the diplomats couch their thoughts, is the belief that war is inevitable. The conviction also is growing that since the Anglo-Americans possess the immediate superiority of armaments, if there is to be a war it would be best to have it now.

How much of this proceeds from hysteria and groundless apprehension, and how much from a genuine and prudent assessment of the realities, requires a careful weighing of many complex facts and conditions. The situation is by no means a simple one.

III

The Soviet Union and the United States of America, though at opposite poles in national outlook and social aims, possess much in common. They are both dynamic and vigorous. Both are young states as far as history goes. Both possess great natural wealth and extensive resources together with numerous, energetic and able populations. Both are the product of revolutionary concepts which were compelled to challenge the old legitimacies in order to achieve power. Both worship at the shrine of science and have become masters of modern industrialism.

What is of even greater importance, both differ from the conventional and outmoded nations of the day in that they are not states at all, but federations of states, expressing vital philosophies of government and representing systems of federal authority capable of vast expansion. Either, if necessary, could embrace within its corporate system the entire globe.

In a world composed of unequal, malfunctioning, shattered and imbalanced states, these two great power systems are like gigantic lodestones, capable of exercising an extreme magnetic attraction on all the small and incomplete economies which fall within the spell of their influence.

Only these two states are capable of surviving the century, though two others, Brazil and China, possess the potential competence to do so.

This brings us to an all-important fact which cannot be too highly stressed, for in the end it will be the single point of reference which will tend to dominate all others. It is this: not only are these great federations the most powerful, but they alone possess the physical attributes which would enable them to make the adjustments called for by the conditions of this age.

By merging their forces with either of these great federal unions, the smaller and economically weak neighbor countries would be able to make good critical deficiencies. They would acquire military and economic security and, within the scope of the common union, become equal participants in the collective fortunes.

Ignoring all questions of social and ethical outlook, by merging their fate with the U.S.S.R., little Lithuania, or Estonia, acquire whatever economic stability and security the Marxist system is able to offer. They cease to exist as imbalanced fragments and take on the attributes of the wider universe around them. Much the same is true of Hawaii, or Florida, in their relation to the United States.

At this point, the analogy ends. The United States is a union of politically democratic states whose economy is founded on the assumption that the rights of the individual take precedence over the power of the state. This involves not only the freedom to own property and engage in trade, but title to free opinion, and in other respects an independence from all but nominal interference by central authority.

While these rights do not exist in the Soviet Union, this does not mean that the United States is necessarily good and the U.S.S.R. bad. It simply means that the American setup in theory admits only a political area of jurisdiction on the part of government; while in the Soviet Union the concept of political democracy is considered to be a barbaric relic of a dying social system. The Soviets have substituted in its place what they describe as economic democracy.

The single item of socialization of property on which we

concentrate attention in making our estimates of the U.S.S.R. does not explain the Russian political philosophy or social view. It is important to realize that this philosophy is not alone alien and antagonistic to our own, but that it categorically rejects every premise on which Western culture is based. The two outlooks are not so much hostile as they are mutually exclusive.

There thus exists, in these two colliding worlds, diametrically opposed concepts of the citizen's role in relation to the state, as well as that of peoples to universal organization.

The unalloyed doctrine as it is held by orthodox Communism is given by Stalin in his book, *Leninism*, as "the domination of the proletariat over the bourgeoisie, untrammeled by law, based on violence, and enjoying the sympathy and support of the toiling masses. . . . Democracy under the capitalist system is . . . the democracy of an exploiting minority. . . . Democracy under proletarian dictatorship is . . . a democracy of the exploited majority."

When we speak of democracy and of introducing it into the conquered parts of Europe and Asia, we mean one thing; when the Russians speak of it they mean something totally different.

We mean the effective spirit of political compromise as divorced as possible from the economic aspects of our national life.

The assumption of Western democracy is that if the Russias could move to confiscate the food supplies of the three million recalcitrant kulaks so as to condemn them to death by starvation over a single winter, or were able as a precautionary measure to remove the entire population of the Volga German republic from its historic home in European Russia into central Siberia, such a system could move with equal power against redheaded men, or against the very symbols of God and truth themselves.

The essence of what we mean by democracy is contained in Thomas Jefferson's comment that "all the powers of government, legislative, executive, and judiciary, result to the legislative body; the concentrating of these in the same hands, is precisely the definition of despotic government."

Obviously this pattern does not promote efficiency. It leaves room for many inequalities; but it is the very core of what we mean by liberty. It is here, as well as in the purposes of government, that our system stems off from that of the Russians and places us at automatic odds with them.

In the U.S.S.R., the individual has no rights as we visualize them, in the shape of inalienable safeguards to protect him against the tyranny of the state itself. He is subject to a police power from whose decisions he practically has no recourse.

This must not be taken to mean however that Communist outlook is fundamentally antisocial and predatory as were the social doctrines of the Nazis, to whose system otherwise Sovietism bears a considerable likeness.

There is a marked difference in social ideals between the two. Nazism avows a total contempt for universal culture, and for the aspirations of men. It constitutes a rationalization of the raiding and despoliation tactics of the old racial horde, adjusted to the mechanics of modern enterprise.

The Soviets profess, at least in the character of their objectives, a deep attachment to the noblest ideals of the Greco-Roman cultural tradition. They have not broken with the cultural continuity of man, as did the Nazis. Whatever reservations may be made in reference to the Russians and their system—the denial of civil liberties and the bloodcurdling brutality the march to Soviet goals has involved—this must be acknowledged: they are the only young massive force engaged in the world struggle which pretends to be actuated by humanism, by a regard for the happiness and welfare of men.

The Communist doctrine demands absolute equality of races, as well as the leveling off of classes.

If the great attractiveness which this system unquestionably holds to a large portion of the earth's inhabitants is to be capsulated into a single sentence, it is this: it is a system which essays to provide security to the worker rather than liberty; and which offers him the prospect of a safe and arranged life, free of the periodic crises to which he has become accustomed under a capitalist economy.

Stalin stated the view in his discussion of the new Soviet Draft Constitution. "Bourgeoisie constitutions," he asserted, "tacitly proceed from the premise that society consists of antagonistic classes [and] . . . that a constitution is needed for the purpose of consolidating a social order desired by and beneficial to the propertied classes." This, he averred, means exploitation of the many by the few.

In contrast, he claimed the Constitution of the U.S.R.R. proceeds from the proposition that all people have equal rights, "irrespective of their past and present position, or of their strength and weakness; [and] should enjoy equal rights in all spheres of the economic, social, political and cultural life of society." Staunchly defending the absence of political liberty in the Soviet system, Stalin declared: "Bourgeois constitutions usually confine themselves to stating the formal rights of citizens, without bothering about the conditions for the exercise of these rights. . . .What distinguishes the draft of the new constitution is the fact that it does not confine itself to stating the formal rights of citizens, but stresses the guarantees of these rights, the means by which they can be exercised. It does not merely proclaim equality of rights for citizens . . . but legislatively ensures them by providing definite material resources." These Stalin enumerates as "the right of every citizen to receive guaranteed employment; the right to rest and leisure; the right to education, etc."

The Soviets are contemptuous of what Stalin refers to as "rotten liberalism"; there is no freedom of speech, press or political organization as we know it. However, education and technical efficiency are encouraged by the government of the U.S.S.R. as in few other places. This is part of the long-time plan by which the Soviets seek to prepare the Russian people to assume a leading place in world affairs. Books are published in editions running into millions. There is no district or area, no matter how far away, which does not have its own newspaper in its own language.

Citizens have the right to education straight up through the universities at the expense of the state. Workers receive paid vacations, free medical aid and social insurance of various types. Though it is true that the level of living standards is still far below that provided in the West, great progress has been made in these directions under the Soviet regime.

While there is no free press in the Western sense, this possibility cannot exist in a country where an organized bureaucracy retains an effective monopoly over all the means of production and distribution, as well as control of all news sources. In place of controversial political topics the attention of the individual citizen is diverted through the press to the details of production, marketing and manufacturing problems, on which full discussion is encouraged.

This condition, too, is defended by Soviet spokesmen. "What some countries of the West call freedom of speech," writes the newspaper *Pravda*, "is nothing but a rope on which a capitalist publisher keeps his journalist. . . . Abroad the journalist's profession is a career. With us it is a combat post."[1]

It is certain that we cannot place our relations with the Russias on a basis of sustained moral indignation, on the assumption of an incurable Russian immorality. As we shall observe, even by our own standards, the moralities are not

[1] Issue of September 24, 1945.

altogether on one side. Moreover, the Russians do not care a fig for our moral ideas, which they consider to be the product of a monumental hypocrisy and a ritual by which the continued exploitation of the productive elements of society is justified.

Whatever immorality or antihumanism of which we might accuse the Soviets, the feeling and estimate is returned with interest by them. The Russians accuse Western diplomacy of covering with a mantle of beautiful principle the worst politics its statesmen care to engage in. In his report to the Eighteenth Party Congress on March 10, 1939, Stalin says with biting sarcasm of the free enterprise states: "It would be naive to preach morals to people who recognize no human morality."[2]

The Communists see in their creed the future of the world. They look on those states and regimes which oppose it as backward and barbaric. They therefore consider any means of liquidating the bourgeoisie order as legitimate, including those provided by the quality of the bourgeois ethical code itself.

If there is to be a struggle between the two systems, it is not to be a war between good and evil, the Godhead and devildom. It is rather a contest between two unyielding giants, mutually antagonistic and inflexible in their judgments—each of whom regards the other as cruel, intolerable, bigoted and unhuman.

IV

Since the beginning, Russian existence has been dominated by the situation of Muscovy on the vast inland plain of Eurasia.

[2] He was accusing the Western democracies of attempting "to poison the atmosphere and to provoke a conflict with Germany without any visible grounds."

Until this territory with its peripheral areas fell to a single political ruler, it was the natural arena of plunder and conquest by the wild and savage men of the inclement North and of the Asiatic pastoral fringe. Such legendary characters as Rurik and Genghis Khan left their mark not only on the nature of the country and its institutions, but on the character of its people. These are mystic, generous, intelligent, idealistic, and at the same time, obstinate, immovable and relentlessly savage when aroused to a fever of conviction or anger.

Russia, as we shall see, is like Mars: another world, spiritually inaccessible and structurally almost impermeable to any scheme of assimilation which might seek to consolidate it with the West within a general framework of world law.

The U.S.S.R., as all other states, derives its institutions from its history. It exists as an extension into modern terms of the old Russia, from which it has inherited the great bulk of its motivations. These have matured and have been heavily modified by the revolutionary creed of Marx, a confession of faith unequaled for its impact on European society since the advent of Christianity itself.

Except for a period of a few months under the interim administrations of Prince Lvov and Alexander Kerensky, Russia always has been a dictatorship. Authoritarian rule is normal to the character and experience of almost all the peoples inhabiting its vast sprawling territories.

The history of Russia is a record of a great amorphous growth which developed increasing appetite and absorptive powers as it went along. It is a chronicle of wandering Slavonic tribes, warlike Norsemen, and fierce Tatars, who did not enter into the bustling perspective of history until comparatively recent times.

The Russias survived the terrible battering of the Mongol invasion. They lived through a series of incursions and massacres as merciless and bloody as any contained in human annals. Until two centuries ago, Russia existed in a scarcely penetrable twilight, situated on the very edge of history; a product and expression of oriental cruelty; a land of contraries, of mysticism, struggle, squalor and feudal magnificence, of noble and aesthetic ideals, and of all-pervading imperial absolutism.

As far as European history was concerned, the continent might as well have begun at the Vistula. It was the Polish nation which was considered to be the buffer zone between Western civilization and the enigmatic recesses of the unfathomable East. As late as the last century, Bismarck said of Russia that she had nothing to do with the West, and that there "she only contracted nihilism and other diseases."

The origin of the Russian state is bathed in legend and obscurity. It is generally regarded as having been founded by a Scandinavian freebooter, the legendary Rurik, about the year 826. This roistering prince ruled the areas around what is now Kiev and Novgorod.

A succession of Norse rulers known as the Princes of Kiev made the little state on the Dnieper their stronghold for a series of wide raids and exactions, levied against neighbors as far south as Byzantium.

Then for more than two centuries what had been the beginnings of Russia disappeared. The country was the scene of wild, unending assaults by nomad Mongol and Turanian freebooters, and the prey of unabating civil war. It was not until the middle part of the fifteenth century that the invaders were expelled and internal order restored.

Now began the Russian territorial expansion and consolidation which has continued as a familiar process since, both under the Tsars and the Soviets.

By 1478, the nuclear province of Novgorod was united with the areas of the Moscow Tsar. Under Ivan the Terrible, the great Tartar khanate of Kazan, which reached from the borders of Novgorod to Astrakhan, was occupied, opening up the easy and inevitable road of Russian expansion to the East.

By the early sixteenth century, wars, intrigues, and marriages had mushroomed the Russias in size until they now extended from a hundred miles north of Kiev to the White Sea, and from the Volga to the Urals. By 1566, Russian dominion had reached the Caspian, and by 1620 was already halfway across what is now Siberia.

Under Peter the Great, the Russian march to the sea began to find definite expression. By defeating Sweden, the empire established itself in Finland and on the shores of the Baltic. It began to turn its eyes toward the West, and its ambitions toward the beginning of a new universalism.

The symbol of this Western orientation was the new capital city of St. Petersburg, now Leningrad, built on the very western edge of the empire, as if it represented the whole crushing assurance and weight of Russian ambition in its forward march to the open waters of the Atlantic. Until this time, the only port of consequence in this massive landlocked area was the northern city of Archangel, whose usefulness was limited by the icing conditions which prevailed over a good part of the year.

Under the reign of Catherine the Great, Russian rule was swept into the deep south by a successful invasion of the khanate of Crimea, establishing the Russias on the shores of the Black Sea, from which they looked longingly at the gem city of Constantinople. White Russia, Little Russia and the Ukraine were taken from the Poles. Poland itself was finally partitioned, and two thirds of that once powerful country became a province under the tsars.

A series of wars brought the borders of the empire westward from the Bug to the Dniester, and in 1812 beyond the province of Bessarabia to the Pruth.

Wherever they were stopped in Europe, the Russians turned their eyes again to Asia. In the late eighteenth and nineteenth centuries, the Caucasus and considerable portions of Persian and Turkish territory fell into their hands. Turkestan was swallowed, and soon after, Bokhara and Khiva. In Central Asia, Russian conquests were driven forward to embrace the lower reaches of the Eli, at the expense of China.

In Siberia, pushing into what was almost a resistless vacuum, the Russians finally reached the Pacific, penetrating as far as the northwest corner of America, later to be sold to the United States, as the territory of Alaska. The Amur basin was taken from China and colonized; Sakhalin Island fell, together with the mouth of the Amur.

By occupying Liaotung peninsula and securing title to the key city of Port Arthur, the tsars achieved part of their tenaciously held ambition for egress on the warm waters of the Pacific. Outer Mongolia and northern Manchuria were grasped by the reaching Russian fingers. Korea was threatened, and its government fell under the influence of Russian finance experts and military instructors.

V

The outstanding characteristics of northern and central Asia was its likeness to the great empty plains and virgin forests of America in the early days of the Republic. The distinguishing feature of this enormous area, which was comparable to all of North America in extent, was not only its emptiness, but its isolation. This was the Heartland, on which the English geographer Mackinder had placed such commanding stress.

Approachable only from the West, it was cut off from the south of Asia by the all but impassable Himalayas, the mountains of the Hindu Kush, the huge arid plateau of Iran, the dread deserts of the Gobi and of Chinese Turkestan, and their flanking ranges of almost unexplored wilderness, embracing the rugged Kirghiztien Shan, Altyn Tagh, Altai, and in the east, the forbidding Yablonovoi and Stanovoi mountains.

This tremendous cone of silence buried in the very center of the world's landscape, and peopled only by pastoral tribes and minor agricultural nations, could be approached in no other way than from the European side. Thus, by geographic destiny, the tremendous center of Asia was to become a special and exclusive Russian field of reference.

The attraction this area was to exercise on Russian minds can be judged from the statements of the powerful Russian statesman, Prince Ukhtomsky, chief aide to Tsar Nicholas II. In common with other Russian leaders, Ukhtomsky saw the great Russian future in Asia. He urged young men of enterprise, says the historian Pares, "instead of fuddling their heads with European constitutions, to come to Asia and rule the world."

When the great railway was built with its terminus at Vladivostok, "dreamers saw it at Peking, and even at Shanghai."[3] Russian statesmen and patriots encompassed in their visions a dazzling Russian empire of the East, stretching from the Bay of Bengal to the South China Sea.

Hundreds of thousands of Russians began to pour into eastern Siberia annually, which soon assumed the aspect of a true Slavic extension of the motherland.

By 1896, the Russians had secured the right to build the branch line known as the Chinese Eastern Railway, connecting the Trans-Siberian line across the north Manchurian plains to Vladivostok. Another branch known as the South Manchurian Railway, was built to the Russian-controlled port of Darien.

[3] Robert J. Kerner, "Russian Policy in the Far East," *Yale Review*, September, 1945.

The all-important Trans-Siberian road, instead of taking
the wide detour north of the Amur River, where it remained
precariously outflanked by the cleaving wedge of Manchuria,
now led in a straight line south, directly to the city of Vladivostok.

This surging tide hit its apogee and began to retreat with
Russian defeat in the ill-starred war of 1904 with Japan. The
tsar's government was pushed backward, out of Manchuria
and Korea. It lost Port Arthur, the Liaotung peninsula and
the southern half of Sakhalin Island.

The nadir of Russian imperial destiny came with the Red
Revolution. A combined American, British, French and Japanese expedition occupied Vladivostok and the coastal regions
of Siberia. At Brest Litovsk Russia lost Finland, Poland, the
Baltic republics, Bessarabia, the great granary of the Ukraine
and the border provinces of Anatolia. That part of the Caucasus not directly ceded to Germany, together with the area
of the Don Cossacks, declared its absolute independence of
the Bolshevik regime, as did the big Central Asian territory
of Turkestan.

Russia had been driven into the landlocked interior like a
whipped pariah to his hovel.

At this low ebb in her fortunes, Russia and its new
Bolshevik masters suddenly became the beneficiary of the
collapse of Kaiser Wilhelm's Germany. The Ukraine was
retrieved, as were the lost areas of White Russia and the
Caucasus, the lands of the Don Cossacks, and the territories of
Central Asia and eastern Siberia. For the rest Moscow bided
its time, but did not forget.

VI

In this flailing, dynamic flow of forces, we have a picture
not of a nation in the accustomed sense, but of a huge con-

stellation of power situated as a practical unifying force in the very center of the huge Eurasian land mass. It was a power whose appetite and needs developed as its conquests increased.

The growth of this great coagulation of nations did not fail to attract the enmity and apprehension of other powers situated on its borders. These either were in the pathway of conquest or were destined by their own dynamics to meet in headlong collision with the ambitions of the tsars.

One calls to mind Germany, Austria, Hungary, and Japan; but their antagonisms were itinerant and spasmodic. The great long-term opponent of the Russians was Great Britain, which brought its sea power to bear over two centuries to keep the Muscovite giant confined within his landlocked cage.

After the beginning of the eighteenth century, the British began to see the threat of Russian might directed everywhere against the tenuous lifeline which connected London with its prize possession of India. Even that big peninsula itself was deemed to be an object of secret Russian ambition.

The sharp rivalry between the two empires, and the continuous wrangling which characterized it, is one of the classic duels of history. It continues into the present day, and is one of the deep unseen currents by which the course of prevailing events is given its direction.

England fought five separate wars with Russia to prevent that country from pouring through the Balkans to take control of the Dardanelles. It was for this reason that Britain espoused the Turkey of the sultans when that fanatic and archaic country was known as the "sick man of Europe," and was considered the bounden enemy of all Christians.

It was fear of English designs which caused the tsars to sell Alaska to the United States. In Afghanistan and Persia, British troops put an end to what then had seemed the inexorable march of the Russias southward. In the Far East in 1861, a parade of the British fleet forced the Russian Captain Borilov to disgorge the highly strategic Tsushima islands which patrol the vital Chosen strait separating Japan from Korea. Later Britain lent encouragement to the Japanese in what was regarded as a necessary policing action against the unruly Russian giant.

During the Red Revolution, it was English money and intrigue which backed the White Guards and the Poles. At one juncture British troops occupied the Caucasus, and five different intervention forces were operating simultaneously in Russia.

The centuries-old struggle was patched up at various times when even more formidable and immediate enemies threatened the lives of the two great empires; but after each alliance they again reverted to the old rivalry.

Innumerable treaties, pacts, agreements and engagements were made, but the basic aspects of this duel continued the same. British policy was designed to keep the Russias land-locked and bottled up. The opposing flow of forces within the Muscovite empire was to rend asunder these intolerable bonds and to break onto the Mediterranean, the Atlantic, the Persian Gulf and the warm Pacific.

The major prize in this unabating contest was the Straits city of Constantinople from which Russian eyes have never been diverted.

This fixed ambition dates back to the days of the Norse-Slavonic raiders of the ninth and tenth centuries. Even then there existed a prophecy which said that "in the last days, the Russians shall have Constantinople." The Slavs possessed their own name for the city, calling it Tsarigrad, the city of kings.

The Russian craving for the Straits survived the tsars and the Kerensky government, and is one of the dominant forces actuating present Soviet policy. It has lived through two centuries of intrigue, maneuver and battle between the Russian Bear and the British Lion. Time after time in their insistent drive toward this shining goal the Russians almost had the Dardanelles and the queen city of Constantinople in their hands. Each time it was London and her allies who frustrated Russian hopes.

The great Russian opportunity appeared to come when Turkey joined the Central Powers during World War I. By holding over the heads of her associates the unspoken threat of a separate peace with the two Germanic emperors, Russia was able to force London to reverse its traditional policy. By a secret agreement Britain consented to the annexation by Russia of Constantinople and the territory bordering on the Straits.

This deal was blown sky-high by the coming to power of the Bolsheviks. The promise was negated and never acted upon.

That the Soviets themselves had not lost interest in this traditional concern of the imperial Russias was shown in 1940 shortly after the signing of the Russo-German pact. The Kremlin began to press upon Turkey for special privileges in the Straits.

The Turks refused point-blank to entertain the idea of any concessions under the proffered "mutual assistance pact." Their emissaries left Moscow in an air which was distinctly cold.

Soon after, the Russian Premier Molotov in an angry statement castigating the French and British as warmongers, accused the Turks of having "definitely rejected the cautious policy of neutrality" and of having "decided to enter the orbit of the spreading European war." "It is not, however, for us to guess," he added enigmatically, "whether Turkey will not regret her actions!"

The situation was commuted by the subsequent German assault on Russia; but as soon as it was apparent that the Reich was beaten, Moscow once more resumed the historic Russian march toward the Mediterranean, issuing the specific demands on the Turks to which we already have referred.

VII

Running parallel with this expansion drive toward the Adriatic and the Mediterranean were two closely integrated forces which drew their power from the conditions of eighteenth-nineteenth-century Europe. One was the strong mothering impulse of the Greek Orthodox Church and the schismatic hostility which separated it from the hierarchy at Rome. The second was the new and intense racial and national consciousness which accompanied the growth of industrialism in Europe. Both magnetized Russian steps in the direction of the Balkans.

It was only in Russia that the Greek Orthodox Church possessed access to diplomatic force backed by recognized military power. Elsewhere its communicants were repressed and sometimes persecuted. Moscow became the center of the Greek Orthodox world, just as Byzantium had been in the past, and it was to its minarets and spires that the faithful looked.

The intense anti-Christian persecution which took place in the Balkans under Turkish rule caused the entire peninsula to turn its eyes to the all-powerful Patriarch who sat in the Holy City of Moscow, and to the Little White Father who was Tsar of the Russias. Moscow became the protector of the oppressed Slavic peoples, as well as of the non-Slavic Orthodox Rumanians and Greeks.

The second of these constraining forces was Pan-Slavism.

Throughout southeastern Europe, the Slavs were a subject people. Under their Mohammedan overlords in the Balkans, they were restive and passionately nationalistic. In the North, they had been for centuries the victims of German aggression and were little better than a slave-folk, who, in some areas such as Prussia and eastern Germany, already had lost their identity.

The vague gropings of the Slavic masses were not formulated into a true movement for racial liberation until the early nineteenth century. It was the Slovak poet, Jan Kollar, who formulated out of the writings of the earlier Slav prophets the great principle of Slavic political unity. Kollar, a Lutheran minister, referred to himself as a Slavonian patriot and preached the unity of the Slavs as a counter-force to the rapidly jelling union of the Germans. "What art thou?" he exclaimed: "A Russian? A Serbian? A Pole? My children, unity! Let your answer be, I am a Slavonian."

Kollar was to the Slavs what Isaiah was to the Hebrews. With deep lament, he surveyed the condition of his people in Europe, the most numerous of all nations, but almost all of them bondsmen. "Bohemia, the vanguard of the race, almost German; the Illyrians talking Italian; the Hungarian-Slavonians under the tutelage of the Magyars; Serbia and Bulgaria yet unborn; the cultured classes in Poland, and in Russia, affecting French manners and language."[4]

With insistent prophecy, Kollar wrote in his great poem, "Slavia's Daughter," published in 1842:

> What will become of us Slavs a century hence?
> What aspect will Europe wear then?
> Floodlike, Slavic life will inundate all,
> Expanding its influence everywhere;
> And the tongue which was proclaimed to be
> the speech fit for slaves, according to the
> distorted judgment of the Germans,
> Will resound within the walls of palaces,
> issuing even out of the mouths of its very rivals.

[4] Thomas Capek, *The Slovaks of Hungary*.

• Sciences, too, will flow in Slavic moulds.
The styles, customs, and songs of our people
Will be mighty, alike on the Seine and on the Elbe.

Just as Pan-Germanism was to affect the rising concept of
militant German unity, Pan-Slavism began to exercise a magnetic attraction on the minds of the Slavic races. It became an
important part of Russian expansion policy. The Russian aim
now was to unite all of the Slavs in a single great political unit,
which could not fail to dominate the affairs of Europe.

Under Peter the Great and those who followed him, Slavic
poets and mystics already were speaking of the supreme
destiny of the Slavonians under a common roof. The great
Slovak writer, Paul Josef Safarik, contemporary with Kollar,
did not hesitate to people Hungary, Turkey and Prussia, as
well as Slovakia, Bohemia and the Balkans with Slavonians.

A spate of books, pamphlets and rhetorical addresses took
up the great theme, which only needed a Hitler to generate
it into a *passion fatale*. It did not even seem amiss for the
famous Bohemian author, Josef Jungmann, to assert that
since Russia was the strongest of the Slavic states, all the
Slavonians should form a union and accept the Russian as a
common language.

Just prior to World War I, the Pan-Slavic movement was
at its height. It declined rapidly with the liberation of the
Slav minorities in Central Europe, and with the destruction
of the Greek Catholic Church in Russia by the triumphant
Bolsheviks.

The great shadow thrown by the new Russia over the life
of Europe has brought once more to the fore the spectre of
Pan-Slav ambitions. Pan-Slavism is one of the urgings used to
seduce the Yugoslavs and Bulgars. In Poland, Bohemia and
even parts of Austria, it has proved a useful weapon in the
hands of Soviet spokesmen.

It is in the light of these maturing conditions that the reintroduction into Soviet Russia of the Greek Catholic Church as an extension and ornament of the state, takes on significance.

VIII

These streams of power action all tumbled into a single supreme confluence, the mighty river of unconscious Russian universalism.

It cannot be stressed too strongly that the U.S.S.R., as the imperial Russia which preceded it, is not a nation in the conventional sense, but a dynamic and expanding universe, a coagulation of states—a world like the Roman world, embodying a total system of law and a unifying culture, which from its own exclusive view is justly entitled to the use of the title, "civilization."

It is precisely the all-inclusive quality of Russian expansionism which should warn us against making a too-simple estimate of the character of this state or its potentials for the future. All that may be said is that the Russians are a world apart, a young and aggressive cosmos fired with a sense of its own appointed destiny.

As we have noted, the political unit later to be known as Russia, and finally as the U.S.S.R., had its beginnings at a comparatively late date in history, starting with the merger of an assorted aggregate of Slavic tribes. Since that time, in contact with many diverse and often recalcitrant peoples, the Slavic stream has displayed an immense capacity for the absorption of alien elements in its path of rule. Cossacks, Swedes, Tartars, Germans and many others were assimilated into the common Slavic stem.

This process is represented currently in a rapid digestion by the flow of incoming European Slavs, of the Mongoloid peoples of Siberia and Central Asia in their own home territories. Though under Soviet rule ethnic particularisms are encouraged rather than suppressed, the process of fusion between the peoples of the U.S.S.R. into a series of Slav-dominated types goes religiously forward.

Today, as a result there are hardly more than a million natives of unmixed blood in Soviet Asia.

Though the pattern of Russian policy derives from an intricate tangle of threads, the weave is all in the direction of consolidation into a single federated power whose universal nature is hardly open to challenge. To perfect this purpose and round it out, the absorption of more and more adjoining territories is indispensable.

Whether this performance is elaborated in the name of military security, the need for raw materials, racial and religious affinities, ideological concord, or control of railway exits to warm water ports, makes little difference. The generating forces return always to the same central controls, no matter how intricate and unrelated the machinery of acquisition may seem.

It is possible for the Soviets, for example, to be the power front for a unified Slavonia, and at the same time proclaim the infallibility of the universalist principles of Marx. They simultaneously can demand the annexation of Czecho-Slovak Ruthenia as representing an extension of unredeemed Russian nationalism, though this area has never belonged to Russia in the past. They can invade the fellow-Slav state of Poland in concert with Nazi Germans under the claim that Russia can not "remain indifferent to the fate of its blood brothers, the Ukrainians and the White Russians," who inhabit the eastern part of the country.[5] It is possible, moreover, for the Kremlin to apply itself with righteous ardor to the recovery of the Anatolian districts of Kars and Ardahan, on the score that these had once belonged to imperial Russia under the tsars,

[5] Radio speech by Soviet Premier Molotov, September 17, 1939.

though these provinces contain no Russians, and are inhabited only by Armenian Turks.

Under this complex flow of impulses, it is possible for the Kremlin to operate on many levels of policy without suffering seriously from the tempestuous incongruities which must develop from them. The end result of these exercises is always the same—that of further power consolidations on an expanding territorial base.

To the conventional nation-state, these contemplations force into existence a whole group of questions concerning the nature and terminal view of Soviet political organization. These countries must consider whether it is possible for Russian appetites to be self-limited, and whether the thresholds on which they operate do not necessarily lead to new and wider ones. Especially must the conventional governments ask themselves this: is the Soviet organization in itself completely irreconcilable in terms of the classical world surrounding it; and must it thus be regarded as the spearhead of uncompromisable insurrectionary forces which exist under the surface everywhere? In brief, is not the total quality of Soviet dogma the very center and soul of aggression, as it has been for all great exclusively held philosophies in the past?

Since Communism is dynamic, revolutionary, rigidly intolerant, and professes to be a confession of faith of universal dimensions, can it stop short of its goal, which can be nothing else than universal control? Can its powerful dynamics be caused to expend themselves in directions which will not result in revolutionary collisions and warlike quarrels with other nations? Finally, can the intense Communist energy and proselyting mood be transmuted so as to become an internal force for the peaceful development of the present-day territories of the U.S.S.R., causing the Soviets to become, for practical purposes, an equilibrated counterpart of the orthodox state?

This is by all odds the nuclear query on whose answer more than on the existence of charters, leagues, treaties, promises and conventions will depend the immediate prospect of peace. If the Soviets see the future of mankind as immovably fixed in the predecreed logic of Marxian philosophy, the basic contentions existing between the U.S.S.R. and the outer world cannot be satisfied short of a major world settlement.

Such a conviction on the part of any people by its own existence is a guarantee that whatever the restraints which may be written into peace formulas, war is inevitable. This bleak outlook may be observed in retrospect in the early career of both Orthodox Christianity and Mohammedanism. It may be seen as well in the utter failure of all attempts to contain Hitler and his Nazis by organizational means, and to prevent them from overrunning Europe.

Nevertheless it is useless to descend to the devil theory and to attribute sinister motives to the Russians; or to view their policies as being other than a natural development from primary causes. The opposing view, however, that no danger of conflict exists is equally unsupportable. To neglect on this score a proper analysis of the conditions which motivate Russia's policies is to be blind to the sources of human action and comes under the head of folly.

It is not alone what the Russians say, nor even their actions, to which we must give our most careful attention; for both action and words may be the result of expediency, or some purely transient situation. It is what the Russians are, plus the wide gulf which separates their basic values from our own, which must be examined. It is here that the element of preordination which governs our mutual long-run conduct will be found.

An illustration of the conflicting egos, convictions and emotions involved is aptly given in the self-assurance by which we have contracted to spread American propaganda throughout the world as one of the official activities of the State Department's new Office of Information and Cultural Affairs. We have been urged to interfere in Europe's economy and set up free capitalist republics on our own model, replete with political and social freedom. But we are aghast that the Russians should seek the same kind of enterprise, furnishing not political freedom, of which they are contemptuous, but that planned economy from which their state derives.

If it occurs to us at all, it seems a piece of perverseness that the Soviets should regard our current plan to reform the imperial Japanese Empire into a Western type of democracy as a step backward. Yet from the Communist view, the sole enduring effect of this measure would be to delay the mechanics of the inevitable revolution, for which from their eyes Japan was almost ready.

When the Russians speak of bringing democracy and self-rule to the peoples of Europe, they do not mean our democracy, nor nationalism in the academic sense. Nor does their contemplation embrace a no man's area which is to be neither fish nor fowl, and to exist as a buffer between themselves and the capitalist world, but a true extension of their own system and of their own concepts of universal organization.

This is the only realistic view which can possibly be taken of the situation. When Estonia was rescued from the Germans and reincorporated into the Soviet Union, the triumph was described by A. Weimer, chairman of the Council of People's Commissars of the Estonian S.S.R. as "a struggle which ended in the Autumn of 1944 when the gallant Red Army in whose ranks fought the Estonian National Guard Corps, ejected the German invaders and restored freedom and independence to Estonia."

In much the same vein, Mr. V. Lacis, chairman of the Council of People's Commissars of the Latvian S.S.R., referred disdainfully to "the so-called independent Latvia formed after World War I with the help of the Germans and the Latvian reactionaries." The period of "so-called independence," he assured his hearers, "was in fact the period of liquidation of the Republic's independence."

These circumstances receive additional weight from two important contributing factors, one ascribable to the long pattern of national experience, and the other to the character of Communist doctrine.

The Russians, under whatever regime, always have been noteworthy for their capacity to recede under pressure and then to bound back again in pursuit of their original objectives. The unbending courage and persistence which has characterized their actions on the battlefield is competently mixed with a capacity for shrewd political dissembling and maneuver.

Time and again Russian official policy has renounced goals whose acquisition was implicit to the full success of the Russian economy. Many times, the Muscovites swarmed over the Dniester and the Pruth into the prized Danubian provinces and the Balkans. As often they retired, but the tormented longings which drew their footsteps to these regions remained constant and unaffected.

Under the tsars the evacuation of Manchuria was agreed to on three separate occasions, yet the Russians always were found back again. The Soviets signed away the Chinese Eastern Railway, and, after the defeat of the Japanese, achieved its recovery. Russia has seized, relinquished, and resecured the territories of the Polish nation on many occasions. Russian pressure on the Turks constitutes a continuous though undulating pattern. Demand for egress on the waters of all the warm seas has remained as a constantly recurring element of Soviet policy. Whether in Iran, the Straits, the Adriatic, Manchuria, or Korea, at some favorable point the stream of

Russian expansion will be seen to flow again in the dry beds of the old channels.

This tendency to be guided by the uses of *Realpolitik* has been sharpened by the power theories which underlie the body of Communist doctrine itself. These adjust themselves perfectly to the use of political opportunism as a legitimate expedient. No retreat is considered final, but only strategic.

This principle is visible in Lenin's frank acknowledgement of the conditions connected with Russia's New Economic Policy, the famous Nep, which was universally hailed as representing a Russian swing to the Right. "We are now retreating," said Lenin, "going back as it were; but we are executing this retreat only in preparation for a longer step forward . . . [and] in order to start a persistent advance later."[6]

IX

The Soviet state is a product of a power tactic of the German military during World War I. The democratic revolution which had swept Russia in the early part of 1917 and had forced the abdication of Tsar Nicholas II did not result in the chaos for which Germany had hoped. Under their new social democratic rulers, the Russians remained in the war.

In Switzerland was Lenin and his band of revolutionary Bolsheviks. Though without power or any considerable following, these men were looked on by the German General Staff as dangerous and vicious agitators, exponents of nihilism in its worst form, and as an antisocial force of literally unpredictable power.

They were men whose life had been devoted to revolution. Revolution was their profession. They had thrown bombs, wrecked railways and issued haircurling manifestoes. They had conspired in half the capitals of Europe. For the most

[6] *Lenin's Selected Works*, Vol. IX, p. 376.

part stern intellectuals, they had given up the conventional purposes to which most men in their lifetimes aspire. They had starved and suffered and risked their lives like hunted animals of the field, a hundred times over.

This was a kind of austere, harsh, scintillating and resourceful leadership which Europe had not seen since the days of the French Revolution. It was an ivory tower stuck in the muck of amorality, whose commanders would stop at nothing to achieve their ends. No risk, no violence and no sacrifice was too much if it furthered the cause of the Revolution.

It was the German hope that the disruptive power with which this little band of revolutionary outcasts was charged would precipitate a social crisis in the already wobbling Russian state and throw it into anarchy.

The Germans and the Bolshevik exiles met on what was to prove one of the most fateful occasions in world annals. The proposals were made and accepted. The Russians were to be placed in a sealed train and sent through the Reich to Russia.

In this locked, moving receptacle which no one could leave or enter as it passed through Germany, were thirty of the most accomplished radicals in Europe. Official German psychological warfare tactics envisaged its human cargo as a sort of time bomb prepared against the Reich's enemies.

The Germans had calculated well. They had given the Bolshevik movement in Russia its general staff. Their tactic developed an impact whose proportions were to prove literally ungovernable.

Neither the liberal regent for the provisional constitutional government, Prince Lvov, nor the liberal parliamentarian, Alexander Kerensky, was to prove half a match for the brilliant leadership provided by Lenin, Trotsky, Radek, Zinoviev, and their company, or the iron discipline and purpose which existed in the radical Bolshevik ranks. Maneuvering, combining, dissembling, and propagandizing, taking instant advantage of every opportunity as if they constituted a military machine, Lenin and his Bolsheviks finally controlled a majority of the Congress of Soviets, and overthrew the provisional government by force.

In his strong fingers, Lenin held the direction of a party fanatically devoted to reform. To a man its members could be compared to the French revolutionary, Jean Baptiste Carrier, who is alleged to have told his fellow Jacobins, "We will save France in our own way or leave her a graveyard."

The party itself was a legacy of the ferocious underground which had neither given nor asked quarter in its resistance to the Tsar. Lenin looked on it as a secret and controlling power, a permanent agency of reform which stood like an invisible giant Mafia as a hedge against the political unpredictability of the proletarians themselves.

This structure was duplicated in a parallel mechanism of government which ruled by ruthless terror, enabling the nation to survive its own internal chaos as well as the unremitting hostility of almost the entire civilized world.

The infant Soviet state succeeded beyond any but the wildest dreams of the most sanguine Bolsheviks in meeting every challenge in its path. Today, it possesses a generation which knows nothing else, and which, like the Turkish Janizaries, is uncompromisingly devoted to Communist goals.

The authority and veneration given such writings as Lenin's and Stalin's *Letters on Policy*, can only be compared to that accorded the Biblical epistles. While these adventures into orthodox Marxian dogma may be tiresome and unconvincing enough to the uninitiated Westerner, they have the awful power of finality to the persuaded Marxist. These writings for practical purposes have been enshrined, and are subject neither to investigation nor debate.

This might be seen as early as 1931 in Stalin's biting denunciation of the Soviet publicist, Slutsky, for daring to question the omnipotence of Lenin in a "discussion article." "The question of Lenin's Bolshevism," admonished Stalin, "the question as to whether he did or did not oppose Centrism as a form of opportunism . . . cannot be made the subject of discussion. . . . It is an axiom!"

In a similar vein, denouncing the great Soviet pamphleteer, Bukharin, who had written several years after the death of Lenin that in a minor detail of dialectical controversy with the master, he, Bukharin, had been finally proved in the right, Stalin commented with terrible sarcasm: "Bukharin's claims may seem incredible, Comrades, but it is a fact. Hitherto we have regarded ourselves . . . as Leninists. Now it appears that both Lenin and we, his disciples, are Bukharinists."

X

The tenets of Communism envision not only an ultimate classless society in which all of the instruments of production and distribution will be commonly owned, but a stateless society as well. In the ideal social structure of the future, toward which the Communists are confident they are marching, there are to be no class or race distinctions of any kind, and each is to have his due according to his needs.

As the proposition is stated by Marx and Engels in the first Manifesto of the Communist party, when all class distinctions have disappeared "and all production has been concentrated in the hands of a vast association of the whole community, the public power will lose its political character. Political power, properly so-called, is merely the organized power of one class for oppressing another. . . . In place of the old bourgeois society, with its classes and class antagonisms, we shall have an association, in which the free development of each is the condition for the free development of all."

If Marx was Communism's prophet, Friedrich Engels was

its high priest. He assured the faithful that "the first act in which the state really comes forward as the representative of society as a whole—the taking possession of the means of production in the name of society—is at the same time its last independent act as a state. The interference of the state power in social relations becomes superfluous in one sphere after another, and then ceases of itself. The government of persons is replaced by the administration of things and the direction of the processes of production. *The state is not abolished—it withers away.*"

While it is possible that it is Communist doctrine itself which has withered away, as is inferentially claimed by the establishment of the U.S.S.R. as a respected member of the conventional society of nations, the basic definitions of Communist philosophy offer little in the way of such assurance.

The original Communist party Manifesto issued by Marx and Engels, boldly informed the traditional world that the appointed Communist mission was to destroy it root and branch. "The Communists," proclaimed the Manifesto, "everywhere support every revolutionary movement against the existing social and political order of things. . . . They openly declare that their ends can be attained only by the forcible overthrow of all existing social conditions. Let the ruling classes tremble. . . ."

It must be acknowledged that such violent words have a way of taming themselves when the party which had espoused them reaches power, though this was assumed in the case of the Nazis and proved not to be true.

It is held in responsible quarters in the West that much of this question was decided as a by-product of the quarrel between Trotsky and Stalin, and that the elimination of Trotsky was a victory of the right-wing forces within the Soviet economy.

The reacceptance of the Orthodox Greek Catholic Patriarch as an emblem and adornment of the state is looked on as another significant step in this direction. So is the rediscovery by the Russians of Alexander Nevsky, and of such sanguinary heroes as Ivan the Dread and Peter the Great.

It is assumed, too, that the close co-operation between Moscow and the Western capitals which existed during World War II is further testimony to a general moderating process or swing away from messianic Marxism.

None of these expectations seem to be fully justified.

The Communists themselves do not disdain to hide their views. It is simply we who do not read. In general, the Western democracies, being themselves the product of eternal compromise, are in the habit of believing not what they see and hear but what they wish to believe. In the Information Bulletin issued by the Soviet Embassy at Washington November 20, 1945, Communism is described as "the highest achievement of Russian and world culture, the most advanced ideology of the present day."

In the same issue is a categorical statement from Marshal Stalin declaring that "the masses have become welded into a new political army to create a new revolutionary power, and to make use of it to abolish by force the old system of relations of production and firmly to establish a new system."

In an address delivered to the Central Committee of the Communist party on April 1929, Stalin reiterated the purposes of Communist society. Requoting standard Communist authority, he described the state as: "only a transitional institution which is used in the struggle, in the Revolution, in order to hold down one's adversaries by force. It is pure nonsense to talk about a 'free people's state.' So long as the proletariat still uses the state, *it does not use it in the interests of freedom, but in order to hold down its adversaries. As soon as it becomes possible to speak of freedom, the state, as such, ceases to exist. . . . When there will be freedom, there will be no state. . . .* What distinguishes us from the anarchists is (a) the use of the state *now* and (b) during the proletarian revolution, the dictatorship of the proletariat. . . ."

In his report to the Eighteenth Party Congress on March 10, 1939, Stalin acknowledged that true Communism could be brought about only if it were assumed "that Socialism is already victorious in all countries, or in the majority of countries—that a Socialist encirclement exists instead of a capitalist encirclement."

On the other hand, a socialist economy which was surrounded by a capitalist world cannot abstract itself from the conditions of the international situation. It "must have at its disposal a well-trained army, well-organized punitive organs, and a strong, intelligence service—consequently, must have its own state, strong enough to defend the conquests of Socialism from foreign attack."

At the time of the issuance of the new Soviet Draft Constitution, Stalin told the Extraordinary Eighth Congress of the U.S.S.R. that this constitution differs from bourgeois constitutions because "as a state which is in transition to still another form of economy, the U.S.S.R. is a dictatorship whose purpose is to safeguard the attainment of goals which are still unrealized." In this light, the various phenomena connected with the structure of the Soviet state assume an entirely different significance. *The U.S.S.R. becomes not an established or equilibrated society, but a transitional society, a society in the state of becoming.*

In his report to the Seventeenth Party Congress of January 26, 1934, Stalin, after recounting a dreary story of capitalist failures and contrasting these with Communist economic achievements, cried, "Yes, Comrades, our successes are due to the fact that we have worked and fought under the banner of Marx, Engels and Lenin. Hence, the second conclusion:

we must remain true to the end to the great banner of Marx, Engels and Lenin."

The working class of the U.S.S.R., he went on, was strong not only because of the internal achievements of the Soviet state, but "also because it is supported and assisted by the world proletariat. . . . The workers in the West see that the working class in the U.S.S.R. is the shock brigade of the world proletariat. . . . It imposes upon us the duty of working better and fighting better for the final victory of socialism in our country, in order to attain the victory of socialism in all countries. Hence, the third conclusion: *we must remain true to the end to the cause of proletarian internationalism, to the cause of the fraternal alliance of the proletarians of all countries!*"

The capacity for self-delusion so consistently shown by the West, is no better indicated than in the nature of our reaction to the Trotsky-Stalin feud. It was generally accepted that with the sloughing off of Trotsky and his associates, the real radicalism of the party had departed.

The Trotskyites are believed to have been the advocates of "permanent revolution"; whereas the victorious Stalinites are considered to be a sort of right-wing counterrevolutionary force, seeking to create "socialism within a single country," and to bring about a practical end to the plans of world revolution.

Nothing could be more nonsensical.

Much of the accusation hurled by Stalin against his mortal enemy undoubtedly consisted of pure diatribe and a grotesque distortion of the facts. It cannot be doubted that Trotsky, despite the charges made against him, was a true and convinced revolutionary to whom the accusation of right-wing deviationism must have been an aspersion of the worst kind. Yet this was the indictment rendered against Trotsky and the coterie of old Bolshevik heroes found guilty with him.

Part of our miscalculation has been derived from an amusing misunderstanding of the phrase "permanent revolution," which was supposed to represent the political doctrine of the Trotskyites.

Despite its formidable sound, this charge is one of right-wing opportunism, and not of left-wing radicalism. It is an epithet accusing the Trotskyites of supporting the discredited Mensheviks, who sought to bring about a gradual and painless socialist revolution.

"Trotskyism," Stalin wrote at the height of the famous controversy, "is the vanguard of the counterrevolutionary bourgeoisie." Stalin accused the Trotskyites of being in the pay of the Western capitalists, referring to them as "this Trotsky-Bukharin bunch of spies, murderers, and wreckers, who kotowed to the foreign world, [and] who were possessed of a slavish instinct to grovel before every foreign bigwig. . . ."

Disposing with total disdain of the contention that his regime was engaged in sacrificing the cause of the international revolution in order to achieve "socialism in one country," Stalin roared: "It need hardly be proved that there can be nothing more vulgar and despicable than such an assumption. . . . Even the most vulgar of the Mensheviks are beginning to understand that the Russian Revolution is not the private cause of Russians; that on the contrary, it is the cause of the working class of the whole world, the cause of the world proletarian revolution."

It was the obligation of the Russian Bolsheviks, Stalin announced, to give the fundamental problems of the Russian Revolution, itself, priority: "It was their duty to do so because all these problems were also the fundamental problems of the World Revolution, to whose aims the Bolsheviks subordinated their policy and their tactics."

In common with the other Bolshevik leaders, Stalin is convinced of the predestined mission of the Marxist creed to redeem mankind. "The results of the Five Year Plan," he told a state conference, "have shown that the capitalist system of economy is bankrupt and unstable; that it has become obsolete and must give way to another, a higher, Soviet, Socialist system of economy."

Despite the San Francisco Charter, the convivial backslapping, and the pacts of eternal friendship which the powers have sworn to each other, the Russians still are suspicious, watchful, distant and unbending in their opposition to capitalist civilization. As late as November, 1945, M. Kalinin, the nominal head of the Soviet state, warned a meeting of party delegates: "Even now we cannot forget for a single moment that ours is still the only Socialist state in the world . . . Only the most immediate danger has disappeared."

XI

Viewed in the full parade of its own logic, Communist Russia is a society suffering from the social defects of being perpetually in battle array. Its political structure reflects not the ultimate Communist ideal, but the iron discipline and dictatorial powers required to realize that ideal under the grim conditions of battle.

The blueprint for this piece of architecture in a sense is comparable to the organizational measures undertaken by the United States for war. Even here the dictatorial powers granted the different war agencies cut through the safeguards which normally had protected the liberties of the Republic.

It is from this eminence that the domestic structure of the U.S.S.R. must be observed if all elements of its character are to be seen. In its fixed and inflexible complexion it is understandable only as a continuous mobilization process, which ultimately will be self-liquidating when its purposes have been achieved.

Though a dictatorship in the most extreme sense of the word, the Soviet administration believes that it preserves inviolate within itself the skeletal form of the future idyllic society, of which it considers itself the custodian.

In the sense of becoming, rather than of being, and of representing a process in transition rather than a fixed state economy, the Soviet dictatorship is the most remarkable anomaly in the entire history of political experiment.

If, however, one may judge the nature of power as tending to be self-perpetuating, it may be believed that the Soviet state, despite its declared incentives and goals, has stabilized itself permanently in the guise in which we see it.

This, of course, is a question which does not lend itself accurately to conjecture, and which can be answered only in the retrospective light of history. All that may be established at the moment is that the Soviet Union is a newly grown giant of alien feature and fearsome dimensions, and that it is governed by men of monolithic mind who are in chains to a great vision.

Although the country is known as a Union of Soviet Socialist Republics, final power resides within the Communist party, which is the policeman and watchdog of the Revolution.

The party sits above and beyond the state as a sort of extra-judicial judge, police power and governing agency. It is not the state, but it nevertheless is the greatest power within the state.

The membership of the Communist party is something less than five million, all of whom have been carefully selected for their reliability and devotion to Communist ideals. The party is the only political organization which may legally exist within the Soviet Union. It is probably the most highly disciplined civil body ever to exist in human society.

The authority of its leader is undisputed, and the influence of its ruling hierarchy is such that no policy may be instituted and no individual appointed to high office without party approval. While non-party members do occupy important posts, this is subject always to party tolerance and in no way alters the actual extent of the dictatorship.

As is well known, until recently Marshal Stalin held no post within the government and derived his power solely from the fact that he was Secretary-General of the party.

At the core of the party is the Central Committee which wields the real power, and in which are gathered some seventy-one of the elite.

The supreme authority of the party is supposed to be the All-Union Party Congress. In practice, the Congress meets but once every two years. In the meanwhile, authority is delegated by chain control to the Secretariat of the Central Committee and to the all-important Politbureau, composed of fourteen members selected out of the Central Committee.

Although the members of the Politbureau are named by ballot of the Central Committee, they are said to be actually selected by Marshal Stalin.

As Premier and Commissar of Defense, Stalin has under his control not only the armies, but the dread secret police, the N.K.V.D. (the Soviet Commissariat of Internal Security), a body whose authority is virtually unlimited. Like the Politbureau itself, the N.K.V.D. conducts its affairs *in camera* and makes its decisions known only by decree. It is thoroughly armed in the modern sense, possessing its tanks, airplanes and rifles, as well as having at its disposal a vast intelligence system. It has charge of all prisons and is the real government in untrustworthy or unreliable areas of the Union.

Every member of the Communist party is compelled by his duty to be an unofficial agent of the N.K.V.D. and to keep it informed of all activities which may be dangerous to the dictatorship. Like the German S.S.S., the N.K.V.D. is an armed rival of the army itself, on whom it is part of its duties to keep check.

The nominal government which parallels or is actually subsidiary to the authority of the party, is a tightly woven machine with none of the checks and balances usually provided to confine the sway of government. There is no separation of powers between the judicial, the legislative and the executive branches. All organs of the Soviet administration from the smallest village soviet to the Council of People's Commissars, exercise both executive and legislative powers. This authority extends to jurisdiction over cases of those charged with crimes against the state. Such cases are seldom heard before ordinary tribunals.

The police power of the state is total, though it is in the hands of men who profess to be idealists and who, in this sense, are removed from an otherwise inevitable comparison with the murderously grubby and materialistic Nazi dictatorship. They do not hesitate to use the weapon of merciless terror wherever this may be seen to serve the purposes of the Revolution.

By decree of the Central Executive Committee of the U.S.S.R., even the activities of Soviet citizens abroad are closely controlled. "Refusal of a citizen of the U.S.S.R., or of an official of a state institution or organization of the U.S.S.R. active abroad, to return to within the boundaries of the U.S.S.R. at the suggestion of organs of state authority, is regarded as going over to the camp of enemies of the working class and the peasantry, and is classified as treason." Persons so refusing to return "are declared outside the law."

Such a declaration has as its consequences: "(a) confiscation of all property of the guilty person; (b) shooting of the guilty person within twenty-four hours after the establishment of his identity."[7]

[7] *Criminal Code*, official text with amendments up to September 1, 1943, Moscow, 1943.

Labor has no independent existence, since in the event of a contention it would become the opponent of the state, which is the sole employer. Though strikes are outlawed every worker is compelled to belong to a trade union, which provides the vehicle through which his labor is utilized by the state. Penalties for infraction of discipline are severe.

Within recent years, the authority of factory directors has been increased in an effort to promote better management efficiency, and now is as complete as it is anywhere else in the world.

Management pyramids into the hands of a tightly organized group of great trusts. This in turn feeds into the Council of People's Commissars via the Gosplan, the Economsoviet, the Council of Defense, and the State Bank.

Lesser trusts exist for each activity of Soviet economic, cultural, educational, or other operation.

This arrangement is duplicated in the organizational scheme of the individual republics. The more important industries, however, are controlled directly by the All-Union People's Commissariat without reference to intermediary bureaus.

This immense and complicated machinery is harnessed for the party through individual members judiciously placed. All activities, from that of the highest planning body, the Gosplan, to the operations of the smallest village soviet, form a single co-ordinated apparatus which can be set into motion from top to bottom by the pressing of a single button.

Synchronized with this great mechanism is still another, which together with the Council of the Union merges into the Presidium of the Supreme Council of the U.S.S.R. This is the Council of Nationalities, which represents the different national groups of which the Union is composed.

From this important aspect of its operations, the U.S.S.R. can be described only as a league of nations in miniature. It is, in fact so regarded by the Russians themselves, who see its ultimate destiny as embracing "the toilers of the whole world in one global soviet socialist republic."[8]

When the U.S.S.R. was formed in 1923, all of the organizational conceptions of the old tsarist Russia were dropped. The new state consisted of a federated union of four republics which were united by treaty.

The Soviet Constitution of 1936 saw the country divided into eleven Union republics, federated with each other. Since the annexation of eastern Poland and the Baltic States in 1940, the Union consists of sixteen Union republics. In addition there are a large number of other territorial enclaves and autonomous areas possessing one degree of self-rule or another. Actually, there are some forty-nine recognized nationalities.

XII

Theoretically, any one of the republics can secede from the Union. This right was granted without debate by a unanimous vote of the Supreme Soviet of the U.S.S.R. on February 1, 1944, following a proposal by Foreign Minister Vyacheslav Molotov. Each of the republics now possesses its own foreign commissariat, its theoretically separate military staff, and diplomatic autonomy in dealing with other states. The demands made on Czechoslovakia for Ruthenia, for example, and on the Hungarians for northern Bukovina, were made by the separate constituent republic of the Soviet Ukraine.

The capacity to place this interesting operation into effect in the very midst of war was the final proof of the efficiency and authority of the party itself, and of its total ascendancy over any type of political legalism.

The theoretical ability of any one of the sixteen republics to deal directly with other states raises some very neat ques-

[8] Speech by Stalin during a discussion of the Soviet Draft Constitution of 1922. Cf. David Dallin, *American Mercury*, January, 1946.

tions when it is combined with the cultural nationalism fostered by the Communists as part of their scheme of a federated international society.

Quite different from the tsars or, in fact, from any imperialism of the past, the different peoples of the Union are given every incentive to independent development, and their own creative expressions in literature and the arts, provided these do not result in the intrusion of undesired political and social views.

The formal status of the republics is given in a memorandum covering the Ukrainian Soviet Socialist Republic in the May, 1945 issue of the Information Bulletin of the Embassy of the U.S.S.R. at Washington, D. C. It is announced that the Supreme Soviet of that State "has recovered the right which it formerly had and which it voluntarily ceded to the Union of Soviet Socialist Republics in 1922 to establish direct relations with foreign states, to conclude agreements with them, and to have independent representation at international conferences and bodies set up by the latter." The article comments significantly: *"The Ukrainian Soviet Socialist Republic, with a population of over forty million, is one of the largest European states."*

Similarly, the Byelorussian Soviet Socialist Republic is described "in accordance with its Constitution and the constitutional law of March 24, 1944, as a sovereign state, competent to enter into direct relations with foreign states, to conclude agreements with them [and] to participate in any international conferences, international bodies, etc."

Both these "states" declare their right to participate as equal sovereign governments within the conference of the United Nations.

Each of the sixteen republics of the Union, together with the lesser autonomous regions, possesses religious, cultural, racial and other ties with areas lying across its borders. These unredeemed provinces easily could be considered by the Soviet republics as irredenta territories, to be recovered in the fullness of time and placed under a unified rule.

The possibilities this brings to bear may be conjured into existence from the words of Archbishop Gevorg Chorekchian on his election as Gevorg VI, Supreme Patriarch and Catholicos of the Armenians of the World, on June 22, 1945.[9] "The first problem in our national life," he asserted, " . . . was solved with the establishment of Soviet power twenty-five years ago," when "the Armenians set up their own government administered by Armenians." The second problem, the return and reunion of Armenians abroad, "has not yet been solved. Half of our people are still beyond the borders of their country."

On February 25, 1946, K. Chairkviani, secretary of the Georgian Communist party, demanded in an article in *Pravda* that Turkey "restore" to the Georgian Soviet Socialist Republic territories alleged to be peopled by inhabitants of the Georgian race. "The Georgian people's age-old dream," declared Mr. Chairkviani, "remains unfulfilled—restoration of their territorial integrity. Beyond our borders remain the Georgian lands of Ardahan, Artvin, Olti, Tortum, Bayburt, Ispir, Gumusane and Lazistan!"

Obviously no difference can exist in principle between the pressures placed on Czechoslovakia by the Ukrainian Republic for return of an area described as peopled by Ukrainians, and similar pressures exerted against Turkey on behalf of the Armenian and Georgian republics for regions alleged to be inhabited by their co-racials.

A similarly interesting logic could exist on any one of the widely separated Soviet borders. There is a Soviet republic of Moldavia, which presumably holds more Moldavians within

[9] The archbishop was elected by the Assembly of the Council of the Armenian Church in Etchmiadsin, with 110 out of 111 votes, the only dissenting vote being his own.

its confines than Rumanian Moldavia itself. The Karelo-Finnish Republic could possess aspirations to link to itself officially the peoples of what is now independent Finland.

An even more remarkable situation exists in reference to the Turks. The basis for all Turkish nationalism was the pan-Turanism originated by Mustapha Kemal Pasha when he turned his back on Moslem particularism. This movement is based on the presumed ethnic affinity of the Turks with the sea of Turkish tribes inhabiting the belt of territory reaching from the Bosporus through Central Asia, and reckoning a combined population of some 70,000,000.

During tsarist times this movement to attain political solidarity of the Turkish peoples was utilized as a weapon against Turkey's old enemy, Russia. With the fall of the Romanoffs, the Russian Turanians merged their aspirations with those of the new regime, and Turkey was forced to drop the project for practical reasons.

The unification of the Turks easily could be taken over by the Soviets themselves and become an important element in their political program. The republic of Azerbaijan is composed three-fifths of Turkish people. The Usbek, Turkoman, Kazakh, and Kirghiz republics are predominantly Turkish. The inhabitants of the immense Chinese territory of H'sin-kiang also are for the most part Turanian tribesmen, giving the Soviet Union a far better ethnic claim on this territory than that possessed by China.

Even the reactionary theocratic impulse which seeks to unify the Mohammedan world under a single authority, can be turned to its own account by Moscow. Six of the sixteen Soviet republics are Moslem states. These easily could aspire to perform this imperial operation under the aegis of the common Soviet Socialist federation.

That this is not far-fetched despite the old Soviet antipathy to religion, is indicated in the renewed interest the Russians have taken in Mohammedan affairs. The Soviet Moslems now have their own Sheikh-al-Islam, a Mohammedan patriarch who is sponsored by the Kremlin. Though Russians ordinarily may not leave the country except on official business, Soviet citizens of Mohammedan religion now take the long pilgrimage to Mecca under official Soviet subsidies. Soviet representatives in all the Moslem countries make a great show of their orthodoxy. Despite the incongruity this appears to involve, Stalin is said to be extremely popular among Moslems, as was Hitler before him.

The question of why certain autonomous republics were singled out to be raised to the higher category of Union republics, was answered by Marshal Stalin in his report on the Constitution delivered at the Extraordinary Eighth Congress of the Soviets November 25, 1936. The republic to be so honored, stated Stalin, "must be a border republic, not surrounded on all sides by U.S.S.R. territory. Why? Because since the Union Republics have the right to secede from the U.S.S.R., a republic, on becoming a Union Republic, must be in a position logically and actually to raise the question of secession from the U.S.S.R. *And this question can be raised only by a republic which, say, borders on some foreign state. . . .*"

The conclusion certainly would seem to be justified that when Stalin defined these rights, which presumably would involve a process of merger with co-nationals across the border, parenthetically he must have been thinking that it was a poor street which did not go two ways, and that what was sauce for the goose undoubtedly would prove sauce for the gander.

Chapter Four

PRELUDE TO WORLD WAR III

THE zealotry and true force of present-day revolutionary Communism is the central enigma which attaches to Russian policy. It derives from this question: what is the real vitality of revolutionary Communist dogma; and how great is its hold over the Russian mind? This is the core of the ubiquitous riddle which obsesses the minds of Western statesmen when they ask themselves: just what do the Russians mean by their power actions?

All other aspects of Russian universalism can be understood and dealt with as a matter of the traditional give-and-take of power politics; but the vast dynamics of Communist doctrine, with its unlimited aggressiveness and fanaticism, its intolerance of compromise, and its disconcerting attack techniques, presents just such a problem as must be envisaged as between man himself and the brute creation it has been his destiny to exterminate or enslave. The horror which most wild creatures feel for man is precisely what the fragmentized capitalist and liberal world feels for the growing might of totalitarian enterprise.

The weight of the closely organized Soviet machinery is in its very organizing principles too much for the rest of mankind to cope with except on the emergency basis of war. We have had some foretaste of this in our experience with the relatively small and unendowed Nazi state, whose authoritarian power apparatus and capacity for international conspiracy made its policies so dangerously effective to the other states.

The reaction of the normal state to the presence of the Communist boil on its rump is one of rage. The psychology is that of relative helplessness, of searing hatreds, and nervous fears. It has shown itself in various efforts to crush the Russian state by force, or to excommunicate it from normal human society; and in the domestic phase, to place the Communists out of bounds and to consider them as criminals and outlaws.

Now that the Communist state has become a great military power, local Communist parties everywhere, have acquired some of its new respectability. There is no longer the question of liquidating them by force, or of shattering their acknowledged center by the use of sanctions or military violence. Whatever the mental and emotional repugnance which may be retained for it by the conventional diplomats, Russia now must be conciliated with world society if the nations are to be spared the horror of another all-out war for supremacy.

The very prospect of such a conflict makes Western statesmen shudder. They no longer regard it as a question of Adam Smith and John Stuart Mill versus Karl Marx and Nicolai Lenin, or of free enterprise against public ownership, but as a problem of simple survival.

Confronted with the essential nihilism of Communist doctrine and its relentless appearance as a factor in the internal politics of each of the countries, the traditional Western world is overcome by anxieties it cannot master.

If the Soviet concept is to be considered as a single and universal ideal, its presence in party form in the domestic politics of any of the democratic states is like the existence of a delicately balanced high explosive under the nation's bed.

Irrespective of our regard for the Soviet state and the magnificent role it played on the battlefields of World War II, Communist dogma does not lend itself to the balanced operation of democratic politics. Wherever it shows itself within the political arena of the free countries, it does so not as a constituent portion of the nation's legitimate political enterprise, but as an alien and hostile shape.

Communist thinking does not recognize conventional rules, which it considers as so much claptrap originated to armor the bourgeois edifice. Its goals are total goals involving not the discomfiture and continuing existence of its opponents, but their literal obliteration. Intermediate arrangements of any kind cannot fail to be evaluated for their strategic purpose only.

In Communist dogma, there is no room for such a concept as opposing parties and ideas. The existence of a deliberately sustained domestic opponent, such as is involved in the phrase, "His Majesty's loyal opposition," is to the Communist mind a quaint relic of the defunct capitalist period.

As in war, every activity designed to achieve final triumph is recognized as justifiable, whether it involves the tactics of unlimited duplicity, the shock action of scientifically studied revolutionary propaganda, or the calculated sabotage of the industrial base from which the attacked nation draws its subsistence.

Though Communism often has come to terms with its opponents, in the long run it brooks no rivals and shares power with no one. In the general ideological sense, it is an exclusive article of faith, which bears the same general view toward classical capitalism as the medieval totalitarian church did toward paganism. The compromise factor exists only as it reflects the necessities of the moment, or as it expresses the inability of crusading religion to impose its will and create that uniform and exclusive acceptance of its claims which is fundamental to its universal nature.

Until the rigid views which form the framework of Communist dogma are modified by time and become transmuted into something else, the axiom recited by Hitler in his *Mein*

Kampf may be regarded as accurate. "Political parties," he wrote, "are inclined to compromise; world concepts never. Political parties count on adversaries; world concepts proclaim their infallibility."

These categorical convictions find their voice in the unbridled violence of expression used toward enemies of the movement, or toward schismatic factions within it. These become "assassins," "procurers," "saboteurs" and "criminals." They are accused of talking "like lunatics" or of "gangster-like insolence." Itself often the victim of persecutory talk, official Communism never has hesitated to utilize this instrumentality on its own account.

Within the bodies of the various Communist parties themselves, there are periodic purges. Backsliders are expelled, declare their repentance, and expiate their errors in an atmosphere of almost religious confession.

II

Within the Communist dictatorship itself there is by no means a singleness of view as to the foreign policy which is to be pursued. Strongly dissenting opinions are held among the different factions of the governing Communist elite. There are at least three powerful groups, whose attractional influence on official Soviet policy is exerted and recedes as their respective views are favored by events.

There is the moderate group, of which Maxim Litvinov is the member best known to the West, who would prefer to let socialism take its course by natural development rather than risk a war to establish it. There is the Old Guard, mystic, resolute and unbending in their adherence to the ideals of the Revolution.

Then there are the usual chauvinists who tend to verge to-

ward reaction and a deification of things Russian over things
Communist.

It would be an extremely naive man who would count this
latter aspect of Russia as the Dr. Jekyll side of the Jekyll and
Hyde combination. It may be even the most dangerous of
the Russian factions, for with its activism and power sense it
does not possess the frantic ideals which gave the old Bolshevik Russia a spiritual side unknown to the conventional states.
These men have inherited Hitler's belief that the Western
democracies are relapsing into decadence after a final fling
at power, and will seek peace at any price.

It is widely believed in the West that Stalin is a sick man,
and that his death or retirement would bring into power a
group of military men who would overthrow the ruling
Bolshevist clique. The assumption is that the same antagonisms
of interest exist between the army and the political hierarchy,
as applied in the Nazi Reich between the party and the
Junker generals.

This is a false hope. If the army were to take over, there
would be presaged a more, rather than a less aggressive policy.
The army is as much representative of the Revolution and of
the expansionist dreams of Russia as were the Janizaries of
Osmanli Moslemism. Practical realists, these men would be
sure to demand a thorough exploitation of Russian opportunities.

Western politicians also are inclined to make much of the
hope that Russian discipline is collapsing; and believe that
the Russian soldier will draw a painful contrast between the
police regime at home with its poverty of consumer goods,
and the comforts and liberties he will discover in even the
meanest little country of Europe.

This, too, is a useless contemplation. Stalin's soldiers have
seen Europe at the lowest ebb of its moral and material fortunes. "Many Russians," reports the *London Economist*,

"made their first acquaintance with the outside world through the barbed wire of Hitler's concentration camps and in the shadow of his death factories. The reality of 'capitalist Europe' which they have seen is blacker than any picture that had been portrayed to them by official propaganda at home."[1]

Many thoughtful Russians undoubtedly have been impressed by the higher standard of living in the West and by the new and unaccustomed sense of freedom which applies there, but these will not be sufficient to affect the basic mood of the Russian masses.

Beneath the still surface of solid unity which cloaks the hidden and unknown Russia, it may be accepted that the Soviet state, too, is experiencing its own social troubles though it is in a position to repress their manifestations by force. The rumors of peasant disaffections and of serious dissensions between the Army and the party, for the most part, however, can be discounted, though some very real fire may exist behind the obscuring haze of smoke.

Among encouraging signs from the Western view, has been the reintroduction of the old ranks and disciplines into the Army, and the elimination of political commissars. The Soviet Union appears now to be conscious of the glorious Russian past and of the decalogue of heroes who once graced it. Stalin has made an occasional and ingratiating speech for world consumption, stating the willingness of the U.S.S.R. to co-operate in world affairs. State-sponsored abortion has been disposed of, as has been the practice of free love. In their stead is an advocacy of large families, backed by subventions from the state. The League of the Militant Godless has been dissolved, and the patriarch Sergei, head of the Greek Church, reinstalled as the center of veneration of the Orthodox East.

More important than any of these, the feared, sinister and

[1] Issue of August 25, 1945.

shadow-like Comintern has been liquidated as an official arm
of the Soviet power machine.

A correct appraisal of these developments obviously is of
the greatest importance. They could be looked on either as
a product of expediency or as a rational growth in the direction
of conservative sobriety pleasing to the West.

As for the rapprochement with the Church, it fairly may be
regarded as an adventure in practical politics, directed toward
the Orthodox of the Balkan peninsula. When the League of
the Militant Godless and its aggressive publication, *Bezbozhnik
and Anti-religioznik*, were suspended, and in their stead a
Council for Religion formed under the Council of People's
Commissars, the Russians sealed a gap which they had been
unsuccessfully attempting to bridge during a generation of
propaganda.

The abolition of the Comintern, too, may be regarded as a
concession to proper circumspection at a moment when this
revolutionary adjunct to Soviet power waved like a red flag
before the eyes of a political world which half sympathized
with Hitler's adventure into the Ukraine though it was at
war with him.

The Comintern and its inflammatory slogan, "Workers of
the World, Unite!," made Russian policy disreputable in the
eyes of all other nations. During the crisis provoked by Hitler's
attack, it was of the utmost importance to the Soviet state that
it officially be abandoned.

As long as dialectical materialism remains the world outlook
of the Marxist-Leninist party, it is difficult to see how this
retreat from Marxian principles can be permanent. Whatever
is taking place inside the Soviet Union in respect to the new
adoration of the old Russian heroes, of Russian literature and
art, and of the virtues of virginity and motherhood, the international Communist texts have not changed.

For the most part, those around Stalin, fed on a generation
of unrelieved Communist doctrine, emboldened by a series of

economic and military successes, and eager to take their cue from what they regard as the appointed hour of their destiny, are anxious for new adventure. They see in Europe's chaos and Asia's lumbering movements toward freedom, the great opportunity for which the new Communist order has so long waited.

In the long run it would appear to make little difference who is on top in the ruling circles of the Russias except as a symbol of existing opportunities for men with muscle. The presence in power of Molotov, Zhukov, and Zhdanov, as against Litvinov or Voroshilov, means only the triumph of some special strategy rather than a major change in over-all purposes of the Soviet state.

All factions are unanimous in their belief that time is the ally of Russia. They believe that political pressures and recurring social troubles at home will force the early withdrawal of American armies of occupation, leaving Moscow with a comparatively free hand in Europe, and possibly Asia.

The party itself has emerged from the background shadows into which it had receded during the war, and is now more important than ever as the dominating influence over Soviet affairs. It has been rigidly cleansed of unreliable or lukewarm elements by a series of purges and purifications, seeking to re-establish its old Spartan-like discipline as the shield of the Revolution. It is consciously reverting for its inspiration to the original pure sources of Bolshevik thought. Marx, Engels and Lenin once more are being studied and swallowed whole, without interpretation.

The attitude of the party in any event will be dictated by strategic rather than conventional considerations of respectability. This we are compelled to accept since the party rejects the entire base from which classic Western morality is derived, and therefore cannot recognize its authority as a restraining device.

III

If any reasoned conclusion can be made from the pattern of Soviet activity in the past, the Communists will proceed with characteristic energy to a renewal of their program from where they left off. The point of departure will be marked entirely by the necessities as they apply to the immediate position of the Soviet state itself.

There are plenty of straws in the wind.

In all of the countries, it is patent that the honeymoon is over. The strategy of assisting production has come to an end. Everywhere there is indication of a return to the old class warfare program, though this time an effort is being made to align the still potent middle class with the rampaging proletariat.

In these activities, Russian intermeddling is not directly traceable. If the Kremlin indeed is involved, it has been discreetly circumspect.

To Western statesmen, the world-wide pattern of policy nevertheless appears to be clear. On circumstantial evidence and without additional proof, the grim suspicion must remain that in one way or another, many of the social troubles experienced by the West originate in Moscow.

Today as before, the Communist bodies and their affiliates in the different countries are the Kremlin's most reliable contact. Highly disciplined and devoted, their value to Soviet policy in certain parts of the world can hardly be overestimated.

In theory, the Third Internationale is composed of the representatives of Communist parties from all of the countries. During its official existence, however, it has been dominated totally by the Russian faction and used by the Kremlin as a frank instrument of Russian foreign policy.

In 1934, when Stalin thought that the capitalist states were about to carry through a concerted attack on the Soviet Union, he warned them bluntly that their plan would fail, that "it would be a most dangerous war, not only because the peoples of the U.S.S.R. would fight to the very death to preserve the gains of the Revolution, [but] for the added reason that it also would be waged behind the enemy's lines, as well as at the front. The bourgeoisie," he continued, "need have no doubt that the numerous friends of the working class of the U.S.S.R. in Europe and in Asia will do their best to strike a blow in the rear at their oppressors who start a criminal war against the fatherland of the working class of all countries."[2]

What else was in the Soviet mind, at least at that time, was frankly conceded by Stalin, apropos of his confident allegation that in the capitalist countries "a revolutionary crisis is maturing and will continue to mature." He admonished his hearers: "Some Comrades think that once there is a revolutionary crisis, the bourgeoisie must be in a hopeless position; that its end is therefore predetermined; that the victory of the Revolution is thus assured; and that all they have to do is to wait for the fall of the bourgeoisie and to draw up victorious resolutions.

"This is a profound mistake. *The victory of the Revolution never comes by itself. It must be prepared for and won. And only a strong proletarian revolutionary party can prepare for and win victory.*"

To prove his point, Stalin quoted Lenin, repeating the advice given by that great founding father of Sovietism when Europe once before was in turmoil: "The Revolutionary Parties [everywhere] must now prove by their practical actions that they are intelligent and organized enough, are in contact enough with the exploited masses, are determined and skillful enough, to utilize this crisis for a successful and victorious revolution."

Stalin's claim to the devotion of Communist parties every-

---

[2] Report to the Seventeenth Party Congress, January 26, 1934.

where has proved no idle boast. Their discipline and allegiance to the "cause of the world proletariat" has left little to be desired.

When Moscow made its startling switch to the side of Nazi Germany in 1939, Communist parties wherever they existed made the leap with it. Up to this time, they had unqualifiedly denounced Hitler as the world enemy, referring to him in uninhibited terms as a "mad dog." The second World War which broke out immediately after, was described by world communism as being "not a war against Fascism," but "a Second Imperialistic War," in which if anything, France and England were ethically in the wrong. After the demise of Poland, the subsequent Molotov-Ribbentrop pact pledged the Nazi and Soviet governments "to pool their efforts to liquidate the war." "Should the efforts of both Governments fail," the pact continues, "then the fact will be established that England and France are responsible for the continuation of the war, and the Governments of Germany and the U.S.S.R. will consult as to necessary measures."

In 1939, the Communist members were ordered out of the French Chamber of Deputies, as being collaborationist and pro-German. The American Communist party ceaselessly denounced the "capitalists' war," but maintained silence in reference to Hitler's aggressions. It opposed the Selective Service Act and was foremost in the isolationist and antipreparedness parade. In China, the important Communist sector volubly echoed this opinion, and denounced the French, English and Americans as "robber barons."

Within a matter of hours after Hitler invaded the Soviet Union, the legions of world Communism changed their tack again. The war now became a crusade of "democracy" against the Fascist beasts. In every country, the Communists were foremost in their demands for a total and aggressively waged war. The slogans of world revolution suddenly disappeared.

The Communist technique for inciting strikes and industrial turmoil came to an abrupt halt. Now it was only the "irresponsibles" and non-party men who were accountable for these activities in the unions. Throughout the West the Communists became a model of collaborative conduct in the interests of the democratic cause. Even in India, a focal point of Communist attack, the local party withdrew its assistance to the revolutionary program.

Today, the party's new line is best expressed by the French comrade, Jacques Duclos: "We are the champions and defenders of the middle class."

When we see the Soviets line themselves up also on behalf of agrarian reform in the Orient and eastern Europe, in short for peasant ownership of land, we are compelled to believe that this is a tactic and not a policy.

Both Lenin and Stalin insisted that the peasantry was "the last capitalist class," a class "whose economy is based on private property and small commodity production." Therefore, warned Stalin, the peasantry, as long as it owns the land or has access to free trade, "will breed capitalists in its ranks, and cannot help breeding them, constantly and continuously. This is of decisive importance in the question of our Marxian attitude to the problem. . . ."[3]

The possibility of a permanent alliance between Moscow and the social democracies is not a very promising one. Eliminating for the moment the Russo-phobia which exists among powerful elements in the free enterprise states, we discover in Communist credo itself the implicit conviction that social democracy is the most powerful of all the forces which Communism must buck in its path to power. Any permanent arrangement with the free democracies is considered in the nature of a disastrous compromise.

[3] Address before the Central Committee of the Communist party of the Soviet Union, April, 1929.

Assailing those whom he alleged to be right-wing spokesmen within his own party, Stalin, in an address on October 19, 1928, asserted that any deal with the social democracies could only mean "the strengthening and consolidation of capitalism, *for Social Democracy is the main support of capitalism in the working class. Hence, a victory of the Right Deviation in the Communists' Parties in capitalist countries would add to the conditions necessary for the preservation of capitalism.*"

Until the very moment of German invasion in 1940, Russian leaders had expressed themselves frankly as awaiting the time "of mortal conflict between the two world-powerful groups of imperialist robbers" (a category in which they placed the United States as well as Great Britain), as being the time for the world proletarian revolt. Stalin himself commented in reference to such a war that "it is sure to unleash a revolution and jeopardize the very existence of capitalism in a number of countries, as was the case in the course of the First Imperialist War."

It would be no more wise or sensible to draw solid long-term conclusions from the warmth with which Presidents Roosevelt and Truman were received at the Yalta, Berlin and Moscow conferences, than to make the same assumptions from an identical engaging hospitality which was shown to Von Ribbentrop a few years earlier. The same toasts were drunk, though this time to Hitler, Von Ribbentrop and the Nazi state.

In April, 1929, Stalin told the Central Committee of the Communist party that the main task in all countries was not against Fascism, but of "intensifying the fight against Social Democracy, and primarily against its left wing, which is the social prop of capitalism." At another time he wrote: "In the period of the struggle against Tsarism [1905-16] . . . the most dangerous social support of Tsarism was the liberal-monarchist party, the Cadet party. Why? Because it was the compromising party, the party of compromise between Tsarism and the majority of the people. . . . Naturally, the Party at that time directed its main blows at the Cadets, for unless the Cadets were isolated, there could be no hope of a rupture between the peasantry and Tsarism; and unless this rupture was insured, there could be no hope of the Revolution achieving victory. . . ."

Throughout Communist doctrine and philosophical writings there is an acknowledgement of the propriety of this type of strategy. The first Manifesto of the Communist Internationale states quite frankly that "the working class of all countries in its historic development has taken advantage of the regime of democracy in order to organize against capital. . . ."

IV

An appraisal of the present extent of Communist world influence reveals a dual condition, in which enormous Communist gains tend to be offset by ensuing losses. Except in those places where it may be suspected that Communist authority is being imposed by force, the old experience which followed the rank growth of radicalism after World War I is largely being re-enacted.

On the Communist side of the ledger, are important and even spectacular gains. In France the Communists have become the leading party. In the Low Countries and throughout the Balkans and Central Europe, their strength must be reckoned with in any election.

In Italy where the party chief, Palmiro Togliatti, is now Minister of Justice, the all-powerful trade unions are virtually Communist controlled, though the rank and file have been only partially touched by this philosophy. Whole troops of Fascist youths are said to have been taken over bodily into the Communist organizations.

In North China, the Communists control outright almost 100,000,000 people. They have taken an important part in the nationalist movements of southeast Asia. In India, even though only a small proletarian class exists, they have become a potent political force, ranking next to the Congress, itself, and the Moslem League.

In Latin American countries, such as Cuba and Mexico, once considered immune to Marxist philosophy, Communist leaders have won strong positions. In Brazil, after years of suppression, their growth has been spectacular. In Chile and Peru their increase, while not comparable to that which has taken place in Europe and Asia, is nevertheless of no mean consequence.

Throughout Latin America, however, the growth of Soviet ideology is complicated by the old factional ruckus between the Trotskyites and Stalinists, and is apt to be overrated through the penchant of the *hacendado* and clerical classes for labeling all progressive elements as Reds.

On the other side, all the natural protective devices of the existing order again have been galvanized for a last-ditch defense. World centripetal forces are focusing on a nationalist victory in China and have at their disposal such superior strength that the Communists do not at the moment dare risk a struggle for decision and have had no choice but to retreat. Unexpected opposition has developed to the Red program all over Europe, not only from its natural enemies of the Church and propertied classes, but from the peasants and proletariat as well.

The Russians at the beginning had endeavored to make the most of their opportunities, and were welcomed everywhere by the ordinary rank and file, who at least were in the mood to be proselytized. The British policy of resurrecting the old discredited princelings, and of backing with their guns the broken remnants of the incredibly backward feudal aristocracies, resulted in embittering moderate groups and patriots alike, turning them to support of the Communists, around whom for the moment all of the patriotic elements were rallying.

Soviet propaganda had behind it the apparently invincible power of the Russian war machine, and the might of an industrial society which could justly be stated to have been built literally out of nothing. Many of those otherwise skeptical or hostile were ready to become convinced by this glittering example that Communism was synonymous with security, and that whatever the criticisms made of the Soviet Union and its methods, they were at least effective and a stanch armor against chaos.

When the Russians entered Germany, red flags flew from almost every house in the Wedding district, the Berlin workers' section. Russian propaganda was insistent and compassionate. It was declared publicly that Premier Stalin regarded it as his personal responsibility to see that the German people were taken care of, and that food and even coffee and cigarettes were rushed to Berlin as soon as possible. The solicitude of Comrade Stalin was so great, according to Lieutenant General Berzarin, Russian commander of the Berlin zone, that he had ordered daily reports on the reconstruction work in Berlin sent on to him in Moscow.

Radio loudspeakers were installed, small radio sets freely distributed, and great pictures of Stalin installed with the inevitable inference that here was the new Fuehrer.

Despite these measures, Russian policy miscalculated badly. Europeans did not react well to the police state. The removal, as reparations, of industrial machinery into the interior of Russia angered them. They were frightened by the wholesale suppression of the underground, which had come to consider itself as the new elite, as well as by the continued liquidation of what remained of the traditional intellectual classes. The transportation of great numbers of able-bodied workers to the center of the U.S.S.R. to satisfy the drastic shortage in Soviet manpower, also produced an unpleasant effect.

Of still more serious consequence to Soviet policy was an unforeseen decline of Red Army discipline. This was accompanied by a great deal of rape, hooliganism and looting which left a bad taste wherever the Russians appeared. In Moscow itself an entire cavalry division had to be called in to suppress these manifestations of outlawism.

The shocked Russian authorities who had not been prepared for this intense reaction to years of war weariness, repressed emotion, and stern military regimentation, suppressed the disorders with an iron hand, but not before they had left a deep impression on the populations of the occupied countries.

The difficulties experienced by bureaucratic inefficiency, and the troubles ordinarily incidental to a new regime, also acted against the Russians.

Moscow overplayed its hand badly on the evident assumption that the situation was running strongly in its favor. The Russian zeal to smother all political opinion contrary to their own extended even beyond the zones directly under their control and produced an unhappy impression. The Soviet government sought to ban the publication of Trotsky's *Life of Lenin* in Italy, on the ground that it was Fascist. They demanded the suppression of the satirical magazine *Cantacchiaro* which had been poking fun at the Communists.

And even more ill-advised action was taken in regard to the Swedish magazine *Obs*, which had a relatively silly story saying of Premier Stalin that he "was never injured by rumors that after a night of heavy feasting and drinking, he had driven back to the Kremlin happily shooting his revolver . . . or that he had let his happy feelings be increased by one or another girl."[4] For this the Kremlin strongly protested in a note to

4 Issue of April 20, 1945.

the Swedish government, admonishing the latter that the *Obs* story was "incompatible with normal relations between Russia and Sweden" and demanding confiscation of the magazine.

Fully as determinative in its effect on the shifting political affections of the populations of Europe was a sudden change in the popular estimate as to the invincible nature of Soviet military power. This accompanied the discovery of the atom bomb and the stiffening of Anglo-American policy which followed the death of Mr. Roosevelt.

Until then the tenor of Russian declarations had been that "the Soviet Union had played the main, decisive part in the achievement of this historic victory"; and that "for three years, the Red Army had single-handedly fought the armed forces of Germany and her satellites."[5]

Until the birth of the atomic bomb dramatically altered the military picture, east Europe had been almost totally shut off from any contact with the West. Life in these states had gone on grimly behind a closed curtain, where according to rumor and report the Russian steamroller was methodically liquidating all opposition. Socialists, social democrats, Fascists, Trotskyites, clericals and anarchists alike were executed, imprisoned or deported. The numbers so affected were said to have amounted in some countries to some 15 per cent of the total population, a figure comparable to the liquidations undertaken by the preceding Germans.

The new swing of world power brought a scarcely veiled challenge by the Anglo-Americans to the policies of the Kremlin. As Anglo-American diplomacy hardened, it lent encouragement to the suppressed opposition, which previously had receded in hopeless resignation from what had appeared to be an invincible revolutionary cause.

Even in little Bulgaria where events were hidden behind a cloak of dread silence and where resistance to the new scheme

[5] Speech by Marshal Zhukov at Moscow, June 25, 1945.

of planned economy involved grave personal risk, the genuine opposition parties now boldly refused to participate in the elections.

In most of the other countries, the Communist tide appears to have been definitely stemmed. In some it either has been greatly overestimated or is in the process of dismal recession. The Continent is still very much to the Left, but it is not Communist.

As a result of the first early encounters for the soul of Europe, there is every evidence that ultimate staying power is in the hands of the moderate and much despised Socialists. It is clear that the battle far from being over has just begun, and that in their estimates of potential opponents, the Communists have been shrewdly accurate in selecting as the most enduring the right-wing Marxist groups.

Soon after the war's end, Europe's Socialists were beaten and unregarded in the scramble for power. Today they are supremely confident. "The Communists," announced Léon Blum, "have missed the boat."

The elections in Hungary chalked up an unexpected landslide victory for the Small Landowners party. A coalition of the Communists and social democrats managed to achieve only 43 per cent of the total vote. In Germany at the early polling the Communists trailed badly. The Austrian elections showed an actual swing to the Right, with the conservative People's party winning a clear majority over the Socialists and Communists together. In France, although they proved to be the largest of the many parties, the apparently irresistible mushrooming growth of the Communists was stopped.

Similar tests of strength everywhere indicate that the first great rush of the Communist tidal wave has spent itself.

Even more important in this assessment of relative powers, is the newly grown aloofness of the moderate left-wing groups and their cooling attitude toward the Communists. In Italy, where 70% of the Italian socialists once had voted for a political fusion with the Reds, the plan finally was renounced due to rapidly dwindling socialist support. The French socialist party rejected a similar proposal by an almost unanimous vote at its Thirty-seventh Congress, though the balloting had been expected to go the other way.

It is evident that the Russians who came into eastern Europe determined to win over the local populations, or at least the broad working classes, have forfeited the initiative wherever they are unable to apply the pressures of naked force. By having failed to grasp the tide of events at its height, they have lost prestige strongly with great groups that once had been fascinated or overawed by their doctrine and the power of their arms. This certainly is the case in Europe.

In Asia, the weight of Communist influence will depend on the course which will be pursued by the United States. Asia does not need Communism to survive, and will turn to this mystic creed of liberation only as a reaction to the humiliations, grinding misery, ignorance and poverty imposed on her by her enslavement to the imperial West.

Chapter Five

THE BEAR WHO WALKS LIKE A MAN

BENEATH the polite dissimulations with which the diplomats engage each other, there shines hard and clear the new conditions of power as well as the identity of the competing forces which wield it. Wherever the two great federal systems impinge on each other, tentative preparations are being made for a day of eventual reckoning.

The Far Eastern naval bases sought by the Americans can have only one object: to encircle Russian Asia and to neutralize it. The Russians, in turn, are fortifying the Kuriles, which places them within effective striking distance of the North American continent, though their announced purpose is that of securing "protection against renewed Japanese aggression."

From the Elbe to Trieste, and ending at the Greek border, Europe has divided into two worlds, each imbued with a deep conflict of purpose and of policy. Along the Elbe, the Americans and British plan to install permanently stationed air forces. In the strategic Middle East, the jittery British have inveigled the United States into maintaining strong military establishments as a measure of insurance against any possible Russian action in this quarter. The struggles between British, Arabs and Jews for possession of Palestine, between Britain and France over Syria, between Russia and the Anglo-Americans for Iran, the support given by the democracies to such reactionaries as Salazar of Portugal and the despotic

Arab kings, and the expedients, wrangling and machinations which have poisoned the sessions of the U.N.O., all are linked to this single cause.

It is in the Near and Middle East that this situation is seen in all its grotesque clarity. This area is one of the glittering prizes of the world. It is in the hands of minor and barbaric peoples among whom corruption is rife, and who are easily impressed by a show of power. It holds immense quantities of oil.[1] In the valleys of the Tigris and Euphrates are some of the richest agricultural lands known. These territories are the strategic pathway between three continents, a veritable cross-roads of the world, which has been fought over by world conquerors since the days of the earliest recorded kings.

Old causes and long-abandoned slogans have reappeared to add to the tangle provided by the usual propaganda, power intrigues, and traditional activities of the *agents provocateurs*. Moscow, after its rapprochement with the Greek Orthodox Church, has taken over the ancient Greek Catholic position in the Middle East as the protector of the faithful, and now supervises orthodox control of the holy places. Diplomats from the Mohammedan Soviet republics have appeared in the courts of the Arab kings. Even in British-dominated Egypt it is said that strikers prefer to lay their case before the Soviet Minister rather than any agency provided by the government or their own unions.

The Russians also have managed to identify themselves with the anti-imperialist movements and the cause of human progress in the countries of the Middle East. Dallin gives the Communist party membership in Iran as over one hundred thou-

[1] According to the DeGolyer Report made to the United States Government in 1943, a preliminary estimate indicates that Iran has in crude reserves six billion barrels, Kuwait and Iraq four billion barrels each, Saudi Arabia and Bahrein two billion barrels together, and Qatar about half a billion barrels. Other reserves of even greater magnitude are suspected, particularly in Saudi Arabia.

sand, a literally enormous figure in view of the political conditions in that country.[2]

Balancing off the scales is the outright military and economic control exercised by Great Britain. London holds Palestine, Syria, Iraq and the Hadramaut in fee simple though the fiction exists of mandates, and in the case of Iraq, of independent government.

Under the British political wing is the Arab League, a synthetic creation which was the brainchild of the late Lord Moyne, former British Resident Minister in the Middle East. Its present Secretary General, Abdul Rahman Pasha Alazzam, is reputed to be a British intelligence agent. All of the countries composing the league are in one way or another under British imperial rule.

An American military mission now is stationed in Saudi Arabia, where it is to be permanently established. The deficits of this barbaric country for long years have been underwritten by the British treasury. Today, the United States has taken a hand in the game. Soon after the European war was over, it made a beginning by presenting Ibn Saud with ten million dollars in Lend-Lease, though his country had not participated in the conflict.

In Iran, the old rivalries between the British and Russians again have become explosive. This backward theocratic state not only contains great quantities of oil, but it lies directly athwart the British lifeline to India while at the same time representing the natural path of Russian access to southern waters.

A battle royal has gone on periodically over this territory since the early 1800's.

The present occupation by the Russians, British and Americans was designed to remove the former pro-German ruler, Riza Khan, and to provide a roadway for American war

[2] *The Big Three*, p. 186.

material intended for the Russian armies. By treaty arrangement, the troops of the Big Three were to have been evacuated immediately after the end of the war. The troops were not evacuated.

In the expected maneuvers for position which ensued, an American colonel found himself in charge of the important Teheran police. The Anglo-Americans occupied strategic points in the oil economy of the country and provided the Iranian court with its economic and financial advisers.

The Russians countered with the practical measures for which they are known. By a sudden forced march one night they occupied the vital Teheran airfield which had been nervously conceded by each of the armies to be no man's territory. The Kremlin resolutely planted its feet on the extended Anglo-American neck by setting up a demand for oil on its own account.

A proletarian party known as the Tudeh (meaning "mass party") came into existence. It was compounded of a great many moderate and liberal elements, as well as Communists, though the latter, as in many of the European undergrounds, furnished the active leadership.

In the zone under Russian occupation, Tudeh became an almost exclusive power like Tito Broz in Yugoslavia. In the provinces of Azerbaijan, Gilan and Mazanderan, it is said that a Persian could not even visit the baths or ride in a public conveyance unless he produced a Tudeh party membership card.

The coup by which Azerbaijan secured its autonomy from the Iranian crown has left Iran in a sort of vacuum, its rich agricultural provinces separated by an iron line from the industrial areas of the south.

The new regime, which is under the leadership of the Tudeh party, is expected to result eventually in a merger with Soviet Azerbaijan. From now on these provinces will be an exclusive Soviet sphere of interest despite their nominal ties with Teheran. Since the rebel territory borders on northern Iraq it exposes that country also to further Russian pressure. Some foretaste of what may happen is glimpsed in the insurrectionary pro-Kurdish movement in Iraq which the Soviets are accused of promoting and which seeks to unite the Kurds of three countries into a single autonomy.

Another quarter of this giant sector, the nation of the Greeks, on the surface is recognized by the Kremlin as an exclusive British zone of interest. Beneath this formal agreement, the vicious contest between London and Moscow has gone on unabated. A strong Communist faction exists in Greece which is said to be growing rapidly as the conditions of British occupation drive many intermediate elements into the arms of radical reaction. A preview of what may be expected when the time comes is given in the plain reference by the newspaper *Izvestia* to the British occupation as an "open Fascist terror";[3] and more recently to the irritated demand by the Russians in sessions of the U.N.O. for an "investigation" of British activities in that forlorn little country.

The British have been fully as explicit. Both Churchill and Bevin have issued thinly veiled pronouncements which have drawn a deadly parallel between the current actions of the Russians on the Continent and their predecessor totalitarians, the German Nazis. Recently this challenge has tended to drop even the existing thin veil which conceals its movements.

II

The position of Britain in the rancorous contest is potentially a desperate one. It is impossible to omit the observation that age finally has caught up with the Empire as it did

[3] Moscow, August 23, 1945.

with Genoa and Austria before it, and that it no longer is possible for a small nation of forty-five million to occupy the privileged imperial position which has been Britain's fortune during the past several hundred years.

In the agony of her watching, Britain sees not only the rapid deterioration of her own situation, but a corresponding enhancement in that of the Russians. Britain is like an old bull seal which has succeeded in collecting the greater part of the eligible females on his bit of rock, and who insists on maintaining and even adding to his harem though the physical strength which created his supremacy no longer exists. The price for such ambition has always been challenge, and a renewed battle to the death.

The seriously impaired British economy cannot possibly sustain the immense drains being made upon it, yet as the fabric of empire fades, it must patch up the rents with still new adventures to match those of its growing rival.

In order to keep up the pretension to being one of the great powers, and to maintain its roadway to India and the Orient, Great Britain has been forced into the greatest per capita military expenditure of any nation. As a small state with limited resources and population, Britain not only must maintain land, sea and air establishments comparable to those of Russia and the United States, but in a strength capable of coping with the widespread diversity of her interests.

Adding to these troubles, Britain is not recuperating from the effects of the war as is the U.S.S.R., or the United States, and is becoming more and more mired in economic difficulties.

Great Britain's military and economic hold everywhere is in jeopardy. In addition to the U.S.S.R. she faces a host of minor enemies with whose ambitions she is at some point in active opposition.

The extent of British holdings now is greater than at any time in her history, a fact in strange contradiction to her present and ever growing weakness in the world power firmament.

The peak of British power was reached after World War I when the Russian empire appeared to have collapsed. The former German colonies in Africa had been seized. Southern China and the Yangtze Valley were under active British influence. The great port city of Shanghai, together with its services and major industries was virtually a monopoly of the British Sassoon family. Arabia was occupied by British troops. General Dunsterville was at Baku. The Transcaspian republics, Armenia, Georgia, Azerbaijan and the Caspian-Tashkent Railway were in English hands. An expeditionary column had established itself in Persia. A British force occupied Constantinople; the Sultan was a practical captive, and a puppet government had been formed under British tutelage. What is now Soviet Central Asia was coupled to the British system through still other puppet rulers.

With the exception of France and the United States, Britain stood without a rival, the great imperial balance point of the world, and the very symbol of the civilizing instincts of man backed by the agencies of force.

Today the Empire faces the bitter prospect of organic failure.

In the armed truce which exists between Britain and the Russias it is plain that both want the same things, and that by the simplest rule of logic both cannot have them.

The true positions of the two empires now are so heavily weighted in favor of the Russians that the Empire and perhaps Britain herself can be prevented from passing out of history only through the economic assistance and armed support of the United States. Britain no longer can maintain the equilibrium by the old method of coalition, since no coalition is possible on the Eurasian continent equal in power to the forces at the disposal of the Russians.

In order to maintain their global position we observe the British compelled to act far out of proportion to their real strength. We see them forced to add to their already swollen holdings still others; and thus to plague themselves with a Pandora's box of ever increasing problems.

We find Great Britain saving Indonesia for the Dutch and Indo-China for the French, with the aid of Japanese troops, machine-gunning insurrectory natives whom Britain suspects its imperial partners no longer can handle. We see British troops in *de facto* possession of North Africa, and reducing Ethiopia, another of the casual allies of the war, to a dependency. We see her take over bodily in Siam the controls once exercised by the Japanese; quietly supervising the banking, business and political administration of that country under the muzzles of her guns.

The British imposed harsh conditions. Siam pays reparations in the form of an "occupation tax" of approximately one hundred thousand badts a day; all British rights in that country are restored, together with an indemnity for all British losses during the war, with interest at banking rates. Siam agrees to go under British military control as a puppet state. It is prohibited from building a canal across the Kra Peninsula to join the Bay of Bengal with the South China Sea, in the interests of the British base at Singapore. The country agrees to place its tin, tea, rubber and other export products under the control of British dominated cartels.

On the ideological front in Asia, the war with Russia is fairly out in the open. The British are moving directly, as in Greece, to wipe out Communists and other radicals by the use of tanks, airplanes and field pieces.

London is seeking to build a *cordon sanitaire* around the Russians on a global scale under the guise of a strengthened U.N.O. equipped with military force. Except for occasional tempestuous outbursts, both sides are attempting to avoid the appearance of provocation in their direct relations with each other. London officially maintains on the whole a polite and eminently correct tone toward the Russians. Moscow in turn has been wary and has refrained from any overt action in respect to British interests in southeast Asia, in particular, which might be construed as aggressive. This was pointedly noticeable in the grim silence maintained by the Kremlin after the besieged Javanese publicly called on the U.S.S.R. to save them.

Under this smothering blanket of diplomatic respectability lies a tinder which already has caught fire and which no longer can be extinguished. Throughout southeast Asia, events are playing into the hands of the Russians. When British punitive expeditions burn Javanese towns in retaliation for individual acts of patriotic violence, the effect on oriental thought is no different from that had on the Czechs when the Germans destroyed the Czech village of Lidice. Russian protestations of racial equality, of class freedom, and of free national development, find willing ears among these people, who readily associate the Red doctrine with the cause of oriental freedom.

Years of insistent Japanese indoctrination also have prepared the way for Communist ideology, though contrary to Tokyo's expectations. This skilled net of propaganda has surrounded the imperial whites in a mesh of enduring hatreds, and at the same time demolished the legend of their invincibility.

Even in free China the animosities held toward Great Britain are fierce and unbending. They are sure to show themselves in serious encounters as the Chinese achieve power with which to accomplish their aims.

The British hold Hongkong which they show no intention of relinquishing. They have established control over Tibet. In spite of nominal Chinese ownership of this region they have prevented Chinese troops from entering it, just as the

Russians have stopped Iranian soldiers at the borders of Azerbaijan. On the economic side, Britain is fighting resolutely against American asssistance to Chinese industry, whose competition London feels would be deadly to British interests in the Orient.

The result, as we shall see, may be that of throwing nationalist China directly into the arms of the Moscow hierarchy, despite the basic incongruities and disharmonies which act to separate them.

The all-pervasive quality of the Russian challenge was felt in another and unlooked for quarter, involving the scramble for possession of the Italian colonies in Africa and the Mediterranean. Here the British had expected to have a free hand except for some minor opposition from the French. The latter they had hoped to take care of through the manipulation of that puppet of the Cairo Office, the Arab League, which had shown its usefulness not only in putting a good face on the removal of the French from Syria and checkmating the Zionists in Palestine, but in promoting a violent anti-European rebellion in French Algeria which Paris had to put down in blood.

When the Kremlin made the startling suggestion that it would be interested in a Russian mandate over African territory, London was aghast. The Russians inferred that they would like to have Tripoli, Eritrea, and perhaps the Dodecanese Islands, which guard the entrance to the Dardanelles. They demanded also an equal participation with the other European powers in control of the vital Tangier zone.

III

The most pressing and immediate problem to Great Britain concerns the fate of Europe. Here the situation is disquieting in the extreme. Historic British interests have made it mandatory that the Continent be kept in a state of political disequilibrium, and that no single power become great enough to impose its will there.

Today such a power exists. It is the U.S.S.R.

To prevent an extension of the Russias, or of the revolutionary ideology which precedes Russian political infiltration, Britain is almost certain to fight a war, no matter against what desperate odds.

This determination, as well as the irresoluble differences between the two powers, is of the most dramatic interest to our own nation, since we are committed to the real policy of sustaining British position. Without this backlog the British could not move, and their foreign policy would be bankrupt.

This unofficial though very real Anglo-American axis, which is backed by America's huge industrial resources and the atom bomb, has compelled the Russians to move softly in western Europe. Until the military situation is equalized again, they will depend on subtler means to advance their interests there.

Though it lacks the physical power to rule the situation adequately except in a few minor areas such as Greece, London has worked hard to build up a counterweight in the European West to the power of Russia in the East. The British have utilized the coercive weight of the Sterling Bloc in Belgium, France and the Scandinavian countries. In Italy, they have aligned themselves with the House of Savoy and possess access to the persuasion of military occupation. Here they are in the unique position of backing ex-enemy Italy against ex-ally Yugoslavia for possession of Trieste and Venezia Giulia. To stimulate Italian friendship London has changed its tack in Sicily and Sardinia, plumping for Italian unity where formerly Britain had encouraged separatist movements to be like Iraq and Egypt under British political tutelage.

The weakness of British position on the Continent is manifest. The vassal kings and reactionary regimes supported by London are not in tune with the normal flow of forces activating Europe. In espousing such worthies as King George of Greece and Victor Emmanuel of Italy, Great Britain is attempting to move against the current of events. She, hence, unavoidably has become the symbol of exploiting tyranny to the greater part of the peoples concerned, a view recited by the Italian liberal, Gaetano Salvemini, in a caustic denunciation which accuses the British government of furthering a policy by which "the 'natives' in Europe are to have no peace: A second India has become necessary in Europe."

While the Anglo-Americans are allying themselves with archaic, if not antisocial, forces on the Continent, the Russians are attempting to move with the popular current. In each country, the Communist machine is compact and closely organized, possessing its intelligence as well as propaganda branch, and operating under a disciplined control which is almost more military than political in its efficiency. In many of the European states the Communist party possesses its own secret armed forces. Above all, it has a goal and a dynamic program, which its competitors sadly lack. Such men as Bierut in Poland, Pieck in Germany, the master strategist Grieco in Italy, the redoubtable Dmitrov in Bulgaria, Thorez of France, and Marshal Tito in Yugoslavia, are Russian trained—instructed with fanatic resolution for just such an emergency as this.

These men are prepared to swing with the tide, to alter their policies daily, to utilize strong-arm methods where they will serve the cause of the Revolution, or like Hitler, to attempt the seizure of control by legal means where this appears desirable.

IV

The single set of considerations which characterizes the actions of both the great allies in Europe is their utter lack of either conscience or scruple where power goals are concerned.

All of this is clearly depicted in the construction of the so-called Russian security zone in Europe.

Soon after the collapse of Germany, it was apparent that the Russians were proceeding to assimilate border areas into their system. This occurred under much the same progressive procedures which resulted in the earlier destruction of the three Baltic republics.

Everywhere the Russians acted without reference to their obligations or previous assurances.

The first warning of Russian intentions came in the case of Bulgaria.

During the entire period of the European war the U.S.S.R. had been at peace with this little country. When the military failure of the Axis became a foregone conclusion, Bulgaria decided to surrender to the Anglo-American authorities, with whom a state of hostilities had long existed. In the hours before this surrender could take effect, Moscow suddenly declared war, and in a lightning thrust proceeded to occupy Bulgaria alone.

Thus the U.S.S.R. presented its allies with a *coup de main* calculated in its own interest, though keeping nicely within the letter of the agreement to which it was committed. This nicety ceased, however, with the Russian failure to implement the armistice arrangement, to which each of the Big Three had agreed, by which there was to be established in former enemy states an Allied Control Commission to "regulate and supervise the execution of the armistice terms under the chairmanship of the representative of the Allied-High Command, and with the participation of representatives of the United States and the United Kingdom." This "participation" the Soviet authorities by one means or another prevented.

A veritable Chinese Wall of silence was erected around the countries of central and eastern Europe, which remained tightly sealed to outside penetration until determined Anglo-

American pressure succeeded in correcting the situation in part.

The three Baltic states were swallowed outright and without pretense. For other countries differing patterns of control were created. In Yugoslavia and Poland, the one-party system is frankly in the saddle, though lip-service is being paid to the principle of an elective party system. In Austria, makeweight has been provided by some socialists, Catholics and social democrats, one of whom at least, Leopold Kunschak, was known to have had strong anti-Semitic leanings.

In Hungary ultimate power is wielded not by the provisional government, which is unreliable, but by the Russian Marshal Voroshilov. In Rumania the Communist leader, Petru Groza, must rely on the Soviet Vice-Commissar for Foreign Affairs, Andrei Vishinsky, a situation which caused the aged leader of the Peasant party, Juliu Maniu, to remark that "the only difference between the Russian and German occupation is that when the Germans were here we had a Rumanian dictator. Now, instead of Antonescu we have Vishinsky."

Through this variable weave of political techniques a great many similarities of design are visible. The foundation in each case is a patriotic front, in which the initiative is taken by the Communists. In the ensuing "coalition" government, Communist appointees take over the ministries of Justice and the Interior, giving them control of the police and the economic machinery of the state. Where they are able, as in Austria and Bulgaria, they also take charge of the important Ministry of Education.

As soon as the government has been firmly installed, a ruthless liquidation of so-called enemies of the state follows. There are widespread imprisonments, shootings and deportations, in which the same kind of people who are elevated to office in the American and British zones are liquidated as Fascists in the Russian.

To give a picture of what has taken place, among those executed as Fascists in Poland were the two leaders of the mildly radical Jewish Socialist party, Erlich and Alter.

For the moment, the old enemies of Communism, the aristocrats, bankers and industrialists, are not interfered with; though the leaders of the social revolutionary parties, the Trotskyites, liberals, intelligentsia, army officers and dissenting politicians, in one way or another are silenced. The attitude was recited bluntly by the Czechoslovak Minister of Information, Kopecky. "Whoever is against the Communists," he charged, "is a German agent and an enemy of the Republic. Former political parties, particularly the Agrarians and the National Democrats, which our Government has forbidden, will never revive."

In Poland, Czechoslovakia, Yugoslavia, Hungary and elsewhere, the organization, armament and training of the army has been made identical with that of the Red armies. Poland was presented with twenty vessels to serve as a nucleus for its new navy, a fleet which remained under command of the Russian Rear Admiral, Kilotay Abramov.

In some countries, nationalization has proceeded at a fairly rapid rate. This has been the case with Poland, Yugoslavia and Czechoslovakia. The latter country has announced that its future economy is to be synchronized with Russia's next five-year economic plan.

In German, Hungarian and other territories, the socialization process has been as assured, but not as apparent. Basic industry has been nationalized, but there has been no collectivization of the land. Instead there have been so-called land reforms in which the land has been distributed among the individual peasants. This tactic furnishes the regime with the immediate good will of the peasants. It also bears an important relation to the fact that the tractors and oil necessary for large-scale mechanized agriculture will not be available for some years.

Wherever it fulfilled the purposes of Communist policy, the weapon of drastic terror has been introduced. In Yugoslavia, it has been under the control of the local militia. In unreliable areas such as parts of Poland, and in Hungary, the job was undertaken by the N.K.V.D. or the Red Army itself, acting against opponents invariably described as "local banditti."

Wherever it has seemed politically advantageous as a stop-gap measure the Russians did not hesitate to deal with the most reactionary blackguards of Europe.

When Soviet troops entered Germany, the Kremlin had in readiness the potential structure of a German government-in-exile. Its most curious characteristic was that it was composed for the most part of German army officers with a sprinkling of old-time Communists. At its head was the German Junker General von Paulus, a thoroughly unregenerate German militarist who before his capture had been known as the Butcher of Kharkov. These men are still being held in readiness by the Kremlin as against some unforeseen eventuality. They wear their old uniforms, have their own orderlies, and live in comparative freedom in Moscow.

In Bulgaria the Soviet-sponsored government was headed by Kimon Gheorghieff and Damian Veltcheff, two of the worst reactionaries on the Continent. In Austria the Russian occupation appointed as Foreign Minister, Dr. Karl Renner, an ex-labor leader who in 1938 had been an ardent partisan of collaboration with Hitler. In Italy, Moscow suddenly recognized the fascist General Badoglio, much to the consternation of the Anglo-Americans who had continued to keep him dangling in uncertainty. The price was the acceptance into the government, as Vice-Premier, of the veteran Communist agitator, Togliatti.

In a similar unilateral action in Rumania the Soviets recognized a government under the tutelage of the notorious Iron Guardist, General Nicolai Radescu. After a short period of grace, Radescu himself was overthrown, and had to flee for his life to the British Embassy at Bucharest. The Communist, Petru Groza, now found himself snugly seated at the head of the government.

To make the transition more palatable to the historically jingoistic Rumanians, the Rumanian Nazi, Georges Tatarescu, was appointed Vice-Premier, and the province of Transylvania was transferred by decree to Rumania from its former possessor, Hungary.

In this tissue of settlements and power actions no other ally was consulted. This was despite the "sacred obligations" Moscow had assumed together with each of the other big powers to "maintain and strengthen in the peace to come, that unity of purpose and of action which has made victory possible."

Though each of these regimes was accounted to embrace all of the so-called "democratic" factions, it is notable that in every case it was the Communists who held the whiphand. The type of "democracy" which exists in Yugoslavia may be seen from Marshal Tito's criticism of the Western democratic system, which he described as nothing but a social vacuum "harboring reactionaries, exploiters and Fascists, and giving them the opportunity to undermine true democratic institutions."

A single-party system after the Russian model pertains in the Yugoslav federation. At the elections, Marshal Tito's list of candidates was presented for vote with no opponents. The National Liberation Front is the only political organization which legally may exist.

In Yugoslavia, all the curious mixture of Russian policy meets in combination. Tito himself is a professional Communist who has been a soldier in the Russian Army. He has appointed in charge of the Department of Internal Affairs a Greek Orthodox priest. A Yugoslav Moslem is Commissar for Communications. Although an orthodox Marxist, Tito makes a passionate display of his adherence to Pan-Slavism. "Yugoslavia," he cried on one occasion, "no longer is alone as she was in 1941. Today she has her big sister, Soviet Russia, as an ally . . . Today, Yugoslavia also has intimate ties with her Slav brothers of Poland, Czechoslovakia, Bulgaria and Albania!"

A comparatively free elective system exists in Hungary and Austria, though the results have not been known to change the executive operations of either government.

In Finland the government shows some signs of reflecting the opinions of the total electorate. Finland, for some reason, is allowed to function with a real semblance of national independence, with the social democrats and right-wing elements possessing the great majority of the parliamentary seats.

Despite their numerical weakness, however, the Communists have control of the police, and hold some important posts in the cabinet.

V

If a great trial for world supremacy is to occur, the modern plains of Megiddo on which it will begin will be found either in the Middle East, Germany, or China.

It is in the captive German Reich that the widely divergent programs followed by the Russians and the Anglo-Americans are most liable to meet in collision.

By dividing the Reich into four different administrations, the Allies made a practical acknowledgement of the gross suspicions, and unbridgeable differences of purpose which exist between them.

In the city of Berlin, as in Vienna, joint occupation by all of the major allies was provided for from the beginning, but no such joint occupation occurred. An impenetrable news blackout, shoddy excuses, a vast entanglement of red tape, or dead Soviet silence greeted every effort of the Anglo-Americans to clear the situation.

Until the forceful representations which resulted in the Potsdam Conference, no American or British officials were admitted into those zones. Whether due in part to the successful atomic experiments in New Mexico or to other reasons, the present areas of agreement on the knotty German and Austrian questions have dated from this time. Until then it had appeared that just as that section of Germany east of the Oder had become part of the Polish extension of the Kremlin's shadow, the portion extending to the Elbe also would be incorporated into the Soviet empire.

When the thunder of Russian boots sounded the victorious entrance of the Muscovite legions into Germany, the Soviet authorities drew a careful distinction between Germany and the Hitlerite Reich. They came not as avengers but as politicians. Russian propaganda was intensive and involved all of the paraphernalia of a great promotion campaign, including radio broadcasts, controlled newspaper stories, and great street pictures of a friendly and smiling Stalin.

From the beginning, the Russians rejected the nonfraternization policy to which the Anglo-Americans were committed.

The newly revived Communist party in Germany attempted the same compromise interim policy followed by Red parties elsewhere in Europe. The big estates were to be divided among the landless peasants; a strong effort was made to win over the middle class by an announced policy of moderation, especially in the realm of small enterprise. Private ownership was to be continued; the Committee of Generals, decked out in the full gold braid of their office, was ready.

The Russian attempt to win over the people of Germany

to Soviet policy, notably has failed. Nevertheless Russians remember what everyone else tends to forget: despite the Hitlerite episode in her national life, Germany was the home of Marx and of Marxism. It bears the same mystic relation to the Revolution that Austria did to the rising might of the Third Reich.

It was socialist Germany which prepared the way for Hitlerite Germany. When the conversion occurred, the intermeshing social machinery of the Reich and the buttons which controlled it remained intact. There was a change in uniform and the addition of the great ingredient of racial megalomania. That was all. In the election of November, 1932, the Communist party had received 5,794,000 votes; the Socialists, 7,247,000. The National Socialist party which itself contained powerful and fanatic left-wing elements, polled 11,000,000. There were some 9,500,000 votes additional, divided among a miscellany of other parties.

According to prophetic Marxist texts the great world revolt of the proletariat was to have started in Germany, where the conditions allegedly were ripe for it.

Under the Hitler regime, the socialist phase was far more advanced than is commonly realized. Had the Nazis won the war, the scheme for a planned economy, though primarily servicing the needs of the German racial elite, undoubtedly would have been implemented to the hilt. In the latter days Naziism claimed stentoriously that it had broken the control of international finance in Europe, and that it was a true philosophy of equalitarianism. America and Britain were described as vicious "pluto-democracies," and the Anglo-American leaders derisively referred to as "those capitalist hyenas."

The long Russian memory hearkens back to one other fact: from the day of Bismarck and through to the geopoliticians headed by Haushofer, the German military mind has seen the future of the Reich in a collaboration with the Russian East. "Germany will have to decide," wrote Haushofer, "whether she is to be a satellite of the Anglo-Saxon powers and their super-capitalism . . . or whether she will be a powerful ally of the pan-Asiatic union against Europe and America."

With characteristic ego the Germans have looked upon Russia as their own special sphere of influence. They do not think that present Russian power will last any more than it has lasted in the past. They hope ultimately to neutralize the U.S.S.R. by alliance, and at the same time to corrupt the United States to German purposes for the next war.

However one might discount this expression of swollen German ego, the U.S.S.R. may not prove immune to the contagion of Brown Bolshevism. By a few simple rationalizations it would be possible for both of these revolutionary ideologies to meet on a plateau of common interests. Though this may be but a macabre dream, the Reich conceivably could promote it in a last convulsive effort to generate the new strength needed to continue on its march to power.

An infiltration of former Nazis into German politics is certain. To some degree these people are sure to bring some remnant of their former ideology with them. The German Communist party officially has welcomed into its ranks "penitent, nominal Nazis who have seen the error of their ways," though in the American zone these people are prohibited from engaging in politics, and have lost the right of suffrage.

To the Russians, it is obvious that the German Reich with its skilled industrial population, its manufacturing cities, its coal, iron and other raw materials, and its unparalleled position on the Continent, will continue to be a decisive factor in the world balance of power. Within five years, according to a report by the Kilgore Committee, "Germany could be far better prepared for war . . . than she was in 1939." With the exception of the key industries destroyed by bombing, Ger-

man industrial production in 1944 was at the highest level
in its history.

The Reich would be a rich prize. Were the Communists
firmly established in control even of their present zone, Soviet
dominion would reach from a distance comparable to that
between San Francisco and Berlin. At its greatest depth in
Asia, it would be as far as between Montreal, Canada, and
Caracas, Venezuela.

The only access to this Brobdingnagian empire, flanked on
all sides by impassable deserts, mountains, and frozen tundras,
would be by air or through the narrow German plain. The
old wide-open line reaching from the Pripet Marshes to the
Pruth and Dniester, would give way to an easily held defense
resting on the Carpathian Mountains to the south and the
enclosed sea of the Baltic to the north.

Under any circumstance, the Russians regard it as mandatory to their policy that the mighty industrial power of Central Europe never again be part of an anti-Soviet coalition.
If it cannot be incorporated in the Soviet empire, this area
must be neutralized. This is the plan.

The presence of the Anglo-Americans in Germany has
brought about mixed results—all of them anathema to the
Russians.

The Americans and English are accused of preaching
democracy, but not practicing it. Both are alleged to have
staffed their zones with reactionary administrators in whom
hatred of the Soviets is so deep-seated as to constitute an
actual sickness. In the British zone, the defeated German army
remains free of restraint. German troops not only retain their
military status, but are granted increased rations over civilians.
German functionaries belonging to the old regime remain.
So do the ubiquitous industrialists. In both the English and
American zones there are no social democrats or liberals in
top positions, and no Communists in any position.

In the Russian zone on the other hand, Communists hold all of the key positions.

When the Russians use the term "de-nazification process," they mean something entirely different than when the Anglo-Americans use it. In the American zone, war prisoners are treated to a course in re-education culled from the writings of Abraham Lincoln, the American Constitution, and Commager's *Pocket History of the United States*. To the representatives of the Soviet Union such teachings are a pure perversion of the future, at total variance with their own conceptions.

London and Washington suspect that Russian ambitions are without limitation; and that the Soviets are waiting their policy out against the inevitable hour when pressures at home will force the Anglo-Americans to withdraw their troops. As if in preparation for such an eventuality, Walter Ulbricht, Deputy Leader of the Communist party in the Russian-occupied zone, announced the Communist intention of extending their Four-Party United Front throughout the Reich. American authorities noted uneasily that this was in defiance of General Eisenhower's prohibition of such political blocs in their zone.

The Germans have not been slow to take advantage of this rivalry, if they are not assiduously promoting it. There has been a great deal of carefully worked out flattery and entertainment, aimed especially at the Americans. The skilled political executives and propaganda operators who escaped the ruin of the Third Reich are everywhere in evidence. The new collective line of attack is patient and even obsequious. It is designed to excite compassion for the defeated Reich and an understanding of the "provocations" which caused it to erupt. The German people are painted as being "much like the Americans" in their cleanliness, efficiency and even kindness. German music, beer drinking, simple home life, and the traditional thick sentimentality, have been given almost the controlled sequence of a movie script.

This is war in another form. Even the general low state of sexual morality fostered by the Nazis has been utilized. German females have given themselves freely to American soldiers. The influence of these women is often large, causing the reportorial remark that to "many a discerning GI, the U. S. occupation rule of Germany and Austria was being called 'the government of interpreters and mistresses.'"[4]

It cannot be denied that a growing softness is visible on the part of Americans and English toward the Germans, as well as a very real sympathy for them. This sentiment has been quickened by underlying British policy, which again sees the Reich as a bulwark against Russian aggression in the West. London has been instrumental in the present hardening of America's view toward the U.S.S.R., and the general mitigation of American opinion toward Germany.

The tendency now is to ameliorate the harsh, punitive terms of economic demobilization which the Anglo-Americans once proclaimed as their set policy. This solicitation for the welfare of our former enemies has gone to the point of granting them a better winter food allotment than we have allowed even our former allies on the Continent.

What will come of all this is anyone's guess. It is certain that it constitutes a policy which the Russians will test by force on the first occasion they feel themselves able. It is certain, too, that the century-old policy of Disraeli and the Pitts of keeping the Continent in a perpetual state of imbalance so that Britain could maintain herself in the role of balancer, has failed.

Eastern Europe reaching from Stettin to Trieste has disappeared from the European trading map, and undoubtedly will be merged with the collectivist world of Eurasia. As far

[4] *Time*, October 15, 1945.

as western Europe is concerned, the world of free enterprise may merely have gained a breathing spell.

The Nazis had reorganized the Continent into a single, working economy identified with German military needs. Under this management, the economic life of Europe had been rationalized and reordered. Europe was not happy, but it existed and functioned.

The wreckage which followed the German defeat, and the subsequent re-Balkanization of the European map, has returned the economic life of the Continent to an orderless wilderness.

The states of western Europe have lost their old manufacturing and marketing relationship to each other and with the world at large. Their present individually severed economies cannot continue in the present vacuum, and in the end must be the prey of severe dislocations with which the conventional West will be unable to cope. The questions of war and peace, of interchange of trade, manufacture, resources and markets, demand either a rational solution or ultimate chaos. The entire political framework of the Continent with its parochial chauvinisms, its trade walls and economic barriers, its inland waterway transport systems, and the uneven distribution of its coal, iron and manufacturing industries, makes a common pattern of administration mandatory.

Unless the Anglo-Americans can find a way to accomplish this object, we must be prepared to write off western Europe, too, as lost to inevitable Soviet penetration.

During the period when the U.S.S.R. was engaged in the early phases of its mortal struggle with Germany, by concessions which allowed Moscow full access to the big seas we might have been able to declare a unified Europe in existence. However, the statesmanship which could have provided so sensible a policy was wanting. Today it is more than doubtful whether such a cause could be espoused in good discretion by the Western statesmen.

Stalin is certain to oppose this project. To the U.S.S.R., which nurses its own dream of a great Soviet Europe, the big subcontinent is merely a noisy, dynamic, aggressive and alien body, of which Hitlerite Germany merely happens to be the most obnoxious part. It is a competing universe which has devoted much of its energies to a recurring invasion of the territories of Holy Mother Russia, under the leadership of now one, and then another, nation.

Stalin has inherited Hitler's determination never to allow the creation of a strong military power on his frontiers. If he cannot control Europe outright, he will seek to insulate the U.S.S.R. and its economy by the creation of a series of managed twilight zones around its borders.

Above all, Russia will not agree to a western Europe under British tutelage. To the Kremlin this could not fail to mean the formation of an anti-Russian coalition.

The Russians can afford to wait. They will not welcome serious social disturbances in non-Soviet Europe since they have no taste for an unmanageable crisis which might precipitate another ruinous war. Moscow prefers to gain its ends by more graduated and peaceful means, which from the Marxist view constitutes an ineluctable maturing of historic forces.

In any case, the position of Great Britain as an offset island less than thirty miles away from the Continental mainland is not an enviable one. It must occur to all that the day when America and Great Britain discovered a way to invade the *Festung Europa*, there was discovered also the way by which England herself could be invaded.

Chapter Six

MATRIX FOR WORLD WAR III

EXCEPT for the sixteen-year period of political ostracism by which we attempted to show our condemnation of Soviet social policies, the relations of the United States with Russia have been uniformly friendly.

The two nations never have had a serious quarrel. Such differences as we have had with the Russian empire always have been based on the existence of opposing social systems, even under the tsars, whose despotisms and pogroms were anathema to us.

The interests of the United States and Russia never have collided to the point where armed conflict threatened as a means of settlement. We have had no territorial disputes with the Russians, and no clashes over mercantile ambitions.

On the whole the intercourse between the two countries has been characterized by their remoteness from each other. As far as any material effects on either state were concerned, the other might as well have been on the moon.

Today the word "remoteness" no longer can describe their dealings. The elbow room which each possessed as an isolated universe has disappeared. The two states have awakened to the fact that they now are neighbors, and that each possesses qualities which are disagreeable to the other.

Notwithstanding the differences of social outlook which distinguish the two Titans, there are no areas of conflict between them directly anchored in their historic needs as commonwealths.

Eliminating our suspicions of the Trojan-horse policy of Moscow, there is only one potential source of trouble between the two countries which must be weighed by the United States as an inescapable precursor to war. This derives from the acknowledged fact that it is only these two powers which can determine the fate of the world, and that the rest of the political firmament consists of a Balkanized area possessing no decisive power potential whatever.

The problem, hence, is not one of achieving a delicate state of balance between a large number of national pygmies whose merging forces determine the issue, but of measuring the size and production potential of the two primary giants.

To the United States, the logic of these events is unmistakable. Stated simply it is this: no other nation-state (i.e., the U.S.S.R.) can be allowed to grow so powerful as to present us with the problem of its literal invincibility in the event of a contest between us.

As a matter of derivative reasoning, if we are to remain as we are within the confines of our present territorial limits, and if the U.S.S.R. is to continue the surging process of growth which now characterizes it, a time will come when Russia will outweigh us in every department, forcing on us an inevitable tutelage as mistress of the world. If the U.S.S.R. continues her expansion, this result is insured by the opportunities provided in her Eurasian setting alone. This enormous land mass when seen as a single unit embraces fifteen-sixteenths of all humanity, and a comparable proportion of the world's natural wealth.

Haunted by such a prospect, the United States could not afford to remain a passive spectator in any activity which might lead to complete Russian dominance of the Old World. We would have to examine carefully every Russian gain with a weather eye open to its effect on her own world position.

To the United States, the key to Russian expansion policy on the Eurasian continent is not contained in Europe except where a war would arise involving Great Britain, which with her sister islands to the north is still the pivot to our security in the North Atlantic.

Europe has fulfilled its destiny as mistress of the world, and will become from the viewpoint of influence and power what it is geographically, a peninsular extension of the great Eurasian land pile.

To the United States the real crux of the global balance is what happens to the more than one billion people of Asia and the territories they inhabit. It seems certain that as a result of the decline of Europe and of the impact of modern industrialism and social ideas on the teeming populations of the Orient, the center of world gravity will shift from the aging Atlantic to the shores of the Pacific, which will become the new sea of destiny.

If European civilization now fails, the East with its deeper grasp of philosophic knowledge, its greater mass of humanity, and its longer continuity of culture, will take over where we have left off.

In India, southeast Asia, and the Chinese coastal plain, are close to half the world's population, an historic force capable of achieving the highest stage of social organization.

For generations the Orient has been caught in a political trough and has foundered at what must be considered the nadir of its energies, giving the West a false conception of its potential powers.

The interaction of trade, the propaganda activity of Japan, the sudden paralyzing weakness of Europe, and the ideological patterns which have accompanied the industrial revolution and have forced all mankind on the march, will make the Orient of increasing potency in human affairs. There is no power which can prevent its ultimate industrialization, or the demoralization and destruction of universal culture if the West chooses to impose by military means its concepts of imperial servitude.

It is physically impossible to thwart the normal processes of development as they apply to a considerable and vigorous people and to condemn them to a slave economy. In a very practical sense, as well as on the level of political idealism, Asia has become the testing ground "for all our theories and ways of doing things." If we fail in Asia there is no hope "for a cooperative world order."[1]

With the perfect sagacity of the downtrodden, Asia senses strength and weakness quickly; and it is contemptuously aware of the serious deficiencies which underlie the pretensions of the European sahib. British prestige can never recover from the mortal blow it suffered when the imperial armies were beaten back by an Asiatic people. Though the British fought well in Burma, Asia is aware that British and Dutch arms had little to do with ultimate victory in the decisive theater of the Pacific; despite the token participation by a few British ships, on which London had insisted for the sake of its prestige effect.[2]

Asia is sullenly conscious that though the European imperials are determined to hold to their privileges on that continent to the end, they no longer may do so by pure power, but only through their influence on American diplomacy.

Whatever friendship America has in Asia will be lost if it is believed that our government is a partner in the effort to revive sahib rule in the colonies. This conviction on the part of Asiatics will cause them to classify us with the hated

[1] Owen Lattimore, *Solution in Asia.*

[2] The American Navy would have preferred to eliminate British and Dutch assistance in this campaign due to the logistical difficulties involved in the supply of separate requirements in shells, repair parts and other war materials.

imperialists no matter how pious our political tracts and explanations of intention may be. Our protestations of good will and democracy already begin to have a shabby ring to sullen, poverty-stricken and victimized people, oppressed by the imperialist designs of small but still powerful European nations whose whole way of life depends on the continued exploitation of others.

These peoples will not be impressed with the advantages of Western democracy as against the rational solutions offered by the Communists as long as the humiliations and abuses of colonial exploitation remain. If a new Spartacide struggle against European imperialism is to ensue, we cannot escape being sucked into the ungovernable maelstrom of events which will follow.

It will be a serious blunder for us to continue viewing the Orient as an amorphous and perpetually unstable piece of creation whose principal róle will be to provide a field for Western financial and mercantile operation.

This part of the globe is certain to develop economically, industrially and militarily in breathtakingly giant strides.

To believe that the Chinese and Indians cannot industrialize, because they have not done so, is foolish.

If one doubts the capacity of Orientals to achieve because their nation is late on the scene of military and political competence, it may be remarked that the Romans from the viewpoint of Egypt and Phoenicia were even later. The very nations of northern Europe which since have led in the economic conquest of nature, were primitive barbarians when Rome already had declined, and until a thousand years ago many of them were almost unknown to history.

The Orient will modernize itself with or without our help. The question will be only one of relative rapidity and painfulness. The basis for enduring human values does not rest with the speculations of the academic economists, as we have discovered in the case of Communist Russia. Without a sound money system and despite the dire predictions of many Western leaders, the Soviets were able to build the great Magnitogorsk and Dnieprostroi works as well as the magnificent factory concentrations in Central Asia and elsewhere.

The Hitlerite Reich also rose like some terrible phoenix from the ashes of an all but incurable bankruptcy which was supposed to have made such a result impossible.

Both the Indians and Chinese have wide and ambitious plans for the economic development of their countries. They combine with these both the will and enthusiasm to carry them out against all obstacles.

The peninsula of India seethes with frustration, hurt dignity and unrequited aspirations.* It possesses the people and natural resources with which to build a modern industrial state. When Britain's century-old deindustrialization policy toward India was reversed due to the desperate situation created by

* The recent British offer of complete independence to India is not taken seriously by the Indians. They regard this proposal with uneasy suspicion as designed to nullify recent world criticism of British actions. They fear that the so-called "independence" which would evolve would be similar to the "independence" of Egypt, Iraq, Poland and Outer Mongolia. The probable result is compared to the recent declaration of an "independent" Transjordan. This territory nevertheless continues to be occupied by British troops, and conducts its affairs under the wing of British "advisers" substantially as before.

The practical fact is that were Britain to lose India she would lose not only her privileged position in Indian markets, but would be subject to the ruinous competition of Indian industry throughout Asia. The offer, it will be noted, is based on the ability of all factions "to get together." Immediately Mr. Jinnah of the Moslem League announced himself in opposition. The six hundred "independent" princely states may also be relied on to take the same position, backed by British airplanes.

The problem is impossible of solution except by the absolute independence demanded by Gandhi, Nehru and other Indian leaders. The alternative plan of turning India into a dominion cannot be applied since it would result in the inevitable Indianization of the Empire by pure force of numbers.

That Britain has no intention of relinquishing her hold on the big peninsula is indicated by London's straining effort to secure its hold over Greece, Palestine and Egypt, and to neutralize Iran and other way stations on the route to India.

World War II, India leaped into sixth place among the world's industrial countries. Her manufactures included steel, airplanes and machine tools as well as such staples as cotton goods.

The fifteen-year goal of the Bombay Plan proposed by leading Indians envisages an enormous growth of heavy industry, and a total increase in industrial output of 500 per cent during this period.

Chinese plans are even more ambitious, with priority given to the development of the chemical and steel industries, and electric power plants. China has all of the resources required to erect a powerful modern machine economy, and will attempt to do so under a program which largely will parallel that of Soviet Russia. The main tasks already have been outlined in a meticulous blueprint issued by China's Supreme Economic Council.

To bridge the gaps in this industrialization chart, China expects to import great quantities of American machinery and other heavy goods. This includes, among other items, half a million new automobiles a year for ten years, and a total of five hundred surplus American ships.

This passionate determination to run their own affairs has become almost an obsession with the Chinese. Recently the various Chinese shipping organizations meeting with the Chinese Chamber of Commerce at Shanghai, produced a startling resolution which demanded of the Central government that it "debar ships flying foreign flags from the privilege of plying Chinese waters."

If the Chinese program is realizable, within the lifetime of some of our present statesmen, China very well might become the foremost industrial and military power of the world.

The great Chinese specter is the antagonism of Great Britain to any major industrial development in the Orient. Chinese leaders believe that Britain is the axis of a Western conspiracy to keep China out of the world markets, and in a semicolonial status.

British power actions in Burma, Siam, Indo-China, Indonesia and Tibet have added greatly to Chinese nervousness. Chungking has a healthy respect for the trained capacities of British officials, and for their skill in any game of international power intrigue.

The Chinese are in deadly fear that in the end British influence over Anglo-American policy will cause America to back London in any quarrel which may develop. They are apprehensive that during the cooling-off period following the end of the war British diplomats will succeed in convincing Americans of the necessity for arresting Chinese industrial growth in the interests of Anglo-American trade and military security in eastern Asia.

The Chinese, on their side, are determined to prevent the re-establishment of colonial privilege in what they regard as their own backyard, and if possible to oust the imperials altogether.

Russia hence is considered to be a providential counterweight to the power of the Anglo-Americans, even though it too pursues a policy fraught with its own dangers to the new China.

The wide prestige the Soviets gained in the Orient as a result of their successful conduct of the war has been a factor of considerable significance. It gave the Russians "face," erasing the derogating memories of Russia's humiliating capitulation to the Japanese in 1904-1905, and the complete collapse which ended Russian participation in World War I.

It should be borne in mind that nationalist China under the Kuomintang is a single-party state. Though he may simulate the forms of Western democracy, there is little likelihood that Chiang will implement the spirit of the agreement into which he was forced, whereby there is to be set up in China a governing Political Council, on which the Kuomintang will be only one of four groups possessing equal representation.[3]

That the Kuomintang will voluntarily abdicate its present all-powerful position is unlikely. Chiang, moreover, is highly suspicious of our demand for a democratic China. He considers that the Republic to be strong, and capable of mastering the difficulties which block the way to its return to greatness, must be under a powerful authoritarian rule.

The Generalissimo is known as a shrewd horse trader. He undoubtedly will attempt to balance off the Western capitalist states against the U.S.S.R. in order to increase his bargaining position. Despite the major suspicions and deep-seated hostilities which exist between nationalist China and revolutionary Russia, there are powerful factors which act to draw them together. One is the strong Communist faction in the Chinese northwest. The bloc of Chinese Communist provinces gives Russia a strong trading point in its dealings with the Chinese Republic. A bargain with Russia which for a time removed the thorny Yenan administration from Chungking's side, could not help but be regarded as a great windfall.

In its efforts to swallow this territory without some *modus vivendi* with the U.S.S.R., nationalist China would bid fair to strangle itself. The alternative would be a forced reliance on the continued presence of foreign military units, a course which must involve Chungking in even graver risks and anxieties. In view of China's sad experiences in the past, even the present American intervention in his favor is bound to fill Chiang with misgivings.

II

The psychology of the Orient toward the white man has been conditioned adversely by two unfortunate circumstances.

[3] These are the Kuomintang, the Communists, the Democratic League and a coalition of various independents.

These are (1) the long-continued race snobbery of the colonials; and (2) the unceasing flood of Japanese propaganda with which Asia has been thoroughly infected. Just as the once democratic French have become imbued with anti-Semitism as a result of Nazi indoctrination, the entire Orient has absorbed many of the persuasions which actuated the Japanese.

This represents a condition whose latent dangers can hardly be exaggerated. There have been clashes between American G.I.'s and Chinese mobs in Chungking, and incidents where menacing crowds have gathered to spit at and stone Chinese girls found with Americans.

In Calcutta, India's largest city, severe rioting took place to protest the treason trials of followers of the late Subhas Chandra Bose,[4] who had been attached to the Japanese Army in units meant to spearhead the planned Nipponese invasion from Burma. In Bombay in a demonstration against the presence of Westerners in India, a mob wearing the uniform of the Royal Indian Navy tore down an American flag and burned it in the streets.

These episodes, though not important in themselves, are laden with warning to the West. The day has long since passed when the principal clubs of Bombay or Calcutta could exclude Indians on principle, or when Chinese notables riding the river boats of the Yangtze could be forced to ride second-class as racial inferiors; or where the major resources and services of any of these great populated Asiatic areas could be turned to the advantage of absentee European owners and ruled by alien rather than native requirements.

What we are having trouble in understanding is that Orientals are not only determined to secure mastery in their own house, and to eject their imperial rulers, but that they also are disdainful of our civilization and its pretenses to superiority. Asia is dangerously close to developing a psychosis

[4] Japanese-sponsored head of the projected "free Indian state."

on the subject of the white man, rejecting him for good or bad as Europe did the Jews.

Japanese propaganda has made China painfully aware of Filipino-baiting in California, of the second-rate status accorded yellow men in the United States, and even of the pillorying of the unfortunate Nisei in the American Pacific Coast states. A bitter story is current in Shanghai and Chungking of a sympathetic remark allegedly made by an American State Department official to the Chinese Ambassador, Dr. Hu Shih, during the early days of Japanese success in China. "Never mind, Dr. Hu," said he: "We'll beat those yellow sons of bitches yet."

China will make it a point of honor to achieve equal treatment of her citizens all over the world. She will want Hongkong returned, and the little Portuguese island colony of Macao. In his book, *China's Destiny*, the Generalissimo has laid claim to Burma, Thailand, and French Indo-China as being ancient Chinese territories inhabited by a kindred people, whose destiny it is to return to the common fold.

The Chinese also will seek to perfect a working arrangement with the Indians covering a program of mutual self-help, and the synchronization of markets and raw material sources. Both Chiang Kai-shek and the Indian leader, Nehru, have expressed themselves to this purpose.

Running parallel with these promptings is the desperate poverty of the Oriental masses. The new nationalism which is gripping them everywhere is merged with the creed of the prophet Marx, which has infiltrated deeply into Asia for a decade.

The attraction of these arguments to the submerged peoples of the Orient is overwhelming. The Soviet program is shrewdly tailored for consumption by Asiatics. As described by Wendell Willkie in his *One World*, it demands "abolition of racial exclusiveness, equality of nations and integrity of their territories, liberation of enslaved nations and restoration of their sovereign rights; the right of every nation to arrange its affairs as it wishes, economic aid to nations that have suffered, and assistance to them in attaining their material welfare."

The strength of Russian influence is based on the same premises which gave it force in Europe: to the underprivileged and degraded masses of Asia, the U.S.S.R. is the only one who proposes anything new at a moment when it is clear that the old is insupportable and must be discarded.

To any disinterested observer, it is not conceivable that the Chinese or any other Asiatic people, will accept a return to the *status quo ante*. The Asiatics, in their war against exploitation, illiteracy, and backwardness, have found a perfect example in the success of Mother Russia, whose arms always have been extended in the most flamboyant gesture of friendship.

Thousands of oriental revolutionaries from China, Korea, Japan and other countries, have been trained in the special propaganda schools of Moscow. Thirty-five thousand Koreans served as a Free Korean contingent in the Soviet army; and similar forces have fought on the side of the Chinese Communists. Following the capitulation of Japan, a large number of young Koreans living in Siberia formed a free Korean movement, with the expectation of moving into their native country and establishing a pro-Soviet government. In Indo-China, the national freedom movement is led by the Communist, Ho Chin Minh.

In Japan the Communist fight is led by Susuku Okano, an old revolutionary campaigner. Before American victory allowed him to return to the land of his ancestors, Okano and his Japanese People's Liberation Alliance had been operating for eighteen months out of Yenan, with some minor success among captured Japanese soldiers.

In China, the Communist development is of such massive proportions and has borne such an intimate relation to the decisive events shaking that unhappy country that it cannot be considered as an isolated phenomenon and may only be described in relation to these events themselves.

III

The real question is not whether the peoples of the Orient ultimately are to come of age and to achieve power. It is rather: what forces are going to control them? The question is whether the Orient is destined to fit into a co-operative world organized to receive it peacefully, or whether it is to become a source of social trauma and disruption, and during the early period of its development, a breeding ground of bloody conspiracies and conflict between the great world rivals for power.

The parallel struggle of social philosophies which attends this contention bids fair to turn the Orient into a new and gigantically enlarged Spain where the major world antagonists will first measure each other's real strength.

Here again the stakes are on a Gargantuan scale.

If the Russians are able to consume Asia or reduce it to a dependency, the world balance which now exists at once would dissolve. The geographic situation of the U.S.S.R., astride the tremendous reaches of the Eurasian plains and protected in every direction but one by almost impenetrable mountain and desert areas, would possess the ultimate in such security as can exist in an age of atomic warfare.

The material resources at the disposal of the Soviet captains would be immeasurably superior to anything we could command.

The great industrial successes already achieved by the Soviets would encourage them to believe that within a short period they not only could equal the industrial concentrations which make the U.S.A. the paramount military power of today, but vastly outmatch them.

These circumstances provide a magnificent setting for a modern air age economy of overpowering proportions. Its massive resources of space, men, and materials would be gigantically enhanced by the fact of Russian possession of the Arctic.

By air line, the shortest distance between all major sectors of the globe is due north. The Arctic is now the very center of the world power compass. Bombers taking off from the European Arctic would find Miami, Florida, Fort Worth, Texas, Salt Lake City, Utah, and Sacramento, California, equidistant from their home base; or operating from Omsk, or Nova Zemlya in Asia, could strike with an almost identical expenditure of fuel at New York, Milwaukee, or Seattle.

America's industrial Middle West is thus as fully exposed to attack as its east and west coasts. In the event of war this would force a costly dispersal of defending forces to guard every important city and installation in the Union.

In view of this pattern of facts, Soviet control of half the Arctic littoral becomes at once significant. The metamorphosis of Siberia from an unmapped wasteland into one of the new industrial centers of the world must be of even more critical interest to our statesmen.

During a single generation, the population of Siberia has leaped from some ten to almost sixty million.

Throughout Soviet Asia, port cities and installations of every kind have been erected, mines dug, industries built and co-operative farms established, where once was only bleak landscape. In the almost feverish tempo of operation, whole industries from Silesia and occupied Germany have been shipped and relocated.

A population increase of more than 18,000,000 is said to

have resulted from the transfer of populations in the path of the Nazi conquest. At Karaganda, in Kazakhstan, once a village of a few tents, today is a city of a quarter of a million. Henry Wallace, on his return from a trip to the Far East, described cities of a million people "so newly built that their names are unknown in other countries."[5]

The Soviet Arctic has participated in this development and has become the site of great fisheries, mining, oil drilling, logging, and other operations. New towns of thirty to fifty thousand people, such as Nardvik, Tiksi, and Igarka, have appeared well within the Arctic Circle itself; and such old ports as Murmansk and Archangel have been greatly enlarged.

As the scope of this enterprise increases and Siberia fills up with people, it will be observed that America instead of being separated from Asia by a cushion of five thousand miles of ocean, actually is only fifty-six miles away from its easternmost tip.

At the present the Soviet maritime provinces are separated from the centers of Soviet population and industry by dense areas of uncharted forests, and by plains and plateaus over which a timeless silence has hung during all the long reach of history. These provinces themselves scarcely can hold more than a few million people; and their industry is insufficient to maintain and service a modern military establishment.

Until the development of the intervening central areas of Siberia is complete, both the Soviet Arctic and the Siberian eastern seaboard are vulnerable to attack from North America. These important territories are joined to the main body of the Russias by a few air-lines, and by the Trans-Siberian Railroad, which though double-tracked part of the way, runs like a thin hair across the great mass of Siberia.

Due to this single item of faulty communications, the Soviet maritime provinces could be taken by assault from America

[5] *Editorial Research Reports No. 16*, November 3, 1945.

with ridiculous ease, cutting off the Soviets from the Pacific, and localizing them behind the Mongolian plateau and Kunlun Mountains. Here, with the exception of such decision as could be obtained by atomic or other bombing operations, any contest between the two giants in Asia would settle into a stalemate.

Under these circumstances, it is mandatory to Soviet policy to achieve, at the minimum, a recovery of the Chinese Eastern railway, together with the Kurile chain of islands which boxes off the Sea of Okhotsk. Moscow also must seek strong bases on the Yellow Sea and its contiguous waters.

A full Soviet security program in the Far East would involve outright possession of H'sin-kiang, Outer and Inner Mongolia, Manchukuo and Korea, establishing direct contact with the one hundred million Chinese Communists, and an open road to the fertile plains and numerous populations of southeastern Asia.

The background sense of these estimates is familiar to military thinkers through the work of the English geographer, Sir Halford Mackinder. The key to control of the Eurasian continent, which he called "the World Island," Mackinder observed was in the great natural fortress which composed its center. This enormous sprawling territory which reached from the Volga River into China, India and the Middle East and thence in a solid mass to the Arctic Ocean, he described as "the Heartland." Mackinder's formula read: "Who rules East Europe commands the Heartland. Who rules the Heartland commands the World Island. Who rules the World Island commands the World."

Both the German and Russian military strategists were heavily impressed with these calculations. The Germans made them the handbook of their world strategy. The Russians, though less obtrusively, also accepted Mackinder's reasoning as military gospel. The Urals and Central Asia became the arch of their security plans. They proceeded to populate and develop these territories by plan, and on a grand scale.

With the elimination of Germany and Japan, the only states capable of offering a physical challenge to paramount Russian power on the world island, the Soviets were presented with unexampled opportunity to perfect their position. If they could hold the Balkans, the eastern Alps, and the arc of the Sudeten Mountains which projects like a sharp knife into the northern plain of Europe, the balance of Europe would become an unimportant appendage to the Soviet empire. Inferior in population, denied vital resources on which its existence depended, and pressed upon by the dominant landmass to the east, Europe could be neutralized and rendered impotent.

In Asia, the approaches to the headwaters of the highly prized Persian Gulf already were in Russian hands. Turkey was vulnerable to the same progressive tactics which had reduced Finland and the Baltic republics. The Near East could be taken whenever the Russian Bear decided to move into it.

The Soviets held Outer Mongolia in all but name. Inner Mongolia and the trackless sweeps of Chinese Turkestan could be taken at will. If Moscow could absorb Manchuria and Korea, all of the preliminary goals of Russian Asiatic policy would be achieved.

Possession of these territories would rectify the weak military position of the Soviet Far East. It would protect the southern flank of the maritime provinces, give the U.S.S.R. unqualified access to the high seas, and provide that unimpeded pathway to the southeastern plains which must be the number one goal of Russian military policy in Asia.

Little in the way of an incursion in force is otherwise possible over the natural barriers provided by the arid deserts of the Gobi, and the all but impassable ranges of the Hindu

Kush, the Tien Shan, Altai, Kunlun, and Himalaya mountains. These weird and all but untraversable barriers have formed the historic wall which has made Central Asia almost a total stranger to the Asiatic Coast.

Neither could the planners in the Kremlin overlook the fact that Manchuria is blessed with fabulous natural wealth, which has allowed it to become the heart of continental Asiatic industry. It possesses a population of approximately one-third that of the United States. Its cities are modern, neat and attractive. Its agriculture is highly productive. Its reserves of iron ore, coal, copper and other raw materials make it a veritable treasure-trove. In the famous Tanaka Memorial, this prize of conquest was described as "unrivaled elsewhere in the world in its wealth of forestry, minerals and agricultural products."

The Japanese utilized these riches as the basis for a modern industrial plant large enough to sustain their great Asiatic armies. Here are chemical, machine tool, synthetic rubber and gasoline reduction plants; great manufactories for turning out every type of machinery; blast furnaces, capital goods industries, and facilities for making airplanes, tractors, munitions and textiles.

Once the central plateaus, together with their funnel outlet to the south along the Manchurian plains, were in Russian hands, no military power now observable could prevent them from overrunning the balance of Asia. As a pure problem of military mechanics, the pincers would squeeze down on China first and then the Middle East, transfixing India in a gigantic claw, to be devoured at leisure.

IV

How far the Soviets could carry on such a plan in the East before finding themselves enmeshed and stultified by the chains of their own ideology is an interesting question. We may conclude that human nature being what it is, Soviet theories are no more constant than democratic theories when they come up against the biological obsessions which have plagued men from the beginning.

The effect of Russian absorption of India alone under the prevalent Marxist interpretations would be not the Russification of India but the Indianization of the Soviet empire. This may be judged not only on the basis of comparative populations, but by rate of demographic growth as well, which is even more favorable to the Indians. India now contains almost four hundred million people, with a net increase of fifty-five million every decade. "If by some miracle India's people could suddenly be freed from want, and her extremely high death rate reduced to that of the United States, her natural increase every ten years would be three times the present figure," and even then "would just be getting a good start."[6]

While the Indians were absorbing Marxism and turning it to their own purposes, the Russian Slavs would find themselves overwhelmed not only by a strange race, but what is more, by a colorful and stubbornly resistant culture, fundamentally alien to everything that is Russian.

The same result, of course, would follow an attempted mass assimilation of the Chinese, and hardly could be prevented.

The Russians as we have seen, have absorbed a great amount of alien blood in a continuing process, beginning with the days of the Tatars and the horsemen of the Great Khan. Yet this genius for assimilation would wear thin and brittle were the Slavic majority to find itself tortured by the fear of becoming a hopeless minority.

At the present, though it is integral to Soviet philosophy that all races possess unequivocable rights of equality, the

[6] Burch and Pendell, *Population Roads to Peace and War*, p. 2.

Russians themselves are heavily in the majority in the U.S.S.R. The Soviet civilization is not only overwhelmingly a Slavic one, but essentially a Russian one as well. Though the U.S.S.R. consists of some eighty-eight nationalities, this figure is apt to be misleading. More than 80 per cent of the total Soviet population is made up of the three great branches of racially akin Slavs, the great Russians, White Russians and Belorussians.

Even now the Russians see themselves in a unique light as "the first among equals." The Soviet historian, Ivan Bulovin, envisages the Russians as a sort of Sir Galahad amongst the Soviet peoples. The Russians are described as having gathered these peoples around them by acting as their protector. In the resistance Muscovy put up against the Tatars, Bulovin discovers "the selfless struggle of the Russian people [which] . . . for the first time performed its universal historical role: *Russia saved European civilization from the menace of the East.*"[7]

Despite their proclaimed ideology it is unlikely that the triumphant Russian ego will willingly acquiesce in its own demise. Neither would these circumstances stay the surging tide of Russian expansionism from its natural course.

What would be apt to occur would be the familiar evolutionary change which overtakes all great movements when they find it necessary to adjust to some new and fixed condition. This undoubtedly would result in some modified aspect of the older imperialism.

Whatever orientation official Communist policy may take, real or posed, it is inevitable that the Kremlin will seek by one means or another to reduce to its own purposes all other potential power factors in Asia.

Moscow realizes that the Orient with its great intelligent population is exactly where Russia was on the eve of Soviet

[7] *Asia and the Americas*, November, 1925, p. 537 (Italics mine).

industrialization, and that the potentialities of the Orient are such as to make it a possible competitor and dangerous rival for the future.

Whether the Kremlin is bent on subduing the entire world to the proletarian revolution or not, its immediate goal must be to make the U.S.S.R. completely independent and secure against Russia's great capitalist adversaries of the West. This demands a sound position in Asia, and a friendly or puppet government in China.

A consolidation of the Russian and Chinese giants, or an effective working agreement between them, would lock in place the last beam in the skeleton structure of Soviet world power. On the broad canvas of global operations, it would leave the United States in a seriously isolated position which the passage of time could not fail to make precarious.

As the cards have been played out, they have fallen with great advantage to the Kremlin.

Among its war gains Moscow has recovered the southern half of Sakhalin Island, as well as the strategically important Kurile chain. The 740,000 square miles and one million nomad inhabitants of the Mongolian People's Republic, the former Chinese Outer Mongolia, in everything but name has become part of the Soviet Union.

In its political and social structure this prairie nation is almost a carbon copy of the Soviet Union's Buriat Mongol Republic, which lies directly across its border. When Moscow declared war on Japan, the armed forces of the Mongolian People's Republic paced the advance as an integral part of the Soviet Armies. At the great plebiscite held following the Chinese-Russian Treaty of Friendship and Alliance of August 14, 1945, the Mongols voted solidly (without a single dissenting ballot) to withdraw from their nominally existing association with China, and to become a "free republic."

To the north of Outer Mongolia, and once forming part of

its territories, is a region which since 1936 has been recognized
as the Independent People's Republic of Tannu Tuva. On
October 29, 1945, without bothering with further dissembling,
Tannu Tuva announced that it will elect two deputies to the
Union of Soviets and the Soviet Council of Nationalities.
Through some machinery whose operations were not ex-
plained, it is to be included in future as an autonomous area
within the Soviet province of Irkutsk.

The immense Central Asian territory of H'sin-kiang also
falls within the sphere of Russian influence, though by desig-
nation it is part of China. Its 4,360,000 people for the most part
are racially allied to the Kazakh tribes, an almost pure Turkish
people who inhabit the nearby Soviet republic of Kazakhstan.
H'sin-kiang also contains a considerable Mongol element
which is easily susceptible to Pan-Mongol propaganda, a line
of attack which could be expected to have its effect in Inner
Mongolia and Tibet as well, whenever the Soviets decide to
press the button which will set it going.

The Russians found H'sin-kiang a world apart, as isolated
and remote from human knowledge as if it had existed on some
other planet. They built airfields, factories and towns, dug
mines and organized a police force. Russian troops were forced
to withdraw in 1942 under Chinese pressure. This was at a
time when the victorious Wehrmacht was sweeping everything before it in its eastern march across the Russian plains.

After the German tide rolled back, active Russian interest
in H'sin-kiang again was suggested, though by indirect means.
In March, 1944, planes of the Mongolian People's Republic
marked with red stars, bombed Chinese troops which had been
sent to H'sin-kiang to put down a rebellion of Moslem tribesmen. The result was to force the substitution of an administration more acceptable to the Kremlin, though the big province
continued to remain Chinese territory.

The ultimate strategic importance of these far-away do-

mains may be great. Within H'sin-kiang's deserts and mountains are said to be fertile, habitable valleys, and great stores
of minerals. The dash of Roy Chapman Andrews and Sven
Hedin across the Central Asian desert in 1934 by motor con-
voy, proved the practicability of motorized advance over these
regions, which may assume considerable military significance
in the future.

H'sin-kiang is the very heart of the Heartland. Its existence
can be ignored by Russian policy only at a moment when
China is weak. A strong nationalist China would regard it as
a prize of potential economic importance, and as the key to the
back door to Europe. A future struggle to control this territory might precipitate a war which literally would blow the
roof off the world.

Similar implications derive from the situation of Korea
which occupies a potential flanking position on both Siberia
and the Central Pacific. The country now is divided in two,
with a Russian-occupied industrial zone in the North, and an
American-held agricultural segment in the South. The partition
of Korea parallels in some degree the partitioning of Germany,
with many of the same problems in evidence. There is practically no liaison between the two administrations, which as
far as normal trade and communications are concerned are
almost completely isolated from each other.

Early in 1946, the General Secretary of the Korean Communist party, Pak Heun Yung, showed which way the wind
blew by unleashing a violent denunciation of American policy
in Korea, and demanding its eventual inclusion in the U.S.S.R.
as a component republic.

V

If the Orient is the historical lock to the door of world
destiny, its key is the situation of China.

Here again, the status is a complicated one, and a result of the strivings of many contending forces.

The most important in its bearing on ultimate events undoubtedly is the autonomous Communist administration in North China.

In the handsome, peasant-born Mao Tse-tung, the North Chinese have a leader of determination and genius, who may be compared to such figures as the Generalissimo himself, or even to Lenin, Trotsky and Stalin. Mao is said to be alert, shrewd, ruthless and at the same time ascetic, rigidly honest, and passionately devoted to the cause of the revolution. He has a talent, rare in China, for securing deep personal devotion from his followers.

American military officers located at Yenan have been much impressed by the discipline and organization of the North Chinese. The Communists undeniably have been the authors of many needed reforms. They have cleansed their areas of old corrosions such as "squeeze," bribery, and conscienceless peasant exploitations, which still are an everyday feature of existence in many other parts of the Orient.

Those who have been in intimate contact with them deride the idea of their revolutionary radicalism, and describe them as a cleansing and moderate element in Chinese society. This mild socialist tone, not more extreme than that adopted in Britain under the Labour party is apt to be confusing. If accepted at its face value, it leads to the most absurd of conclusions.

Mao Tse-tung, the supreme Chinese Communist leader, has been a Comintern agent as well as former member of that body. In his book, *China's New Democracy*, Mao states flatly that "China's revolution is a part of the world revolution." "We cannot," he writes, "separate ourselves from the assistance of the Soviet Union or from the victory of the anti-capitalist struggles of the proletariat of Japan, Great Britain,

the United States, France and Germany." Though he insists
that the revolution must be by stages and cannot be successfully brought off at a single stroke, Mao nevertheless warns
that "whoever prepares to oppose the Communists has to
prepare to be crushed."

On the record, the Chinese Communists have followed
faithfully every deviation of Russian policy. Until its formal
dissolution in 1943, the Permanent Executive Committee of
the Comintern contained at least three representatives from
the Chinese section.

Communist China has maintained its own troops, issued its
own money from its own capital at Yenan, and for practical
purposes kept itself independent of the titular Chinese government at Chungking. The Generalissimo's armies and those
under the command of the Communist general, Chu Teh, have
battled each other even more desperately than they have
fought troops of the invaders. During the war, Chungking
placed a price on General Chu's head of $250,000. When
apprehended, Communists were made short shrift of, and were
machine-gunned in whole companies. Yenan in turn castigated
the Central government as a tool of the Japanese, and of
reactionary Caucasian interests bent on sucking the Chinese
teats dry.

In its concepts, objectives and social organization, Communist China is so totally alien to the Chinese South that the
two cannot possibly be reconciled. Any agreement which may
be reached between them is forced to be in the nature of a
treaty between intrinsically hostile forces.

Notwithstanding the ingrained differences which act to
separate them, Moscow and Chungking managed to come to
a Treaty of Alliance just before the Japanese capitulation in
the late summer of 1945. As soon as this agreement was announced, Yenan renounced its previous hostile attitude toward
the Kuomintang, and threw the mantle of brotherly co-opera-

tion around all Chinese of whatever political description. When soon after, Chiang Kai-shek ordered the Communist troops to remain at their posts, and not to move into the big coastal cities on their own initiative, General Chu Teh bluntly rejected the ultimatum, with the public challenge to Chiang that his order was "only to the advantage of Japanese and traitors who have sold out their country."

The Russo-Chinese Treaty was tribute to the baffling practicality of oriental politics, which manages to conceal under an inscrutable mask a profound appreciation of realizable values. By agreement, the Generalissimo was recognized as the supreme leader of China. The country was to be ruled by a coalition government uniting Chungking and Yenan in a common administration. The Russians were to withdraw such support as they might have given the Chinese Communists and to abstain totally from any intervention in Chinese affairs.

In return, China gave up all claim to Outer Mongolia, and consented to recognize Russian rule over the southern half of Sakhalin and the Kuriles. On its side, the Soviet Union promised to withdraw from Manchuria, luminous goal of all previous Russian policy in the Far East, retaining only a joint ownership along with China of the Chinese Eastern and Southern Manchurian railways. Moscow was to have permanent control, however, of the much-prized Yellow Sea ports of Darien and Port Arthur, which were to become Soviet naval bases.

In general, it is safe to say that both parties to the treaty regard it in the way of a fluid truce, meant to bridge power events of more commanding importance.

In assessing events after the curtain has dropped on the current act, the arrangement appears to be far more favorable to the Kremlin than was at first supposed. British-American diplomacy was beginning to grow testy, and perhaps un-

predictable. There was always in the offing the dramatic
specter of the atomic bomb. In any event Russia was far from
ready for a showdown policy, and needed a respite from any
quarter she could secure it.

Although Moscow seemed to have abandoned Yenan, from
another view she had succeeded in introducing the previously
outcast Communist party as an accepted force into Chinese
coalition politics. The Kremlin had reason to believe that it
had placed a substantial foot in the door of Chinese politics,
secure in the conviction that the future would run against the
brutally hurt economy of orthodox China. The Russians saw
on their side the deadly and uncontrollable inflation which had
been creeping on China like a paralysis, and the expected
failure of the mandarin- and sahib-type of social system
throughout the Orient.

It also was not inconceivable that Chungking was playing
a double game as well as Moscow, and that in return for a
secret Russian promise to abandon Yenan and to give Chiang
large-scale economic aid, China had agreed to turn her back
on the West and cast her lot once more with the Russian Bear.

Perhaps more significant than the treaty itself was a remark
attributed to Chiang Kai-shek at the hour of signing: "We
now can return to the days of 1924." The time to which the
Generalissimo referred was the period when Sun Yat-sen and
the youthful Chiang were building a revolutionary Chinese
army with the active assistance of Borodin, Galen and other
Russian agents; and when the Communist party was an
important and recognized factor in the Kuomintang. This was
three years before the ferocious break between Chiang and
the Communists, and its bloody aftermath in civil war.

If the treaty itself is to be adhered to literally, the Russians,
faced with the possibility of all-out war with the West,
could regard it in the nature of a considerable victory. The
high contracting parties are to "give each other all possible

economic assistance in the post-war period . . ." "Each of the High Contracting Parties . . . [is] not to conclude any alliance whatsoever, and not to take part in any coalition whatsoever, directed against the other Contracting Party."

The threat of a new axis with the Soviet Union also could be used by Chungking as a stout club to counteract British anti-Chinese machinations in Washington, a possibility which certainly has not escaped the astute Chinese leaders.

Though accepting direct American military aid in establishing himself in the North against the Communists, the Generalissimo has sent his son, Chiang Ching-kuo, to Moscow for a series of talks which may of themselves be of critical importance. Young Chiang replaces the older type of conservative Kuomintang representative. He speaks Russian fluently, is married to a Russian, and, while not a Communist, is known to favor a pro-Russian rather than pro-Western orientation for the new China.

Meanwhile, as if to confute any rational interpretation of this confused medley of circumstance, the Chinese political volcano erupted into what threatened to become a large-scale civil war between the nationalists and Reds, hardly a month after the Sino-Russian agreement had been signed. More than a million men were engaged on a long line of battle, with the Communists shifting their headquarters to Kalgan in Inner Mongolia.

Russian occupation forces in Manchuria were showing a reluctance to depart. It was charged that they were dismantling factories and shops, and stripping the country to its dry bones. The great Mukden arsenal was reported to have been given to the Mongol marshal, Choi Bol-san, together with much industrial equipment. As a result, Choi Bol-san will become a military figure of consequence in Asia. The Kremlin also is reported to have demanded extensive new rights in Manchukuo. This includes air fields and a 50 per cent participation in the development of Manchukuo's heavy industries, including coal and iron production. Japanese military leaders and their troops are at liberty, as a possible mercenary army similar to the large German forces maintained by the British in their part of the Reich or the Polish armies kept in Italy.

Among the pieces in this difficult jigsaw puzzle has been the intervention locally by American forces on the side of the Chinese Nationalists. Behind the platitudes which cover this event lies the growing conviction on the part of American military men and politicians that an adventure which took the Soviet Union into Inner Mongolia and North China immediately would create a situation of the utmost peril to the United States.

Powerful American air fleets directed by American officers have moved entire Chinese armies to a line opposite the Communists. The United States Navy has pressed American transports into similar use.

In addition to large quantities of arms transferred to them unofficially, the Chinese Army and Air Force have been parties to formal negotiations for the purchase of surplus American military stores now in the Orient. They are also to receive a quota of improved types of airplanes and other weapons which have come off the American production lines too late to be used in battle.

As far as the Orient is concerned the U.S.S.R. thus has been placed on an unspoken but meaningful notice. This circumstance certainly is not diminished by the current Russian apprehension that London is seeking to re-erect Germany as a strong military buffer in Europe.

Events have disclosed that, shorn of direct Russian support, the Chinese Communists are considerably weaker than had been presumed. Their armies, though well organized, do not exceed 450,000 men, and are woefully short of weapons of all kinds. It also appears that the Communist regime, which had secured its power through glittering promises to Chinese peasants and workers, as well as through the implementation of certain desirable reforms, has existed as a more or less superimposed hegemony in North China, rather than as an authentic expression of mass Chinese opinion.

Outflanked on all sides and facing superior power, Yenan has been forced to accept the logic of the situation, and once more is seeking Chinese harmony. The Chinese Communists hope to retain separate administrative control of the districts they now hold north of the Yellow River, and to incorporate, under Communist leadership, forty-eight divisions of their army within the Chinese nationalist forces.

The first skirmishes of this battle for the Orient seem to indicate that on the whole the Russians though making some small gains have come off second best. Their confident expectation that all Asia would flare up in inextinguishable flames as an outcome of the Second Great Capitalist Crisis, was far from realized. Their power position, on the other hand, for future bouts in this titanic engagement, is unexcelled.

Chapter Seven

MILITARY SECURITY IN THE ATOMIC AGE

IF THE Russians are able to consolidate the territories they now hold east of the Elbe in Europe, together with those which have fallen into the Soviet lap in Asia, the U.S.S.R. will possess an area of 9,647,334 square miles, and a population estimated as of 1970 at approximately 429,000,000. If to this empire eventually can be added H'sin-kiang, Manchukuo and Korea, the Soviets will rule a land space of 11,260,661 square miles, containing an estimated 1970 population of 530,000,000.

At this period, which is a favorite estimating point for the demographers, the United States will hold a population of approximately 156,000,000 in an area of 2,977,128 square miles. This assumes that our present geographic reach on the American continent will remain unchanged.

The dynamic factors which accompany this physical relationship may fairly be said to favor the gradual decline of American power and the growth of that of the U.S.S.R.

The ultimate significance of this relative position is contained in the determination of the Soviets to build the greatest industrial machine ever yet seen.

At the moment the economic structure of the Soviet Union is seriously impaired. Despite the magnificent Russian armies it is doubtful whether the U.S.S.R. today could stand the concussive impact of another major, all-out encounter.

In its death struggle with the invading Germans, the U.S.S.R. suffered terrible losses. The cost to the Russias in human life alone may come to some 25,000,000 people. The greater part of the Soviet Union's industrial set-up in Europe also disappeared as a casualty of war. Railroads were ripped up, mines flooded and factories, dams and power plants dynamited. 1,710 towns, and more than 70,000 villages, were erased together with 32,000 industrial establishments and 98,000 collective farms. 160,000,000 acres of the most fertile Russian land were placed to the torch. Machine equipment was carried away together with farmstock.

Much of what remains standing out of this hurricane of ruin is obsolescent or in such a bad state of repair as to be useless for productive purposes.

The situation undoubtedly is a bad one, but it is not the predicament that many Americans imagine it to be. During the war, the Russians managed to build something of a compensating industry in the Urals and middle Asia. They are accustomed to tightening their belts and to go along without consumer commodities which are a main necessity in other states. They live under a police regime which knows how to wring the last advantage from the most refractory situation, and possesses the indomitable will to do so.

The Russians will squeeze themselves dry, and build if necessary without money or credits, exploiting their native resources on a scale dwarfing anything ever contemplated before. Under the latest blueprint, by 1950 the devastated areas are to be completely rebuilt. The economic structure of the nation is to have a total overhauling and to become the last word in modernity.

The capacity of the Soviet Union to compete on equal terms with the most advanced industrial nations is observable throughout Soviet Asia. As a single instance, at Magnitogorsk in the very midst of the continuing crisis of war, a series of gigantic blast furnaces were built, said to be larger than any in Europe. The mills, furnaces, machine shops and plants of this single mushrooming area are reported to cover more than thirty-two square miles.

Today the Uzbek Republic alone, bordering on the strategic Middle East, is responsible for more industrial production than all of the countries of Asia Minor and the Middle East put together. In nearby Kazakhstan, which stretches from the Caspian Sea to the gates of China, startling developments have taken place. A wide variety of minerals are being mined on a scale sufficient to support major industry.

It would be the part of prudence to believe that the development of the Soviet Union will continue at even a faster pace than has characterized its preparations for the present war. Every element is present which is required to make it the leading power factor on the industrial and military landscape.

Confronted by this pyramiding power growth, the United States would be condemned to a progressive inferiority not only in numbers and geographic position, but even in regard to indispensable raw materials.

The United States, once profligate in its expenditure of a seemingly endless store of natural wealth, rapidly is becoming a have-not nation. Many of its critical materials such as tin, rubber, kapok, quinine and tropical oils, come from abroad. It is possible to substitute for some by synthetic manufacture. Our stockpiles on others are critically low.

On twenty-one of the thirty-three minerals strategically required in our industry, we possess less than a thirty-five-year supply. More than half of the materials contained in an American motor car must be imported, many of them from far-away places. Our reserves of easily accessible, high-grade iron ores will be exhausted in eight years at the present rate of consumption. Our position with reference to asbestos, quartz, lead, zinc and many of the ferroalloys is a poor one. We have practically run out of bauxite, mercury, platinum, chromite, nickel and tungsten.

As the cycle of Russian growth matures, the United States may find itself not only outnumbered and outweighed but strategically surrounded. This envelopment movement would be made complete by the loss of Latin America, a possibility which cannot be wholly discounted.

The preliminary affrays between the two big competitors would take place on economic, political and ideological levels, rather than by bomb and gun-fire. Here the totalitarian system shows to great advantage over that of the democracies. The latter have to prepare suddenly for war and to remake their psychology as well as their material effects. The totalitarians on the other hand are always mobilized and on a wartime basis. By the nature of their dictatorial quality they can blow hot and cold on any proposition the same as could Hitler, turning their policy on and off as if it were a spigot, as their rulers deem expedient.

Neither does the free political system lend itself well to cutthroat economic wars of the modern type. The democracies possess a soft underside like the turtle. They are victimized by pressure groups which operate as states within states, and present disconcerting aspects of weakness in political crisis.

The entire business of power politics is alien to the system of constitutional law with its checks and balances, and its limitations and divisions of authority, by which the lives of the democracies are ordered. Though democracies have proved that they are able to fight a successful war, they invariably have lost all of the preceding battles for position, even against minor despotisms; and have shown little understanding of the nature of the preliminary attacks made upon them.

In an age where the influence of public opinion is extended to affect strategic foreign policy, the free states are under the acute handicap of having to please public opinion at home. The profit system also places certain limitations on functional efficiency and makes for a certain sluggishness in adopting methods, techniques and machinery which would involve business enterprise in material losses. In countries where manufacture and commerce are government monopolies it is possible to discard obsolescent equipment to the junk heap without reference to cost, and based on criteria in which private enterprise could have no possible interest.

With regard to atomic weapons themselves, where we now hold unqualified superiority, our tenure of power may be brief. Potential enemies functioning in the greatest secrecy, might improve greatly on known methods of manufacture and delivery of these weapons, or devise countermeasures to limit their effectiveness. While this question represents a venture into the unknown and undoubtedly is highly debatable, it would be foolhardy to consider our present superiority of military strength a permanent feature of our existence.

It would be as serious a mistake to judge the problem of national security as centering permanently around some single weapon, no matter how terrible its destructive force might be.

Though the current military situation has been changed dramatically by the mutations in strategy resulting from the atomic bomb, the basic premises on which military competition is founded remain much the same, though projected into new dimensions and areas of combat. The superiority of numbers, geographic space, raw materials and manufacturing capacity, not only continues among the dominating influences in war, but, where the social organization and will-to-fight are equal, may be raised to new and undreamed of powers.

A good deal of somewhat loose talk exists about rockets, stratospheric bomb projectiles and other ultra-scientific weapons, as if these inventions destroyed the basic facts of geography and material economic condition. The American frontier now is said to be on the Rhine, in the far Pacific, or even in eastern Asia.

While obviously there is an element of accuracy to these statements, they unfortunately contribute to heavily distorted conclusions.

It would be equally true, for example, if one were to declare that the American frontier now is along the Volga or the Ganges. Every spot on earth today is within some effective striking relation to every other spot. Beyond this, and the revised conditions created by the revolution in weapons, the circumstances connected with waging a successful war remain much the same. They must remain concerned with logistics, strategic situation, raw materials, the quality, numbers and temper of the populations involved, their factory installations, laboratories, industrial know-how and social organization. All of these things affect the nation at war and adjust it to the conditions of modern battle, though this no longer involves localized struggle along linear lines but a large-scale saturation assault aimed directly at the enemy's vitals.

The ability to organize for war, to conduct the necessary scientific investigations, to possess collateral and alternate sources of material and industrial power, together with a strategic location with reference to the enemy's vulnerable points, still is the touchstone of military success.

None of the principles of strategy which have survived the great wars of mankind have been liquidated by the atomic bomb and the other monsters science has let loose on the world. These lessons continue to exist with even more validity than before, though perhaps in new and scarcely recognizable terms. Despite the fantastic triumphs of the Buck Rogers type of weapon, distance still is the enemy of military efficiency. The capacity to concentrate force quickly at the enemy's vulnerable points and to occupy his key citadels before he can regroup his shattered ranks, remains of key importance. The airplane, radar, and the rocket projectiles do not change the role of the forward base as a decisive element in warfare, or lessen the critical value of the transportation pattern by which the nation maintains its communications.

The A-bomb itself must be delivered to its target. Once this objective has been destroyed, the war must assume a new phase, that of physical combat involving considerable mechanized masses of men. For every soldier who is kept overseas some eighty-one tons of supplies must be furnished.

This brings into focus the production and supply lines of the nation which in themselves become important and perhaps decisive enemy objectives.

The lethal efficiency of modern arms has given rise to an almost occult belief in their powers. The prevailing view is expressed by the English expert, Major General J. F. C. Fuller, who states that weapons are 99 per cent, and strategy, generalship and men, only one per cent, of battle.

This concept certainly is exaggerated, and involves a good deal of pure hysteria even on the part of those sensible men who find themselves reciting it. Under any circumstance, modern wars will not be determined by the atomic bomb alone, but by a catalogue of weapons, all of which will be the product of an intensive military system equivalent to the total industry and will to win of the fighting nations.

The impression that modern man has grown obsolete in favor of the impelling quality of the weapons he wields is unsound. Fighting still is done by men, who still control the weapons they use. In particular, the capacity of men for organization, their ability to rally under stress, as did the British and Russians, their doggedness as expressed by the Chinese, and their sheer will to persist and survive, cannot be eliminated from among the decisive elements of history.

We are forced to conclude that as other nations industrialize, and the short period of advantage conferred by our possession of atomic weapons dribbles itself away, the relative size and power of the United States will shrink drastically.

The situation then will revert to the old measurements of relative situation, resources and social organization, and the quality, numbers and will of the competing populations.

II

Whatever absolute importance the A-bomb may possess will be determined by two factors which are as yet unknown. These are: (1) the ability of other nations to penetrate the secret of its manufacture; and (2) the relative cheapness with which it can be manufactured.

The latter circumstance would determine the value of geographic space itself as a smothering agent capable of counteracting the decisive effects of the bomb. If the bomb remains expensive to make, and like radium can be produced only in limited quantities, a decentralization and widespread dispersal of prospective targets would water out its power of decision and limit it to a restricted group of objectives.

In this case the threatened total and instantaneous destruction of all targets, which has been so freely predicted, would involve a cost to the attacker beyond his available resources. In the cost-result ratio would occur that tempering process which always in the chronicles of military management has served finally to limit the power of weapons.

The military situation would alter completely if the bomb could be turned out inexpensively, and in quantity.

The claim is advanced by certain highly regarded scientists that such a result is an inevitable consequence of our present knowledge.

This view is disputed by military men who have worked on this project. They assert that at least in the present phase, only a circumscribed number of bombs can be turned out. Uranium itself is not plentiful, and the separation of the essential U-235 from the uranium body is difficult, expensive, and necessarily limited in quantity. So far, by whatever method the pile has been constructed, the fissionable elements have been the product of this single ore, whose inherent instability lends itself to the processes which have produced the bomb.

Experiments have been undertaken with nitrogen and other elements on the heavy end of the atomic scale, but there is little indication that these will be successful. Trials with Uranium 238, the companion element of Uranium 235, indicate some theoretical promise, but are far removed from any hope of early actuality.

What may be judged, therefore, is that the number of bombs which can be produced is limited, but not so much so as to prevent their accumulation over a period of time. It is safe to assume, however, that enough bombs can be turned out over a long term to obliterate every considerable city at present existing on the planet, if each of these missiles were able to reach its appointed target.

In regard to the capacity of other nations to manufacture the bomb, there also are two points of view. The scientists assert that the basic principles of the bomb are generally known among theoretical physicists the world over, and that those which are not known may easily be discovered by experience and study. These men believe any nation possessing modern scientific laboratories and engineering skill could have the secret of the bomb as well as the bomb itself within a period of from three to five years.

American engineers and military men intimately associated with the manufacture of the bomb believe, however, that this is an inaccurate conception. They point out that the creation of the bomb was the result of one of the greatest organizational ventures in history, of which the scientific end was but a contributing, though all-important, portion. The engineering and construction demands in connection with this enterprise were so difficult that despite the almost unlimited resources at the disposal of American technocracy, each phase was far beyond the capacity of normal American industry when it started. The project is said to have drawn on an almost unlimited number of skills and capacities, a network of mining, research, engineering, manufacturing and experimental operations so vast and multiplex as to be almost impossible to grasp.

Only in wartime, it is claimed, could the scholarship, know-how, resources, management and teamwork required in such a venture, be drawn on.

The military men who have been in charge of this project believe that the only competitor which possibly could engage itself to manufacture the bomb is the U.S.S.R. Their view is that it would take the Russians at least five to seven years if we placed at Moscow's disposal our full records of experiment and operation; and that it would take fifteen to twenty years if Russia attempted to do it in secrecy. In the latter event the drain on her economy would be so great as practically to wreck it.

It may be suspected that the answer lies somewhere in between, but that the conservative appraisal is the more nearly correct one. In such case, the Russians, despite their skilled technicians, industrial managers, and highly organized scientific apparatus, will be a long time in producing the bomb in any quantity sufficient for widespread military use. While small amounts of fissionable material undoubtedly may result from Russian experiments, the gap between this achievement and the final manufacture of the bomb as a working medium of military destruction is far off.

However far the Russians may be from a solution to this problem, they must be acknowledged to possess the scientific tradition, determination, talent, basic industry and capacity for organization which such an engagement would require. We may be sure that after they understand its meaning, they will work feverishly at it. The adoration of science and the machine in the U.S.S.R. practically has become a cult, and is almost an integral part of Marxist dogma.

How far the Russians may have gotten in their attack on this problem is a matter of sheer guesswork. The windows of Russian science are carefully boarded up so that we cannot look into their laboratories and judge the experimental progress which has been made. What we do know is that, in addition to their own research work, the Russians have had access to German records, and have hired a considerable number of German physicists. They have removed into their own country not only data and men, but the experimental laboratories themselves.

Soviet science is organized into a single unified apparatus called the U.S.S.R. Academy of Sciences, which attempts a co-ordinated mass approach to the great problems of investigative knowledge. Although the Russians are far behind the United States in those technical studies in which we excel, they have scored some notable successes and can boast of many brilliant workers. The Russians possess in their own galaxy of nuclear physicists such great names as the Academician, Abraham Joffe, Professor Peter A. Kapitza, and Dr. N. Semyonov.

It is important to observe that at a time when we were recklessly hauling our young university men out of the schools and laboratories in order to induct them in our armed forces, the Soviets made a wise exception in the case of students and apprentices to the sciences. The work of these young people remained uninterrupted during the full period of the war.

Dr. Vannevar Bush has called attention to the all but unrecognized fact that "by taking altogether too many trained young scientists and engineers out of the laboratories and industry, we very nearly wrecked that part of our war effort which consists in keeping the instrumentalities in the hands of our fighting men substantially superior to those of the enemy. We also sacrificed the future to immediate needs . . . by halting our processes of advanced education, thus creating a lack of scientific manpower from which we shall not recover for many years."

The Soviet Union has the further advantage of being fresh and eager, and of possessing no prejudices where the national economy is concerned. Where American colleges and experimental laboratories quite openly show a preference based not on skill and aptitude but on religion and race, instituting a quota basis for their selections which has the effect of keeping out of American science some of its most glowing and capable minds, the Russians underwrite the training of all gifted youngsters irrespective of race or condition.

Among the unknown factors in the Russian situation is the question of access to uranium ore. An attempted answer to this conundrum would be largely speculative. According to the Minerals Yearbook of 1943, the U.S.S.R. Radium Institute is reported to have discovered new deposits of radioactive substances, though their location and type are not specified. There are known ores, however, which occur at Joachimsthal in Bohemia and in Rezbanya in Hungary, and perhaps substantial quantities in Siberia.

III

Though there is much which is yet unclear, the new military processes which range themselves around the atomic bomb lead us to the following conclusions:

1. The present bomb is in the same relatively crude stage that the airplane was during World War I. It is certain to be enormously improved in effectiveness, both as to the destructive energy it releases and the techniques for its manufacture and delivery.

2. The big question of defense is that of stopping the carrier. Electronic contrivances such as the proximity fuse will prevent a large proportion of these from penetrating to their mark, but the wall of interception will be far from complete. Though it now appears unlikely, there may be a development of magnetic and radio devices capable of detonating atomic charges at great distances, or even at their source of production.

3. The peculiar properties of the bomb open up the possibility of entirely new means of military attack. The cities of a selected victim might be destroyed by the planting of bombs in basements or lock boxes. These would be timed for simultaneous explosion at an appointed hour. Since the materials for the bomb are not bulky, and separately in themselves are inert, they conceivably could be smuggled without detection into any country with whom normal diplomatic and commercial relationships existed.

4. The bomb is not just another weapon, but a new stage in the science of mass annihilation. However, other weapons almost as frightful in their import are being experimented with. High on the secret list of a number of nations is the blueprinted means for the mass production and use of deadly microorganisms, directed against men, animals and crops. Trials also have been made with gasses whose terrible killing power may be fully as menacing to human life as the A-bomb itself. These grisly destroyers possess the important military advantage of extirpating only living creatures, leaving all material booty intact. One of the prime objectives of future warfare will be the capture intact of inhabited places, together with their productive facilities, relieving the conqueror of the burden of a barren victory.

5. The importance of the vehicles by which these agencies of destruction are brought to their targets becomes in every sense as critical as that of the weapons themselves. The capacity to deliver an A-bomb in the nose of an accurately driven long-distance rocket may be the decisive factor in exploiting the deadly efficiencies of this weapon. In the top drawer secret lists of all, nations are experiments in jet propulsion, rocket construction, and the manufacture of the fuels to power them.

The invention of the bomb, together with the arsenal of scientific weapons which accompanies it, demands an almost total revamping of accepted organizational procedures in preparing the national defense. One of the greatest military hazards our Republic will face is the possibility that our brilliant victories of World War II will tend to leave a residue of American Gamelins and Weygands who will commit the nation to the military archaisms which contributed to their own strategic triumphs of the past.

The idea of a citizen army parading in platoons and marching to battle to the sound of drums is now ridiculous. The day of drilling and regimented men depending for their efficiency on the massed fire power of small weapons is practically done.

The whole scheme of monstrous armies created by conscription methods has become a dangerous anachronism. Young men are withdrawn from scientific and classroom studies at the most impressionable period of their existence, imposing on them a type of regimentation fatal to the spirit of inquiry and initiative. At the same time in a large percentage of cases, the continuity of their scholastic training is irreparably broken.

This is an unsafe formula which no longer has anything in the way of compensation to offer. The whole meaning of competition in the machine and atomic age lies in the development of scientific, engineering and management personnel, as well as in directed research assisted on a massive scale by government.

The army and the nation in modern war no longer are separate, but identical. The line between civilian and military enterprise no longer is one of basic techniques, or even of special tasks, except as it applies to the relatively small groups who will establish direct contact with the enemy in the theaters of operation.

It is in the organized civilian economy of the nation, its laboratories, mines, farms, factories, universities, foundries and workshops, that the real warmaking machine will be created. It will be directed by an immense central planning staff, which will operate from detailed, collated intelligence reports far from the field of battle. Its job will be that of coordinating the national forces for a total struggle which has little to do with the old concept of military campaigns.

The parading and pageantry inherent in the use of uniforms already is, for practical purposes, antiquated. There is no longer an army in the sense of the old militia: the nation is the army.

Military isolationism, the restricted, self-centered existence on small out-of-the-way posts, no longer can exist in the over-all picture of an efficient armed force. The army of the future will be a professional force of skilled technicians and specialists, and not a refuge for ruffians, ne'er-do-wells or soldiers of fortune. The soldier of the future will be a policeman, an executive, a scientist and administrator. He will be trained meticulously for his special assignment, which will be that of destroying the enemy's productive establishment from afar, or of administering it after its occupation and capture.

The classical scheme of routine, close-order drill, kitchen

police and fatigue will disappear. Tomorrow's soldier will not be a half-trained robot, or a screaming maniac rushing to battle brandishing a saber, but a trained specialist. He will have personal privacy like other men, and opportunities to learn, earn and advance himself, according to his capacity.

The Navy will be part of a single co-ordinated force. Except under special conditions it will be concerned almost altogether with the problem of overseas transportation.

The central military operation will revolve around the airborne, strategic forces. These themselves will be only the final product of a constantly alerted industrial mobilization for war, on which all of the capacity and scientific know-how of the nation will be concentrated.

A necessary part of defense in the pattern of the future will be absolute secrecy as to the location of strategic installations. It may be necessary to locate important factories underground, in forests, or under elaborate camouflage. A widespread diffusion of industry would add greatly to the difficulties of the opposing armies, and would act to render any quick scheme of destruction impossible. This factor would gain tremendously in strategic importance if the nature and location of the national industry itself were unknown in their detail to enemy attackers.

Reliable knowledge of competitor operations will tend to become one of the absolute factors of decision in atomic warfare. This makes necessary an intelligence function in brackets far beyond anything previously conceived. All installations of the potential enemy will be mapped in complete detail, and his slightest acts recorded for study. The strains and pressures which exist in his social economy will be faithfully examined for the purposes of psychological warfare and perhaps a pre-military battle of nerves.

The intelligence pipelines will function in every echelon

of enemy activity so as to give a full working knowledge of every facet of his existence.

This sort of super-spying will be an unavoidable consequence of the atomic age if national sovereignties are to remain. Every nation will be exposed to it, except perhaps the Russians, who may manage to close their economy off completely from outside view. The tremendous secrecy surrounding all Russian operations may make it impossible for us to know the location of their factory sites at all. To secure information on Russian operations similar to that observable by any tourist in the United States, we would need a complicated and difficult espionage system.

It is here as well as in their immensely greater geographic distances that the Russians have an immense advantage over us.

IV

It seems plain that with the new weapons, whether of an atomic, incendiary or chemical nature, the capacity to survive the first blow of assault will be decisive.

This clearly suggests that industrial mobilization after the commencement of hostilities will not be possible. In the atomic age industrial mobilization must be accomplished in advance of the first blow. So must the mobilization of all available military forces.

Every state will be compelled to keep itself on a full wartime footing at all times, since it must reckon with the consequence of being forced to begin a fight without cities. Modern weapons place a maximal premium on aggression and add greatly to the advantage of the offensive. The supreme quality of defense, therefore, will lie in the capacity to retaliate immediately from fully equipped secret installations capable of unleashing the full fury of atomic assault against all known enemy power points.

This peculiar equilibrium, by nullifying the element of surprise, will tend to make the prime purpose of armed forces that of averting wars through studied threat, rather than fighting them.

War would begin in its first phases by a long-drawn-out psychological assault, scientifically calculated to smash the nation's inner defenses and to collapse it into a hopeless medley of jangling parts. Dumping and other overt acts of economic warfare would drag the conflict out in the open.

Finally one of the antagonists would find itself forced into a position which in its judgment could be settled only in the cauldron of armed struggle.

The first blow would be struck without warning and with all the devastating vigor at the command of the aggressor. The full accumulation of atomic weapons gathered for this purpose would be spent at once in a furious effort to force a decision. The major cities and production facilities of the enemy would be dissolved within a day's time. All of his essential communications would be placed under instantaneous fire.

A stream of rockets powered with atomic warheads would streak to their objectives from strategically located bases. If one of the nations believed itself in possession of overwhelming power, the atomic assaults would be scattered and accompanied by leaflet barrages designed for their intimidating effect. If capitulation did not follow, there would be a reign of powerful incendiaries such as the napthalm bomb which raised so much havoc with Japanese cities in the last war.

A huge smothering blanket of the new super gasses would be laid down by plane on selected targets, killing every living thing within the area.

These objectives presumably would be key industrial sites, railroad centers and other communication points. An attempt would be made to occupy them at once so as to disrupt enemy operations at their source and throw him into helpless confusion.

Long trains of air transports suddenly would appear as soon as the assaulted area was safe to enter. An entire army with full equipment would be landed, or would parachute to earth.

If these early efforts to bring the conflict to a determination did not succeed, the war would become a stalemate, and would be continued on other levels and by different means.

Granting that the military capacity of the engaged states was about equal, these staggering losses would result in the theoretical demolition of almost all heavy industry, forcing a reliance on isolated or hidden factories, and accumulated stores of weapons and war material.

A continuation of the contest would make necessary a progressive reorganization of the national war machinery on less lethal levels, with increasing recourse to conventional arms.

The art of camouflage would be brought to a high state of perfection from the beginning, to conceal as much as possible the sources of the national military power; whole decoy cities would be built. Geographic space would take on even more important attributes than before as the great ally of defense.

Such a war would not likely be a short one, but might last for a generation. In this contingency it could become a contest of wills, dragging on interminably in a low but debilitating fever of belligerency, like the ugly Thirty Years' War which once almost wrecked the continent of Europe.

Chapter Eight

WHAT KIND OF AMERICAN FOREIGN POLICY

IF THE United States is not to play the part of Carthage to the growing might of the Eurasian colossus which is rising like a new Rome to dominate the next thousand years of history, it will have to blueprint its peacetime strategy exactly as it did its war policy.

If we are to pursue a course independent of emotional caprice and the clutch of old habit, it can be based on nothing else than a cool estimate of our real situation to which we have to make a sensible adjustment by plan.

The usual unrelated power actions which depend for their motivation on prevalent circumstance, no longer are safe. In an integrated world, a policy without over-all durability is one based on aimless drifting, and on the hope of muddling through by sheer luck and power.

Particularly in a democracy such a course will prove suffocating to the true interests of the state. It will involve the country in alternate irresolution and choleric petulance. In crisis it will produce not the icy clarity the national polity will require, but discordant weakness, and our own crop of Daladiers and Reynauds, men whose feet will be mired in the past and who will see no choice in the deadlock of straitened emergency but to yield to circumstance.

At a surface glance, it would appear that this is the direction in which we are trending.

The existing pattern of our foreign policy is the result of

a deep confusion as to the issues and the nature of the task which confronts the nation. Our statesmanship once disposed to rest on a confident appraisal of the Republic's own powers, has been profoundly shaken by the implications of the new weapons, and by the comfortless predictions of the nuclear physicists.

At a moment when we are strong, well-armed and with the world at our feet, we turn out to have no policy and no goal; we compromise futilely, abandon our proclaimed principles, outlaw our friends, and deal on a basis of equality with petty despots and minor Fascist personalities.

We promote a world organization of unequal, inept and dissonant states which we pretend will apply the much-wanted measures of "international law" to the actions of its members. At the same time, we engage in a quiet though no less sinister struggle with the U.S.S.R. in which we announce that we will not be bound by its formal rules—that "we cannot be indifferent—veto or no veto—to serious controversies between any of the great powers, because such controversies could affect the whole power relationship between all of the great powers."[1] The "power relationship" to which we refer is that between the British and Russian empires. Thus in the specious name of the Charter we commit ourselves to ignoring both its spirit and the letter of its provisions; and announce, by reference, our determination to support the territorial integrity of the British Crown in all its holdings everywhere.

In support of this policy we maintain a line in Europe facing the Russians, and prepare to back Great Britain in the Middle East against her old enemy, locating military depots and establishments there whose effect cannot be much different on Moscow than it would be on Washington were the Russians to duplicate this activity in the territory of our neighbor, Venezuela.

[1] Speech by Secretary of State James Byrnes, New York, February 28, 1946.

We take a harsh stand directed at diminishing Communist influence in China; yet we leave Chungking engulfed in a political and economic vacuum in response to the combined Anglo-American fear that a strong China would be an undesirable world companion.

In the very midst of this play of bitter and unresolvable forces, clearly spiraling toward a new test of strength among the nations, we allow our armies to disintegrate. At the very moment when we are backing up Great Britain in her quarrel with Russia, and when the ferment of international unrest is obviously boiling, the mood of Americans is to destroy their armed forces and to return to the old pacifist sentiment which preceded our entry into World War II.

While we thus are destroying the effective base of our military power, we bait the Russians with threats which we are not prepared to fulfill, and the next moment run hat in hand to Moscow and embroider our diplomatic defeats there to give them the appearance of a substantial "compromise victory."

We reserve the secret of our super-weapon, the atomic bomb, holding it as a final threat against the Russians, and at the same time toy with the idea of giving it to an international organization whose powers are almost completely fictional.

Though we alternately appease, denounce and warn, the situation does not change because it cannot until the basic condition from which it is derived is itself altered. It is at this point that the national outlook becomes fatal to any intelligent solution of the mounting crisis with which we are obliged to deal.

II

Despite the current temporizing, and occasional fits of public optimism, the impression has gained rapidly among a large number of Americans that a conflict with Russia is inevitable, and that it would be better to fight it as a preventive war now while we are strong than later when the power of our position decreases.

It is asserted variously that the Russians are barbarous and rapacious, that they are shamelessly insatiable, and that we live in a period of unparalleled cynicism which disposes of all morality in international relationships. The sole reliable factor by which the future peace can be maintained, it is claimed, is the superior striking power of the United States fighting forces for which the entire world has gained a wholesome respect. If we are to strike, it should be now when a preventive war would be likely to end in our favor. Already, it is argued, the hour is late and we are almost past the peak of our strength.

Those who demand a firm policy backed by the full force of our power, vary from a considerable sprinkling of liberals who have been affronted by Russian operations in eastern Europe, through the old line pro-English partisans in the upper layers of American society and government, to the clericals and hard-shelled reactionaries to whom anti-communism and Russo-phobia is a religion.

There also is a small but influential group which nurses the ambitious belief that should the war party prevail, the United States could conquer the world and maintain the status quo of American industrial superiority forever.

There can be no question that feeling against Russia in the United States has grown rapidly. To some degree it has been stimulated by able British maneuvering to win American public opinion and to create an Anglo-American axis in which Britain would possess the advantage of American military and economic backing. The old capitalist fear of Russia has been strongly intensified in reaction to a rising wave of labor troubles which have raised anew the conviction of sinister Russian intervention in our affairs.

In addition to these people there are others who possess no emotional transfixion on the subject of Russia, but are genuinely alarmed over the turn of events. These include a considerable portion of our best military minds, who see the flow of world power running heavily in the direction of the Soviet Union, despite the present array of striking forces at the disposal of the United States. They are influenced by the claims of the scientists that the Russians will have the atom bomb in not more than three to five years. They consider that the magnetic stream of forces which now favors the U.S.S.R., if uninterrupted and allowed to mature, will allow for the eventual easy triumph of that country as the sole world power.

These men are honestly convinced that a fundamental antagonism exists between the Soviet Union and ourselves which cannot be surmounted. They believe that the differences in purpose, attitude and social organization between the two states are such as to result in ceaseless tension which can be only settled by a final trial of strength on the battlefield.

They do not believe that the earth is large enough to hold both the U.S.A. and the U.S.S.R.; and declare it to be implicit in the totalitarian nature of the Soviet system that its terminal goal be nothing less than world empire.

This is the vision under whose commanding stimulus they believe Moscow has moved. They see Russian power actions as part of a long-range plan to effect these purposes, and to make certain under the excuse of security that the dazzling opportunities which now exist do not slip through the closing fingers of the Russian fist. They tend to consider Russian disclaimers in the same light that Hitler's assurances must now be entertained in retrospect, and to view all Russian action as hopelessly contaminated by this sinister project.

These men believe that unless present drifts are halted, the United States is likely to find itself a capitalist island in a

stormy socialist sea, having at its side only a British ally of
questionable power, and a number of Latin American and
European lackeys loosely tied to the strings of its financial
apron. They suspect that if a successful attempt is to be made
to prevent the political consolidation of all Europe under the
banner of the Russians, it must be made now.

On the other side of these dark speculations are those who
hold a sincere interest in the Russian experiment, and who
regard the U.S.S.R. not as an intolerable tyranny and mortal
danger to the future of free men, but as a great social crucible
which may hold the ultimate hopes of mankind. Still others
believe that Russia has reverted to primitive nationalism, that
having perfected its defenses, the Soviet Union will keep itself
at the worst in peaceful isolation.

On behalf of this view it is argued that though the Russian
is a ferocious fighter on his own soil, external adventure is
foreign to his nature. The Kremlin's vast program of internal
development also is pointed to as being sufficient to absorb
all Soviet energy for long years to come.

Those who profess a friendly feeling for the Russias include in addition to persuaded Communists, some of America's most enlightened and idealistic minds. They are convinced that the Russians are as much sinned against as sinning,
and quote the Kremlin's words on their face value as affirm-
ing Russian willingness to enter as a peaceful partner into
the structure of a co-operative world.

Russia, they point out, has had every reason to look askance
at all efforts at world security based on legal premises alone.
Until the very outbreak of the present war the U.S.S.R. was an
outlaw state, ostracized by almost the entire community of
nations. In the early period of its existence, it was the object
of active intervention and conspiratorial action on the part
of collective capitalist society.

The Munich fiasco these men explain as an effort to spearhead world attack on the Soviet Union, which turned back on its authors.

The contention is advanced that fear and distrust breed in kind, and that if we are to persist in the illusion that the atomic age is to be by concurrent definition the Anglo-Saxon age as well, we shall simply succeed in raising against us the animosity not only of the Russians but of the entire world.

We are defeating our own efforts to create world security, it is argued, by retaining this so-called secret, which the Russians are likely to have in a few years anyway. By holding this axe over Russian heads and not sharing the knowledge of the bomb with them, we have only succeeded in adding fuel to the Russian suspicions, turning them back from the pathway of co-operation which we so ardently desire. If our professions are honestly meant, we as the possessors of the atomic bomb must take the necessary steps to outlaw it, and to place control over its manufacture and use exclusively in the hands of a central world body.

Whatever one might think of the pros and cons of these opinions, there is one conclusion which hardly can be avoided: if we cannot get Russia into a world organization the matter is hopeless—it is a case of *Hamlet* without Hamlet.

III

What may be rationalized out of all this?

It is evident that there is involved a good deal of ugly feeling, as well as wishful thinking, and, perhaps on both sides, some legitimate nervousness and suspicion.

What is abundantly clear is that we are on the horns of a true dilemma. We cannot allow further encroachment by the Russians which would finally weigh the world power balance in their favor. Neither can we safely countenance the jingo demands of the war party, which in certain influential circles is growing by leaps and bounds, to attempt to deal with the Russians on the basis of intimidation.

We may conclude that, whether as a legacy of the drives inherited from the tsars or as a product of the new Soviet dispensation, the very heart of Russian policy is dynamic hunger for expansion and growth. No matter what puttering Soviet leaders may attempt with the prescribed ideals of Marx, the essential definition of the U.S.R.R. as a universe in miniature, seeking by continued accretion to become the macrocosm itself, hardly can be denied.

It also is undeniable, however one faces the situation, that political groups committed to the total destruction of our system and its institutions, exist in expanding form in territories of the greatest strategic importance to us.

In Iceland the Communist party holds ten of the fifty-two seats in the Althing,[2] and on the basis of recent gains is probably the second ranking political organization in the country. In Chile, perhaps the most democratic of the Latin powers, the growth of Communist strength is an acknowledged political fact. In Cuba, it is said that the Communists could paralyze the entire life of the country on a few hours notice by the calling of a general strike.

In Mexico, Lombardo Toledano, the powerful leader of the Latin American Labor Federation, has taken a definite anti-*Yanqui* position. The still influential ex-dictator of Brazil, Getulio Vargas, also has taken an anti-United States line, and is closely identified with Prestas, the Brazilian Communist leader. In his new bid for power as the leader of Brazil's workers and peasants, Vargas is playing a card similar to that of the Argentine dictator, Colonel Perón, who has adopted the slogans and catch-phrases of labor socialism in his quest for power. The two are very friendly, and in the future may be closely associated in a mutual anti-*Yanqui*

2 Icelandic Parliament.

and collectivist program, though the clerical element in Perón's administration would cause it to be in opposition to standard Communism.

On the record the Communist parties in the different countries are more than local political associations devoted to a peculiar set of collectivist principles; but must be judged rather as a manifestation of a general and revolutionary universalism. No matter how friendly one might be toward Communist Russia, it would be a political grotesquerie to ignore these circumstances or to pretend they did not exist.

The simple fact is that wherever a strong local Communist organization exists it will constitute in times of crisis a listening post for whatever side Moscow happens to be on. It also will be a coagulating agent capable of organizing blocs of anti-American sentiment, and to oppose local participation in any war in which we may become engaged.

Neither can there be any doubt of the ominous confidence expressed by Soviet politico-economists in the ultimate bankruptcy of the parliamentary and free trade systems, as if these were antediluvian monsters living far past their appointed time.

The Russians believe that the United States is approaching the worst economic crash in its history, a structural collapse from which our institutions will not be able to crawl out intact. This shattering crisis, says the noted Soviet economist, Professor Eugene Vagin, will begin in from two to four years, following a cycle of overproduction. It will drag all the other capitalist countries down with it, in significant contrast to the U.S.S.R. where an "absence of crisis . . . will *be a beneficent influence on those countries which are linked economically to the U.S.S.R.*" [3]

It is difficult to determine from these expectations just how far the wish may be father to the thought, or just how much

[3] *World Economy and World Politics* (Moscow, U.S.S.R.), May, 1945.

the inner antagonisms parallel the economic logic involved. It is probably enough to remark that the Russians would credit to an active anti-Soviet animosity any assumption on our part that the police state itself is doomed by its own character; that it cannot successfully continue to repress normal human desires indefinitely; and that at some point in their development, social crisis is certain to overtake the immense lumbering bureaus which constitute the machinery of Soviet economic existence, and will find them hopelessly heavy, inert, inefficient, and wanting.

It is manifestly true that if we are to fight the Russians, the time to do so is now. With the overwhelming superiority of armament which exists in our favor, we undoubtedly would succeed at the end of a harrowing contest in trouncing them soundly. Though plain weight of power would give us the victory, it would not be bought cheap. The Russians would fight desperately, and their country would have to be taken village by village. It would not be conquered finally until it had been reduced practically to a desert.

There also would be serious question as to the willingness of our people to bear the exhausting sacrifices this struggle would entail.

Whether a preventive war were justified or not it would be impossible of serious contemplation. Our people would not agree to such a procedure, which they would regard as monstrous. It is in the nature of democracy that the people do not want war, and will not organize for it until it literally has been thrust upon them.

There would be even graver doubts as to the remaining resources at our disposal to sustain so colossal an adventure. The terrible demands which would be made on our already depleted economy would impoverish the nation so that it would not recover for generations.

To achieve our victory and to maintain it, we would have

to evolve a mechanistic order, worshipping at the shrine of scientific materialism and the efficiencies of a co-operative robot society. The result would be an American century, not essentially different from the Nazi new order, or the feared Bolshevik world control, in its effect. The concept of human freedom would fade, and be regarded as a relic of a quaintly backward and inefficient period of human life.

If the Soviets could manage to survive such a war, it conceivably could have its compensations to them. The Russians would prefer to achieve their ends by political means rather than by war, but they are used to paying an expensive price for a desired result. It is inseparable from Marxist dogma that the existing order must be torn down in a huge conflagration of violence if necessary, so that the co-operative world can be built upon its remains.

What would be to us an unqualified disaster might be to the U.S.S.R. a necessary step in the historical evolution of world society.

The Russians, it is true, are poorly prepared for immediate military adventure. They dare not move unless they are certain that they will not have to retreat again and lose face. Once the Kremlin is forced to acknowledge that it can be bludgeoned into compliance, the hold it possesses over the minds of the turbulent masses of the Old World would begin to relax.

Moscow, therefore, would hesitate to anger a political leadership which she regards as inept but cantankerous, at a moment when she suspects that the possession of supreme military power is ours.

From the view of the Russian military commanders, the situation would be something like this: the enemy possesses a weapon of almost unbelievable superiority, against which no adequate defense exists. A small number of attacking planes, or even of automatically operated V-bombs laden with this terror, could wipe out all of the principal cities of the Soviet

Union within a matter of hours. There would be no power in the Russian possession which could prevent the required number of these death missiles from reaching their targets.

No matter what their inner strategy and ultimate objectives might be, good sense compels the Russians to be wary and agreeably correct. Their strategy is compelled to be that of cautious expediency, probing carefully for soft spots as they go along. If they are pushed heavily out of position, they undoubtedly will fight anyway. But as long as they can keep face, every choice they make in accepting opportunity must be with a weather eye out for the presence of the bomb.

The Russian strategists are confident that a waiting policy will see the steady decline of American military power from its present peak. The implications of the existing military unrest have been studied carefully. It is expected that pacifist feeling will gain strongly and that there will be a powerful dissenting opinion from any policy which leaves large bodies of American troops abroad. It is expected that home pressures will cause American armies to be withdrawn from both Europe and Asia, eliminating much of the dangers of ignition from some explosive spark generated by Soviet policy.

Moscow is aware, too, that American military power is being torn down today with the same speed with which it was built.

What is happening to our army is simply expressed in a warning by General of the Army George Marshall "that the military establishment cannot hope to insure the safety of the United States very much longer at the present rate of demobilization," and that the actual disintegration of our armed forces had set in.

Even the O.S.S., the only pretense to an efficient intelligence service possessed by the nation, has been disbanded. What is left of it has been removed from military jurisdiction and located as an "Intelligence Office" in the State Department. The Manhattan Project itself is being quietly liquidated. The scientists are drifting away and both "scientific and technical development of atomic energy has practically come to a standstill."[4]

Under all of the circumstances, turning over the bomb to a world authority does not lend itself to serious contemplation. Whatever our goals, it seems unintelligible to contend that we should give away our defenses. Ordinary discretion would seem to dictate that we do not facilitate the acquisition of technical and military knowledge on the part of potential antagonists until the very hour when it is clearly safe to do so. That hour will arrive only when the complex social, political and economic problems of the age are already within the framework of solution.

IV

It is no secret that the concentration of industry and vital communications in a few large cities makes the United States peculiarly vulnerable to atomic battering.

The Russians also have observed to their satisfaction that the decentralizations required as a means of protection against atomic destruction cannot be achieved by democratic states.

There has been some discussion of a proposed dispersal of American industry into widely distributed, self-contained institutions; of projects looking to the breaking up of our cities; of the location of important manufactories underground, and of the construction of subterranean railroads.

This is a lively piece of conjecture which may have much to recommend it, but the question remains: how can all this be done? What happens to our civic liberties under the type of direction this operation would entail? The only way this

[4] Professor Edward Teller before the Special Senate Committee on Atomic Energy.

gigantic performance could be executed would be through the imposition of rigid controls over every aspect of the American economy. This in essence would be authoritarianism.

The decentralizations effected by such institutions as General Electric are exactly the reverse of those required by military security, and act to make the nation more, rather than less, vulnerable to enemy action. This great concern possesses about twenty-five big branch plants, such as those at Bridgeport, Connecticut, Erie, Pennsylvania, and Pittsfield, Massachusetts. Each of these branches concentrates on the mass production of specialized parts: no one is complete in itself in the sense of creating the entire assembly.

The elimination of any one of these plants would have the effect of knocking out the whole General Electric operation, offering the American economy an almost fatal blow in war. This situation is true not only of the illustration given, but of practically every large American industry.

The Russians see us following a strange compromise of commercial and state policies in respect to essential raw materials, which from their own view is incredibly naive and unreal.

Where the economy of the U.S.S.R. possesses the virtue of being self-contained, the United States relies on distant points of origin for many of its critical materials. The development of sources of supply has been affected more by price arrangements, extensions of favor, and commercial convenience, than by its mass relation to the welfare of the nation. In this sense they represent an almost recklessly haphazard spread often in complete contradiction to our military requirements, threatening to saddle the country at war with an extended, costly and almost indefensible supply line.

At the beginning of World War II American purchasers were caught in the grip of foreign cartel monopolies on such critical products as rubber, tin, copra and quinine, which had to be imported from southeast Asia. The gaps which ensued in our military economy were filled by substitutes and improvised materials, due to a time equation which may not be granted to us in the future. Even then the nation came uncomfortably close to losing the war due to the sudden and unexpected blockade on its indispensable industrial supplies.

American foreign policy tends to be dragged along with the problems of big commercial enterprise, and in fact to be attached to them. Here Great Britain has moved with great shrewdness to involve American interests in British activities throughout the world. We have been granted leases in Ethiopia which today is a British province, insuring our permanent interest there. Similar concessions have been made in the oil fields of Iran and Saudi Arabia, both British-controlled spheres. We find ourselves involved in the oil of Iraq, and through interlocking agreements, in the great African cocoa cartels and the Malayan rubber and tin monopolies.

In Palestine an American corporation, the Trans-Arabian Pipeline Company, has been granted a seventy year concession with rights almost akin to those originally held by the Hudson's Bay Company. Under this remarkable agreement, the company is to be free of all taxes, direct or indirect. Its imports are to be duty free; it need not observe labor laws and may import foreign labor irrespective of existing immigration restrictions. On demand of the company the government is to expropriate privately owned land. The company is to have special port facilities and railway rates, is to pay only nominal rentals for government-owned lands and is to receive government-owned stone and timber free for building purposes. It may own and construct every manner of utility, ranging from roads and airfields to railway, streetcar and telephone lines, to pipe lines and electric power plants.

Our stakes in these far-away places represent a military liability to the extent that they constitute principal or important sources of raw material supply. They cannot be defended except under conditions where the United States possesses an absolute superiority of weapons, and is able to dominate communications over any portion of the globe irrespective of any combination of forces which may be raised against us.

Under normal circumstances of war, where the military strength of the combatants involved was somewhere near equal, our position in the Near and Middle East, in particular, would be indefensible. If we were to rely on Arabian oil for our wartime needs, we should lose it.

Britain's lopsided development as an island workshop dependent on outside markets, has fastened on her statesmen the policy of suppressing local industry in the territories she dominates. In the Middle East, London is chary of the growth of any industrial competitor which later might become even a military rival. This is the cause of much of the Indian trouble, and the reason behind the patient artifices aimed at forestalling Zionist enterprise in Palestine.

Whatever its compensations to them, this program argues against Britain's ultimate ability to hold the Middle East since it faces future British military operations, and our own, with an overriding problem of defense logistics which cannot possibly be met. The establishment of heavy Russian industry in nearby Central Asia makes this conclusion inescapable.

A like risk would apply to our purchase of industrial products from Malaya and Indonesia, where the same ruinous logistical weakness exists.

The idea that we can secure ourselves against this result by holding Okinawa, the Marshalls and a few other isolated island outposts, has little to recommend it.

This type of forward base is a relic of the days of fighting ships, which beyond minor reconditioning required little in the way of servicing over long periods of time except access to some strategically located coaling station. In a maturing air age, this old naval formula becomes a risky one.

Modern battle planes require complicated servicing. Unlike war ships, they represent just the opposite of self-containment. They must continually be doctored, serviced and tended as no other battle instrument in history. They require almost unlimited quantities of matériel, parts, gasoline and stores of different kinds; and great numbers of radio operators, mechanics, executives and other skilled personnel. This makes necessary a large establishment, including required foods, hospitalization, housing, and sanitary and amusement facilities.

The modern forward base therefore is compelled to depend on a mobilized industrial hinterland. If this hinterland is far away, all the old questions of logistics and supply lines reappear in full force.

Distant bases which must be served from a far-away mainland extension, lend themselves poorly to defense in an air age. Such spots as Okinawa or Iwo Jima could be annihilated in a matter of hours by a concentration of enemy short-range aircraft operating from nearby industrial areas. Such bases are valuable to get in the first, possibly decisive blows. They would provide important launching sites for rockets, whose accurate range still is greatly limited.

To be defensible, modern bases must not be isolated barbaric outposts, but a genuine extension of the mainland economy to which they are tied. They must be organized in depth as part of the general scheme of continental defense. This requires that they be part of a solid pattern dotting a wide area, and that they be capable of supporting a civilian economy which in part at least, produces the industrial paraphernalia needed to wage war.

If any large water sector is to be held, possession must be had of every island territory within its circumference. The connective lines must be secure and uninterrupted. In the

Arctic, for example, all the islands of any great half or quarter section must be secured in their entirety.

All of the strategic island zones in our hemisphere, including the Greenland, Iceland, Baffinland group, and the stepping-stone islands which lead to Australasia, derive their importance not only from their individual location but also from the general pattern of their relation to each other.

The future fate of these regions, which we shall touch on later, must be of the most critical interest to us in any contemplation of the future.

V

Out of this miscellany of questions, problems and situations a number of general propositions may be visualized as preliminary to any policy of rational settlement:

1. It is essential that we retreat from the present pointless and piecemeal diplomacy and adopt a consistent foreign policy devoted to clear objectives. This policy should bear a sensible relation to our own military and economic future, as well as to that of others. It should be carefully weighed on all levels, and not confined by the iron warrant of the atom bomb, which already in the West has assumed the proportions of Black Mask diabolism.

2. It should be a prime purpose of our foreign relations to establish a healthy footing with the U.S.S.R. A stop-Russia policy, with no other creative end, represents a negative political philosophy which is both unworkable and unfitted to our dignity as a great nation.

3. Although we may not be able to merge into a single world society with Russia, we shall have to exist on the same globe with her. Therefore we should attempt by

direct discussions to arrive at an understanding with the U.S.S.R. based on our mutual interests as well as on the whole question of ultimate human unity. At the same time we must *seek a new world equilibrium of power, in which the U.S.A. will follow a line of development paralleling that of the U.S.S.R.* As we shall observe, this means a reversal of our present policy, and a practical end to the small state. In making an estimate of the hazards this course will involve, it is necessary to realize that as long as the present groupings of small, weak, anarchic and ruined states exist they will constitute a political and military vacuum toward which the forces of the U.S.S.R. and the U.S.A. will be irresistibly drawn, if only by the power of their own converging fears.

4. The United States should avoid entanglement in the maneuvers, power conspiracies and ambitions of others, who either under the guise of practical expediency or lofty idealism seek to utilize our weight in their own interests. Above all we should get out from the middle of the present Russian-British imbroglio and follow a policy which relates directly to our own interests. If we decide to go with the Britain of Empire and the policy of world unsettlement this involves, we must be prepared for war with the Soviet Union, and ultimately with the Orient.

5. Though our first duty is clearly that of guaranteeing the survival of our own nation, it cannot be on the cynical power terms with which the world is unhappily familiar. It is important for us to realize that in addition to being an independent nation we are a part of general humanity. We cannot castigate the dynamic, proselyting quality of the Russian experiment while ourselves occupying a void. Therefore in addition to seeking our national ends it is up to us *to make our social system work.* If we can-

not do so we have nothing to offer either our own people or others but the complaints and vain posturings of querulous old age.

The question we must consider is not whether an antagonism of purpose exists between the Russian Soviets and ourselves. Such an antagonism does exist.

It is no good preaching to the Russians, or condemning them. What we must attempt to bring about is an intelligent world settlement with the Russians which lays at rest for all time both the fears and the opportunities which exist for conflict.

What we must seek most to gain is time. If we can secure another quarter century of peace, time itself may wear many of the present critical issues thin.

Scientific progress in an age of cheap power and cheap materials is certain to make possible a plethora of everything for all the peoples, so that the economic causes of war at least can be dissolved. Even under bad social organization all men can possess a reasonable degree of leisure and comfort once the existing political vacuum has been eliminated.

Under the mellowing influence of time it may be assumed that many issues which now form impassable obstacles to world harmony will disappear. At this point the United States, the last stronghold of free capital, and Russia, the center of authoritarian rule, undoubtedly will have moved toward each other, merging their principal differences in the over-all problems of the age.

VI

Among the circumstances which would serve to defeat this policy is the failing economic and military economy of our British associate, to whose fortunes we are closely linked.

Time is running against the British Empire. Opposed to the new imperialism of the Soviet type, devoted to full industrialization and a total exploitation of human labor, the old limited colonial imperialism, with its levies on barbarous native chiefs and repression of manufacturing processes, has no chance whatsoever. In the ultimate contest of strength which must ensue, it finally will disappear from the scene of history, and even today only can survive so long as it possesses unqualified American backing.

The major fact which we must consider in relation to these quarrels is that any war in which Great Britain may be engaged will involve the United States and its interests. Britain is the new "sick man of the universe" who must be propped up to prevent disconcerting alterations in the *status quo*. Whether we wish it so or not, we have drifted more or less unconsciously into a position where we are compelled to back her wherever she appears to be in serious jeopardy.

Granted this providential protection for its aims British policy is certain to employ every possible artifice to rescue the Empire from the imminent menace which threatens it with disintegration. Those shrewd manipulators of events, the statesmen and permanent officials of Whitehall and Westminster, will seek to utilize the time allotted to them to its utmost advantage. They will use their intimate relationship with us to the full in an effort to turn the tables on Russia and make Britain's world-wide routes of Empire as secure and durable as possible.

London will attempt to cement its hold on the Levant and Africa, and to push the Russians out of the Balkans and Central Europe, where their presence gives British officialdom a nightmare. Britain will proceed with her scheme for a solidly organized group of Arab states under British military and economic tutelage, and when the termination of the present crisis makes further temporizing unnecessary, will adopt a firmer hand toward India, moving relentlessly to exploit the differences between the Mohammedan and Hindu sections. China also will experience the effect of British power action quietly

applied in the finance and economic realms, again presumably
with the backing of the United States. Wherever the Chinese
turn in their efforts to become a world power, they will feel
the weight of British resistance.

British diplomacy is at the same time skittish, apprehensive
and astute, and inclined to seek a showdown with Moscow
while the U.S.S.R. is still uninclined to risk a war into which
America might be drawn.

The British are a brave and obstinate people, who are
perspicacious enough where their vital interests are concerned. They are sure to take full political advantage of the
partnership they share with us in the atom bomb researches.
This recognized circumstance caused the Turkish newspaper,
Vakit, to write, under date of August 11, 1945, referring
obliquely to the pressures exerted by Russia on the Turkish
nation: "The atomic bomb saved mankind."

British policy does not operate to create an absolute Anglo-
American front, but a far looser arrangement in which the
primary interests of the two English-speaking states will run
parallel at every point of dangerous contact with the Soviets,
but cease to do so at other points.

Though Anglo-American unity can be rationalized on a
number of satisfactory levels, the basic interests of the two
countries, where they operate as separate and independent
governments, demand totally different approaches. The interests of America require a world of absolute stability and fixed
power equilibriums, in which we ourselves are one of the two
great opposing weights. British interests, on the other hand,
prescribe a liquid and changeable power balance, permitting
Britain as the island hub of a great empire, to remain one of
the international balancers.

One of the very real dangers to which America is exposed
by this battle for position results from the developing science
of public relations, now frankly utilized by both Britain and

the U.S.S.R. in an effort to influence the weight of American opinion in their own behalf. American sympathy and support is a choice plum for which not only the British and Russians, but the Chinese and many lesser lights, will make a powerful bid.

The character of American democracy makes it peculiarly vulnerable to directed efforts of this type.

The American people in consequence have become the object of one of the most intensive public relations campaigns ever undertaken, sometimes functioning in secret, sometimes in the open. The propaganda of organized foreign interests flourishes on any number of levels, aimed not only at influencing the upper layers of government, but the great masses as well.

The British operate for the most part in the higher social spheres, through lecturers, student exchanges, and interlocking American interests which they either control or are in a position to grant considerable favors. Their public relations office in the United States is headed by an official of acknowledged rank. Britain also relies on its control of important news sources in such portions of the world as India, Palestine and Greece, acting as do the Russians to give the news a carefully perverted twist, over- or under-stressing it as the individual occasion may make desirable.

According to estimated figures for 1944, official British expenditures for propaganda in the United States are estimated to be around $2,500,000 a year. To this must be added other considerable amounts spent indirectly or secretly, as those which are being expended by the office of the Arab League in Washington.

Both the Russian and British Ambassador receive a salary equal to that of the President of the United States. Both possess an unlimited spending account for the purposes of entertaining. Both nations have their partisans and sym-

pathizers within the American government itself, by which
pressures of one kind or another may be subtly applied, as
well as reliable publishing connections. Both maintain a large
number of intelligence agents, particularly in Washington.

The Russians specialize in various "front" organizations,
whose proclaimed viewpoint is that of humanitarianism and
international liberalism. Their influence among the labor
groups is noteworthy, and among the Colored race, very
large.

This type of strategic publicity operation is not limited
in its field to the United States alone. It operates in all other
countries whose democratic character exposes them to this
type of penetration. Even the great British news monopoly,
Reuters, has been accused of acting as an unofficial agency
of the British government abroad, coloring the news in British
interests, or selling it at a loss to secure desired outlets,[5] though
the charge has been denied.

The English operation on the whole is more skillful and
experienced, and less obvious than that of the Russians. In
this country the effectiveness of British public relations work
is indicated in the general support London always manages
to secure for its current politics despite the strong under-
current of anti-British prejudice which exists here.

The major British public relations object in America today
is to sell the American people on the following propositions:

1. That the commercial prosperity of Britain is an absolute necessity to the commercial prosperity of the
   United States, and that the two must act as a cartelized
   unit in the stabilization of world trade;

2. That Russian imperialism is immoral and contrary to

[5] Memorandum on the Post-war International Information Program of the
United States, by Dr. Arthur W. MacMahon, pp. 19-20, published by U. S.
Department of State.

the human conscience, but that British imperialism is a civilizing influence which cannot be dispensed with in the present stage of international development.

3. That a showdown must be had with the Russians as quickly as possible. The policy, capsulated, is expressed as follows: "You Americans already are almost past the summit of your power. If you are to save yourselves and the world, you must act now."

This desire to make a stand and bring the present gnawing crisis to a head is tribute to the shrewd wisdom of British politics and the mettle of British statesmen. The determination to explore this avenue out of Britain's agonizing dilemma accounts for the calculated violence of Foreign Secretary Bevin's public indictment of Russian policy. Russia is to be placed within brackets and either forced into a stand which she lacks the immediate physical power to sustain, or is to be forced to retreat, fastening on the Russians a costly loss of prestige and dynamiting the new Eurasian legend of Russian steamroller invincibility.

London is seeking also to line up the smaller powers in a solid world bloc enclosing the U.S.S.R. Moral sanction thus is to be given Anglo-American power pressures, by parallel measures undertaken through the agency of the United Nations Organization.

This is a difficult tightrope for the British government to tread. Though on the whole, when divested of Britain's imperial anxieties, the British program may seem justified in the interests of the different capitalist states, all of them show a real reluctance to antagonize Russia to the point where she will collapse the U.N.O. by walking out of it.

The British are aware that Russia will be unimpressed by noble speeches of remonstrance hurled against her policy by capitalist statesmen. If actual force cannot be exerted on the

Russians they will continue on their present course, with the result that Britain, though enjoying the oral support of the nations, will in fact find herself surrounded by an iron ring of isolation, which is even now being forged around her. Britain's whole future now rests on the ability of English diplomats to cause American policy to follow channels concurrent with her own.

In the past the amount of influence British statesmen have been able to exercise over American judgments has been large. Our policies were inexperienced, strongly isolationist, and were implemented by political appointees to whom diplomacy was an honorarium rather than a profession.

To most Americans the external world was a strange place from which we happily were separated by wide seas. American interests were confined mostly to the development of the country's rich internal domains. British statesmanship was experienced and long-sighted, and British control of the seas added to the impregnability of our own shores. Despite an occasional quarrel, the quality of British world judgment was estimated highly by our officials; and the two countries by mutual acceptance and sympathy gravitated naturally into alliance with each other during periods of world stress.

As late as the early 1940's we find the influence of the British Prime Minister of signal importance in determining our own policy. Though we then were not yet partners in war, the association was intimate and close.

Though undoubtedly our difficulties with Japan ultimately would have had to be settled by recourse to arms, the crisis which began in the late summer of 1941 was one which threatened the existence of the British Empire rather than immediate interests of our own.

The Japanese statesmen were endeavoring to consolidate their opportunities in eastern Asia and the Pacific, and judging by the record, at least for the time being were attempting to avoid a war with America. Had Japan been able to forestall such a conflict for another eighteen months its militarists undoubtedly would have been in a far sounder position to meet this final and most powerful of their enemies.

Mr. Churchill counseled an immediate showdown. This he said could come only from the United States.

A deep glimpse into these events is contained in a State Department Memorandum of Conversation dated August 10, 1941, and signed by Mr. Sumner Welles, then Under Secretary of State. It reads: "As I was leaving the ship to accompany the President back to his flagship, Mr. Churchill said to me that he had likewise given the President copies of these documents. He impressed upon me his belief that some declaration of the kind he had drafted with respect to Japan was in his opinion in the highest degree important; and that he did not think that there was much hope left unless the United States made such a clear-cut declaration, of preventing Japan from expanding further to the South, in which event the prevention of war between Great Britain and Japan appeared to be hopeless. He said in the most emphatic manner that if war did break out between Great Britain and Japan, Japan immediately would be in a position through the use of her large number of cruisers to seize or to destroy all of the British merchant shipping in the Indian Ocean and in the Pacific, and to cut the lifelines between the British Dominions and the British Isles unless the United States herself entered the war. He pled with me that a declaration of this character participated in by the United States, Great Britain, the Dominions, the Netherlands and possibly the Soviet Union, would definitely restrain Japan. If this were not done, the blow to the British Government might be almost decisive."

The messages which our government sent to the imperial Japanese government apparently were drafted by the British. Mr. Welles's memorandum goes on: "Sir Alexander Cadogan told me before lunch that in accordance with the conversation which was had between the President, the Prime Minister,

Sir Alexander and myself at the President's dinner last night, he had made two tentative drafts covering proposed parallel and simultaneous declarations by the United States and British Governments relating to Japanese policy in the Pacific. . . . The two drafts read as follows:

" 'Draft of Parallel Communications to the Japanese Government.

" 'Declaration by the United States Government that:

" '1. Any further encroachment by Japan in the Southwestern Pacific would produce a situation in which the United States Government would be compelled to take countermeasures even though these might lead to war between the United States and Japan.

" '2. If any Third Power becomes the object of aggression by Japan in consequence of such countermeasures or of their support of them, the President would have the intention to seek authority from Congress to give aid to such Power.' "

The Japanese attempted a desperate play for time. The usual diplomatic double talk ensued in which Tokyo endeavored to give assurances of its peaceful intentions toward the United States.

The President was obdurate. The Japanese envoys were informed that "the country is replete with anti-Japanese sentiment." The impression was left that only the President and those immediately around him were holding out for peace.

The conversations were finally broken off, and the Japanese vainly attempted to resume them.

Mr. Roosevelt's telegram to Churchill of August 18, 1941, reads in part:

"On August 17 I sent for the Japanese Ambassador, and the Secretary of State and I received him. I made to him a statement covering the position of this Government with respect to the taking by Japan of further steps in the direction of military domination by force, along the lines of the proposed statement such as you and I had discussed. The statement I made to him was no less vigorous than and was substantially similar to the statement we had discussed."

Under date of August 26, the Japanese Prime Minister, Prince Konoye, wired the President urging a personal meeting "between you and me." Hawaii was suggested as the place.

The President refused on plea that "Hawaii is out of the question, for according to the Constitution the President must sign bills passed through the Houses of Congress within ten days and I cannot have the Vice-President do it for me."

Soon after, an all-out military government took charge of Japan's destinies, and the result, as we know, was Pearl Harbor.

The inevitable question these conversations bring into being is not that of the justification for our war with the Imperial Japanese Empire. Churchill's advice was sound, and his urgings the product of a deep sense of wisdom. It undoubtedly would have been to the disadvantage of the United States had we waited until Japan had a chance to exploit her new conquests for the benefit of her war machine. What must concern us is that the trigger mechanisms which set these events off were more intimately connected with British interests than our own.

It is in the sense that the tail wags the dog—that the divergent interests of the smaller part dominated the processes of the larger—that this situation becomes undesirable and unsound.

What our relations with Britain have amounted to has been an alliance based on personal terms, and a continuing rapport between the British Foreign Office and the American State

Department. It constituted a sort of closed corporation from which even Britain's wartime allies were more or less excluded.

Mr. Welles's "Memorandum of August 11, 1941," covering his conversations with Sir Alexander Cadogan, British Permanent Under Secretary of State for Foreign Affairs, enlightens us on this point. "We discussed," he says, "the desirability of informing the Chinese of the steps which the United States Government in the person of the President was taking in regard to Japan."

Finally it was decided to tell the Chinese nothing.

The memorandum continues: "Sir Alexander said . . . [that] of course, I realized how terribly persistent the Chinese were and that the present Ambassador in London, Dr. Wellington Koo, would undoubtedly press him day in and day out to know what had transpired at the meeting between the Prime Minister and the President with regard to China. He said that he felt that the best solution was for him merely to say in general terms that the two Governments had agreed that every step should be taken that was practicable at this time for China and its defense and avoid going into any details."

In the postwar period it was intended that this close association of power was to continue. Mr. Welles's memorandum again speaks for itself. Replying to Mr. Roosevelt's remark that "nothing could be more futile than the reconstitution of a body such as the Assembly of the League of Nations," Mr. Welles writes: "I said to the President that it seemed to me that if he conceived of the need for a transition period upon the termination of the war during which period Great Britain and the United States would undertake the policing of the world, it seemed to me that it would be enormously desirable for the smaller powers to have available to them an Assembly in which they would all be represented and in which they could make their complaints known and join in recommendations as to the policy to be pursued by the major powers who were doing the police work. I said it seemed to me that an organization of that kind *would be the most effective safety valve that could be devised.*[6]

"The President said that he agreed fully. . . . I further said that while from the practical standpoint I was in agreement that the United States and Great Britain were the only Powers which could or would exercise the police trusteeship, that it seemed to me that it would be impossible if such a trusteeship were set up to exclude therefrom the other American Republics or for that matter the countries at present occupied such as Norway, the Netherlands, and even Belgium. The President said that he felt that a solution for this difficulty could possibly be found through the ostensible joining with Great Britain and the United States of those powers, but that it would have to be recognized that it would be ostensible since none of the nations mentioned would have the practical means of taking any effective or, at least, considerable part in the task involved."

It will be noted at once that this Anglo-Saxon condominium would in fact dictate the affairs of the world, as well as guarantee against disruption the future of the British Empire. There is no mention of the Soviet Union. The attitude toward the purposes of the league indicates in the full that such a body as this can never escape the backstairs maneuver and political jugglery and deceits with which international politics in the past has been burdened.

Despite the undesirable features which have attended it, the United States does and will require an enduring partnership with Great Britain and her Dominions. This, however, cannot be a partnership subject to separate influences, and deriving from separate interests and conceptions of the future.

[6] Italics mine.

Chapter Nine

WORLD ORDER

THE task of containing the rapidly deteriorating world situation and of placing it under some type of effective control, evidently cannot be performed by the machinery evolved at the San Francisco Conference. It hardly appears that further reliance may be placed on the outcome of these propositions. If in its ordinary foreshortened accounts, history mentions them at all, it will be as an unsubstantial vision of the night, sponsored by men whose purpose was superior to the logic which produced it.

Before proceeding with our survey of the course open to the United States at this crossroads crisis of history, it is well to define the nature of the universal problem. At bottom it appears to be this: since science and machine production have turned the world into an interlocking entity, it grows more and more difficult for it to live separately in its parts. It no longer is an amoebalike character, self-contained in its smallest natural unit, but a related group of specialized tissues which increasingly depend upon their natural synchronization with each other.

As long as one state is capable of controlling the outlets of rivers navigated by others, or possesses raw materials required in the industry of its neighbors, or holds the key to their military defense or the natural balance of their production and distribution economy, its internal affairs become peculiarly the business of all. The independence of such a

276

state from its neighbors will be fictional to the degree that their vital interests impinge on it.

The impairment of sovereign health which derives from an incomplete or insufficient economy can only be described under the name of abnormality. Insofar as nations do not possess the required physical base which would enable them to exist in organic health, they will feel impelled to resort to such means as they are able to safeguard what they must regard as their vital needs. Both in conspicuous need or debilitating weakness the situation of such states will constitute a standing invitation to aggression.

The strength of both Fascist and Communist doctrine is that they recognize the power of these major trends. It is the universalist aspect of these creeds, and their willingness to sweep out the conventional deadwood which clutters the machinery of organized life, that has attracted to them so many vigorous, resolute and adventuresome minds.

As each of the countries comes more and more to fit into the world pattern, its people will take an increasingly revolutionary attitude toward all impedimenta, whether of a social, political or geographic nature, which would place their economy under competitive disadvantage.

The present fright which consumes society is similar to that which has always prefaced some violent and revolutionary change in the human economy. A static state of mind exists where a dynamic one is necessary. Men cannot conceive of the fundamental changes which already have taken place and find themselves in the ridiculous position of opposing their manifestations.

In particular is this true of those who possess substantial holdings in the prevailing order. They are like a man who is riding on a train seat backwards: he sees everything after it has happened, and usually after it is too late.

Beyond the great moral bases from which organized life

derives the meaning it is to express, we are compelled to follow a course based on the objective logic offered by circumstances themselves, rather than to adjust our policy to formal legalisms in whose real authority no one actually believes. Otherwise, we shall be in a physical position to settle nothing, since we will not possess the machinery to do so.

These are the deep realities which we must have the courage to see and face.

II

Good sense must cause us to dispense with the idea that security can be bought cheaply, or a cure for our organizational ills result from the application of some easy poultice.

The apparatus for peace must not only hypothetically outlaw war but render it impractical, unprofitable and unattractive. Above all it must articulate the needs of the earth's inhabitants in respect to their actual relations with each other.

Law cannot be superimposed on a body alien to the conceptions it proclaims. Rules formally expressed, but without the sanction of historical authority, possess no capacity for enforcement.

Law, in human experience always has been the product of government, which means the state. In most of their aspects, the state and society are compelled to be identical. The one is a mechanism for the orderly expression of the other.

The function of law is to rule, not to advise or suggest. The existence of law requires the simultaneous existence of a community which it regulates.

Before reverting again to this subject, it is well to acknowledge that the present international emergency in no sense of the word lends itself to simple cure. It is the product of multiple circumstances and hence by its nature will not subscribe to a single solution. There are many questions, and many related factors. In addition to political, social and doctrinal problems, there are questions of moral view, without which society cannot exist altogether, as well as those which deal with the equated distribution of the products of industry to the great population masses who create them.

While all of this is true enough, it is pointed out only to denote that it exists. The burden of our argument is with the political side alone; for as long as government determines the climate in which social and economic systems must function, politics must be the first concern of men.

The question is not one of overcoming the laws of nature by force in order to provide good government and international harmony, but rather of constructing a society organically capable of the minimum function required of it.

If only by reason of the dramatic transformation in the nature of weapons, and in the world's industrial outlook, a corresponding change in the international political structure is inevitable. All great inventions and discoveries, whether of gunpowder, the blast furnace, the internal combustion engine, or of new and unoccupied territories such as America and Australia, have mirrored not only new achievements in science, economics and war, but the approaching shadow of political change.

An antiquated political system cannot exist side by side with a revolutionary technology. Government to be meaningful is compelled to express the evolutionary quality of the times.

The new world of mechanical mastery obviously demands new political approaches to the problems of our day.

Science has changed the nature of the world question completely. It no longer is one of insufficient grazing grounds, or overpopulation. The fact is that modern civilization requires large and dense populations in order to function well. An area which will not support ten thousand aborigines on a low standard of living may give a comfortable livelihood to many millions of Europeans.

The machinery, means and processes which science is placing in our hands would enable the agricultural state of Texas alone, if intensively farmed, to feed all the people of this Continent. With the new sources of energy and synthetic materials which it is possible to derive from such sources as seawater, cornstalks and sawdust, there is no practicable limit to the capacity of this planet to feed and clothe its children. It is a question not of insufficiency, but of production and organization.

The scientific age has left no further reason for poverty and endemic orgies of mass murder and destruction than the unworthiness of man himself. Man has made himself master of a rich garden. He can enjoy it and ennoble his life with its boundless treasures, or he can destroy himself in a hideous nightmare compounded no longer of hard realities but of his own delusions.

III

Theoretically, the grand result of modern science, discovery and invention, must be a federation of the world.

We are in fact told that there are only a few years left, that a desperate race against time exists, that it is either to be the world state or world suicide.

That some type of organic world order must be secured is obvious. That it can be achieved through the sheer fright accompanying the birth of the bomb is a meretricious piece of reasoning which has little to recommend it.

The approach to this great object is generally conceived to be through the organizational means already provided by the United Nations Organization.

The plan is to "strengthen" the U.N.O. by granting it actual powers of sovereign jurisdiction over the nations.

The world organization, however, will only be a government in the sense that it is entrusted with limited powers centering around the problem of keeping the peace. It will not be able to levy taxes, regulate commerce or govern the conditions under which the individual citizen in each of the states is to live. The old absurdities are to be crowned with newer and bigger ones. The old pretences are to be elaborated on a bigger and more convincing scale; but behind these shadows the old prerogatives and privileges are to remain as before.

It is proposed that the General Assembly of the United Nations be formed into a world parliament, answerable to a "constitution under which all the peoples and nations will participate upon a basis of balanced representation, which will take account of natural and industrial resources and other factors as well as population."[1]

It will be noted that though the veto power now enjoyed by the great states is to be done away with, it is to be substituted for by a weighted type of representation which would secure power in its present hands permanently. Thus China with its five hundred million people would have a representation not greater than that of England, and materially inferior to that of Britain and her Dominions together. India presumably would have no voice at all except as it flowed through the familiar channels of British control. The same would be true of Egypt, Africa and Indonesia, whose function would be that of manipulated puppets moving under the coercive power of imperial direction.

When both Mr. Eden and Mr. Bevin, representing the rounded shape of official British opinion, voice the conviction that in order to be safe from atomic power "we all must abate our present ideas of sovereignty" and "devise a fran-

[1] Declaration for a World Government at the Dublin Conference, a non-official gathering of American intellectual leaders at Dublin, New Hampshire; October 16, 1945.

chise or constitution for a world assembly" which will constitute "a new Parliament of Man," the declaration must be looked on with one eye to the fact that Mr. Bevin's soldiers are using their guns on helpless Javanese natives, shooting down patriots in Greece and Egypt, holding India in bondage, and in similar ways comporting themselves in other parts of the world in a frank admission of self-interest.

What this amounts to is another of the attempts to freeze the existing power balance, and to place an estoppal order on all movements of change, whether by revolution or the military intervention of some powerful rival.

In any free association of peoples based on the principles of democracy, the rights of each individual under its jurisdiction must be equal to that of every other individual, irrespective of race, condition or nationality. Ultimate power would be wielded by those states which are the most populous. Their influence would be exerted direct and without intermediacy on the world authority itself, and would constitute an almost irresistible form of pressure.

In every federal structure it is the mass weight of people who determine the course of events. It is their total power exerted on the machinery of politics which makes all government finally but an expression of their will.

This brings us to the fact that the population mass of either of the two great oriental states immediately would outweigh all the Western countries combined. The effect on world politics would be incalculable and decisive.

If a single federal union were to be brought about, its final consequence would be its domination by the Orient, a solution for which the West is far from ready.

Under any kind of government, the right of free movement by all the peoples of the world would have to be implicit. The movement of citizens from Europe or America into Africa, South America, Canada, or Oceania, could not be favored as against restrictions placed upon those from Asia.

Continued action which cooped up the five hundred million Chinese and four hundred million Indians in their giant ghettos would be resisted. The world society shortly would degenerate into huge blocs like those which led to the American Civil War over the slave question.

No one can gainsay the fact that a free world society must mean the freedom of Asia from European imperial subjection. The cynicism, hypocrisy and unyielding privilege exercised by the colonial powers there cannot continue in the same breath with the demand for world government.

If Asia's economy is to remain in the hands of Western oil barons and financiers, and her territories occupied by the armies of alien usurpers determined to keep the native peoples in subjection and ignorance, Asia's brute struggles for freedom will continue. The result finally will be to enmesh this planet in the most gigantic of all wars.

The mere fact of formal stipulations existing on legal levels will not prevent this inevitable clash. Within our own experience it occurred in the American Civil War, and in the Revolutionary War against Great Britain. We also are acquainted with this phenomenon in the wars of the Latin American states against Spain. In pursuit of a cause which concerns both their passions and material welfare, men at a certain point will risk anything, and will not be deterred by the existence of some legal sanction, or even by the atomic bomb.

For a world government to exist in all honesty, Holland, France and England would have to strip themselves of their possessions and become small European states of no consequence to the future world power scheme. No matter how unavoidable this outcome might be, it is not likely to occur as a free act of renunciation on the part of the imperial powers, but rather as the result of some overburdened situation with which they no longer can cope.

At least one other main obstacle exists to the attainment of a single federated world society. This is the total difference in social feature between the U.S.S.R. and the free trade countries, marking them off into diametrically opposed worlds. There is not the slightest possibility of a workable union of peoples containing an immense revolutionary and totalitarian order responsive to a single will, and at the same time numerous other states which are vulnerable to every maneuver and pressure of their highly organized federal companion.

The result of such a union would be to place the non-totalitarian states at a desperate and cumulative disadvantage which could end only in their overthrow, or in a savage war of annihilation against the Soviets. The two systems cannot coexist within the same legal framework, a situation we see with crystal clarity in the events now unfolding in China. There is no possible means by which the two may be placed under the jurisdiction of a common law expressing the character and aims of both.

Whether a single world government is sound or not, it is undesirable. Under the conditions of this century, it offers the opportunity of making totalitarian oppression complete, and would become the most terrible instrument for the suppression of human liberties ever designed by man. A single world order would tend to remove all competitive spirit, and subdue all attempt at political experiment. There would be no sanctuary anywhere for the dissident mind, and no haven of sympathy for the courageous and the incorruptible.

In the world state, the rebel, the initiator, and the independent thinker simply cannot exist, but must succumb to the crushing weight of internationally organized social bureaucracy. The Thomas Paines and Trotskys, or even the Henry Georges and Léon Blums, would become dangerous enemies of society whose fate would be extermination.

The unrestricted power growths represented by the bureaus of the world government would be responsible eventually to no opinion but their own. There would be no need for placating the public opinion of some outside state; and the temptation to seize control of the central power apparatus would be overwhelming.

The trend of this age is toward more and more monopolistic control of every aspect of the social firmament, so that the suppression of liberty and freedom becomes not so much calculated as almost automatic. This circumstance is unavoidable as long as human affairs remain complex and require regulation, and is inherent in the type of social organization which the scientific age is helping to bring about.

The hope of being able to prevent evil men from seizing power is more a pious wish than a serious contemplation of events. The history of the world is a history of benign social structures falling into the hands of ruthless and ambitious men. Hammurabi gave way to a long list of conquerors. The French Revolution bred the Emperor Napoleon. Even labor unions often find themselves under the dictatorship of cold self-seeking leaders who use them for their own advantage.

In respect to the demand for a world state, one may repeat the words of Queen Christiana of Denmark, who, being urged by her ministers to marry that the country might have an heir, replied: "I could as easily bring forth a Nero as an Augustus."

In any event it must be concluded that the movement for world unity is not moving. Everyone pays lip service to it, but no one is willing to face the consequences of it.

IV

An alternative set of ideas has been offered by the American political writer, Clarence Streit, which argue for the establishment of a world union based on ideological grounds. This extremely attractive project when under close scrutiny shows discrepancies which appear to make it impracticable.

Were the world to federalize based on democratic principles alone, we would find ourselves with extensions of our federal system in Europe and Asia which we could not defend; while many of our own vital peripherial areas would remain outside of our jurisdiction.

An action which placed us permanently in Europe, and perhaps Asia, could not fail to be regarded by the Russians as a *casus belli*, exactly as would be the case with us were one or more Soviet republics to be established on our continent.

It must be observed, too, that those states which now are democracies have not always been so, whereas other states now in the totalitarian column were formerly in the democratic ranks. This is true of such countries as Brazil and the Argentine. Spain once was a democracy. Russia itself for a short time had the constitutional Kerensky government. Austria possessed a highly developed socialist rule, devoted to the humanities, before Dollfuss and Schushnigg took over. France was a republic twice, a monarchy three times, functioned once under the revolutionary Communes, and once was an oligarchic extension of the Nazi state.

On the record, it is hopeless to argue that those states which are now democracies will remain so indefinitely. That would be to ignore the dynamic content of history, without which it has neither sense nor meaning.

If it is a condition for international harmony that the Soviets all become democratic, or that the Indians and Chinese adopt the social ideals, religion and attitudes of the Western democracies, every plan for a rational settlement of the present world crisis must fail.

Such an enterprise is based on estimates which are not borne out historically.

The progress of government by its nature is one of territorial integration, and springs from economic, military, social and trade necessities. The political union merely expresses an antecedent condition of already existing interests between the peoples concerned.

The whole of history can be summed up in the progressive integration of human families, tribes, feudal provinces, nations, and finally, federations of nations.

In the structural form of the United States, the precinct, ward, county, city, state and national systems are an expression of the same progressive integration of human values, proceeding in ordered sequences from one civic level to another.

In the past there have been great empires which violated this principle of healthy organic growth. One recalls the vast realms of Genghis Khan, Alexander, and Cyrus; but all of these were wrought by the sword and died with the eminence of the men who created them.

The single noteworthy exception is Rome. Though the Roman dominions consisted of a melange of states, kingdoms and republics knit together through a common acknowledgement of Roman authority, both the Republic and Empire extended the privilege of Roman citizenship to individuals among the conquered peoples. The latter also were dominated by the superior quality of Roman law and the civilization it expressed. This they made their own, creating the only extended period of political tranquility the Western world has seen.

The processes and meaning of federal growth may be gleaned from a study of such states as Switzerland, or Great Britain itself.

In the case of the Swiss, the Federation originally was based on common religion, language, and economic interests. At its inception in the thirteenth century it consisted of the cantons of Uri, Schwyz and Unterwalden. Then industrial cities such as Zurich and Lucerne were taken in. Military, trade and social necessities forced an expansion to absorb an assortment of others, whether by their voluntary request or the bald use of force. Sometimes both mutual interests and deadly conflicts existed side by side contending with each other for priority. This is expressed in the vicious wars which were fought between the Protestant and Catholic cantons, as well as in other rivalries.

The beginnings of modern England are seen in the rise of West Saxon supremacy under King Egbert in the ninth century. He reduced to his sway the kingdoms of East Anglia, Mercia, Kent and Northumbria, together with the people of Wales.

Under Egbert's grandson, Alfred the Great, the kingdoms of Sussex, Essex and Surrey were added. Later Scotland, Ireland and parts of French Europe were joined under the British Crown; and still later the colonies and great Dominions.

In those parts of the Empire such as the domains of the Crown in France, where no real community of interests existed, there was a continuous effort to break away from a rule which assumed the appearance of an intolerable alien overlordship. The present Dominions as they begin to attain maturity have shown the same tendency to drift off, and to consider their connection with the Crown as purely nominal.

Germany, Italy, France and Spain, as well as the newer countries, Brazil, Canada, Australia and the United States, are the product of just such a community growth. They represent the spirit of regional development of that intermediate type suitable to the age which bore them.

In each case the federal evolution followed a set of principles exactly opposed to those set forth in the late League of Nations and the new United Nations Organization.

Whether in the case of republican France with its combination of Burgundians, Bretons, Basques, Gascons and

others, or monarchist Spain with its Catalonia, Aragon, An-
dalucia, Castile, Navarre, Galicia and Asturias, the conditions
governing the federated process were always the same. They
are:

1. A similar geographic location and synchronized set of
    material interests.
2. The extension of the federal authority directly to the
    persons of the individual citizens inhabiting each of the
    previously independent states.

In that great compilation, *The Federalist*, which should be
compulsory reading for every American statesman and legis-
lator, Alexander Hamilton laid down the eternal principles
by which orderly government can be effected. It is to the
sagacity and penetration of this American genius, together
with his associates, Jay, Madison, Jefferson, and Washington,
that we must turn for much of the political wisdom which
will enable us to cope with the conditions of our day.

If America was to have law and order, asserted Hamilton,
and was not to consist of a set of independent states "in simple
alliance with each other, alternately friends and enemies as
mutual jealousies and rivalries decreed, *we must resolve to
incorporate into our plan those ingredients which may be
considered as forming the characteristic difference between a
league and a government; we must extend the authority of the
Union to the persons of the citizens—the only proper objects
of government.*"

"A sovereignty over sovereigns, a government over governments, a legislation for communities, as contradistinguished
from individuals," Hamilton continued, "is subversive of the
law and end of civil polity, by substituting violence in place
of law, or the destructive coercion of the sword in place of
the mild and salutary coercion of the magistrate."

Only by these means could there be insured a transference

of authority from the provincial state to the common union, and the rule of actual organic law brought into existence.

Something of the same wisdom was perceived by the great English Queen Anne. In her inspired letter to the Scottish Parliament on July 1, 1706, she observed of the union then in process between England and Scotland that "an entire and perfect Union will be the solid foundation of lasting peace: it will secure your religion, liberty and property; remove the animosities amongst ourselves, and the jealousies and differences betwixt our two kingdoms . . . and by this Union the whole Island, being joined in affection and freed from all apprehensions of different interests, will be enabled to resist all its enemies."

The second principle on which orderly government must rest is based on the inter-relation of interests existing between various members of the same natural community.

As civilization has advanced under the magic touch of scientific knowledge, the regional interrelationship of agriculture and industry, production and markets, has been increasingly manifest. It is a factor which touches upon the actual lives of the peoples inhabiting the region irrespective of the political jurisdictions into which it happens to be carved.

The assumption that political and economic geography is wrong, simply because it was grasped by the Germans and bent to their own ambitions, is as foolish as would be the belief that the airplane is necessarily evil because the Germans first subdued it to the purpose of aggressive war.

No matter how the subject is argued, it is impossible to circumvent the fact that a modern industrial economy requires a production and marketing base far larger than that which can be provided by the parochial state.

A large number of political corporations with their competitive tariffs, currencies, and military establishments cutting across a single self-contained regional unit, runs counter to every principle of modern production, distribution, transportation and trade.

The frantic efforts of such a nation as Portugal or Hungary to be self-sufficient and to compete with Russia, China and the United States as small but complete editions of the latter, is not only silly but anachronistic and dangerous. Suppose, for example, that the agricultural state of Iowa insisted on the creation of balanced industries and demanded plant facilities rendering it at least to a degree independent of Pittsburgh, Gary, Detroit and the great airplane plants of southern California. Suppose it wished not only to regulate these activities, but to protect them, so that they would not be strangled in their infancy; and suppose it objected to the migration of the poverty-stricken Okies or to movements of money and industry operated from the eastern seaboard.

The result would be political as well as economic demoralization, and is obviously unthinkable.

The picture may be seen in clear perspective by noting that the American state of New York does not need or possess armies, navies, currency systems or batteries of diplomats. Its relationship with its neighbors is not determined by treaty or by some consultative device but is fixed in place by federal law, which is the supreme authority of the Union.

Whatever differences may exist between the various members of a given region in the way of race, language, religion, wealth, opportunity or condition, a normal concern for their own well-being makes necessary a common plan of defense, a common policy and a common acceptance of the forms and practices by which the good of the whole is governed. This presupposes a common political order which does not attempt to eliminate the factors of power and competition between the states, but to regulate them.

The process of organic evolution cannot be dispensed with by the introduction of some short-cut scheme of world order which presumes that the relationship of Bulgaria to San Salvador is the same as its relationship to Germany or the Soviet Union. This is a patent absurdity which assumes that no interests based on a common geographic location exist, intervening between the nation-states and the proposed world super-state.

An effort to bring a totally unrelated group of states under the roof of a single government is illogical. It skips one necessary step in the sequence.

The interdependence of the Russias geographically, economically, and socially, makes them not merely a collection of sixteen republics allied with various lesser regions, but an organic and identifiable unit on the earth's surface. The same is the case with the Orient, and with the countries of the Western Hemisphere, where a no less true community of natural interests exists.

To disregard this sectional construction of the world's economy is politically unsound and economically nonsensical. In the case of, let us say, Italy, such a conclusion ignores the real problems and material interests which link that country first to Europe, and only secondarily to the greater world economy. It makes a fetish of the atomic bomb and the destructive power it is acknowledged to represent. It tends to negate the natural structural relationship of productive interests which differentiate the problems of the great geographic regions from each other.

V

Even the United States, which to a degree seems independent of these circumstances, must find its policies directly accountable to them.

The American community of interests no longer is isolated to the forty-eight states of the Union, as it was in the year 1856 when it took almost a full month to cross the United States by rail and stage. It now is far wider than the acknowledged political community, and takes in the entire Western Hemisphere, from its most eastern extension at Great Britain to its southwest periphery in Australia.

From the military view alone, we cannot successfully defend the Americas from Europe without possession of Greenland and Iceland, and the co-operation of Brazil and the British Isles. If Asia were to come to industrial maturity, our Continent could not be shielded from assault from this quarter unless it held and developed the islands of Australasia, Indonesia and the South Seas.

In the fall of 1944, when my earlier book, *The Gentlemen Talk of Peace*, was issued, I pointed out that the then existing world fell naturally into five great interlocking communities, each of which was a universe in miniature, possessing all of the necessary resources for a balanced, autarchus and secure existence. These were:

1. The Union of Soviet Socialist Republics, which though already existing, required some rectification of its frontiers, principally in the way of securing free outlets to warm water.

2. A European union, gathered around the Mediterranean as its dead center, and extending into Africa so as to give it access to tropical materials.

3. A union of the West, consisting of the entire Western Hemisphere.

4. A union of the Orient, including India, China, Korea, Japan and southeast Asia.

5. The mandated territory of Africa, by which the more than two hundred millions of the black race would be enabled to possess a geographic center in which to fulfill their destiny.

The virtual disappearance of an integral Europe and the loss of the initiative provided by wartime conditions makes an orderly regrouping of the world along these lines impossible of achievement. The logic of the situation, however, remains, though it now must be restated in other terms. It suggests that once the political world were reshaped so as to conform to the existing outlines of military and economic condition, the resulting handful of political corporations would have little difficulty in associating themselves together to create a body of world law applicable to their needs, where they could not possibly do so in the present power-driven universe of inequalities, chronic imbalances and temptations to raw opportunism.

Sitting in common council together, as would be inevitable, such a limited group of federations could find an answer to problems which otherwise are so tortuous and complex as to be ungovernable altogether. Commanding questions which now agitate the policies of the nations and give them the urgency of life and death itself, would shrivel up and disappear; questions of markets, of food and raw materials, of areas for human settlement, of access to the seas, of river and air routes, of defense, and of competitive advantage in all of the various spheres in which it shows itself.

The present reliance on pure force and its background use of power politics then would be inapplicable, not only for moral reasons but because of a change in the nature of the problem.

It appeared unsound to assume that the existence of five great householders in the world was incompatible with the existence of the bomb, and that someone would be sure to go berserk if no total police authority existed capable of exercising global supremacy. It was this central repression, which to be effective must be the final word in tyranny, which seemed to represent the very principle against which men have fought since the dawn of history.

A world containing a limited number of balanced regions

could come to an arrangement involving total disarmament, and the outlawing not only of the atomic bomb, which is impractical, but of all war machinery. It appeared unlikely in the extreme that large, well-situated, autarchus powers would deliberately risk suicide by challenging well-armed opponents for no reason. In each of them, the constrictions and imbalances which formerly existed to impoverish their citizens or render their security doubtful, would have been swept away. The temptations to attack minor neighbors would have disappeared with the exit from history of the conventional nation-state itself.

While it was true that the will of wicked men to power and aggression would always continue, it was also true that in a world without economic distortions and without the abnormalities resulting from continued political disorganization, both the temptations and opportunities to war would be much reduced. It would have to be assumed also that a normal relationship based on the physical well being of all the peoples, would breed a normal psychological outlook, which in the present situation cannot exist.

Such a political development would not constitute a panacea capable of doing away with all wars. The assumption that the natural dynamisms which characterize life can be brought into regulation by some static device is the most grave error of politics. There is always a point in society where wars theoretically are possible no matter what the organizational plan is. To presume that an absolute end can be put to wars for any cause would require the abolition of human nature itself and the introduction of a millennium of disembodied purity.

The nature of armed struggle would be the same whether it passed under the name of rebellion or of war. Where a cause is sufficiently great, a war will result. The American Constitution did not prevent a civil war in the United States.

Generations of English experience with liberty did not avert a civil war in England.

The best that can be achieved by political organization is the elimination of self-evident frictions which are certain in themselves to generate conflict, and to remove causes which manifestly are breeders of war.

It is useless to strain after hopeless Utopias by which the interests of diverse groups of men can be so merged as to eliminate all possible clashes of interest.

In any political body consisting of diverse peoples, it is conceivable that a conflict between them could reach the point of military struggle. All that we can assure ourselves is that the likelihood is reduced to the utmost minimum.

The Swiss, as well as the Russians, have showed us that deep social divisions based on race, religion or language are not a fatal obstacle to federal union. The Swiss cantons are divided into religious, racial, and language groups which speak French, Italian, German, and a Latin dialect, the Rhaeto-Romansh.

In present-day Switzerland, generally held up as a model of democratic rule, the harmony which prevails is by no means perfect. "Not only outsiders," comments a Swiss writer, "but even thinking men in Switzerland are often startled by the rivalry, the mutual indifference to one another's welfare, even verging on hostility and obstructionism, which prevails internally among the members of the Confederation."[2] What redeems the situation is the capacity of the Swiss at critical moments to rally in defense of those integrities to which they are devoted.

A similar picture is seen in the administration of our neighbor, Canada. French Canada possesses in its language, culture and institutions little in common with those of its Anglo-Saxon neighbor. For these reasons, and perhaps others, serious tensions often arise between the two peoples; but they never

[2] Hans Rudolf Schmidt, *Switzerland*.

give way to unbridgeable violence. They do not involve issues which it is necessary to settle in blood, or which must be circumvented by some dangerous treaty or the circuitous wiles of the diplomats. There are no armies resting on the borders of Quebec or Ontario, no tariff walls, no currency difficulties, no arrangements which might be to the disadvantage of one people as against the other. Each maintains its own schools and its own culture and has access to the common benefits of the united Dominion.

Even extreme differences in living standards are not necessarily fatal to union. In different parts of the United States itself, wages vary greatly. The median wage in Michigan in 1939 was $1,128, or three times that of Mississippi's $386. "The income of the typical white family in the larger cities of the North Central States averaged $1,720 in 1935-36. This compared with $480 for the typical Negro family in Southern rural communities."[3]

The creation of regional spheres of influence dominated by one powerful party or another cannot possibly answer as an adequate substitute for actual organic merger.

The difference is simple. Federation implies equality. The over-all federal system reaches to each of the citizens or organized groups without reservation or favoritism. Power, theoretically at least, is equally distributed as it is in the United States, and is not the property of a single ruling national group, whose own special interests must take precedence.

A sphere of influence implies a strong central control wielded by some imperial ruler. There is no true merging of interests, or equal development of powers. At the best it is the patronage doled out by the *padrone*; and, more often, the repression exercised by the military state gratifying its appetites by whatever means it considers legitimate.

The sphere of influence is not democratic, nor is it per-

[3] Maxwell S. Stewart, "Public Affairs Pamphlet No. 99" (1945), p .14 .

manent. It is contrary to human progress, and is not a fair expression of the needs of the peoples concerned. Above all, such a system has no social goal except the material interests of the big and powerful. It assumes the world to be a jungle in which the large predatory animals sate their hunger and maneuver against each other for possession.

By subject nations retaining some of the elements of sovereignty, spheres of interest invite a clash wherever the privileges of the overlord state meet those of some other strong competitor. One witnesses this feature in Iran and in Greece. It will prove a fertile source of conflict wherever the sphere of influence exists.

VI

Far from being ready for world government, men continue to hug closely all of the pitiful mechanics of the old dispensation. They will not voluntarily yield their privileges even in the interests of that regional order which is the first and primary prerequisite to any rational world decision.

When confronted with the actual task of placing such a plan in effect the worst possible obstacles and drawbacks are seen. It is resisted because of racial and religious repugnancies; because of immediate economic interests, differing living standards, or because of long-continued habit. Or moral flaws are found in the proposal, relating to the right of the individual states to remain as they are, isolated and independent of the general regional community.

The big sweep and somewhat esoteric quality of the blueprint for world government tends to rescue it from these disqualifications. No one yet considers such measures in terms of hard reality, but rather as an adventure into the pleasantly abstruse.

The gigantic changes which are implied in these proposals cannot be brought about by spontaneous and voluntary means.

They require a revolutionary disregard for the existing legitimacies, or the active aid of some powerful and interested party. We have seen this to be true in regard to Russian activities in Asia and eastern Europe. It was in part true of the very acts which brought into existence the American Constitution.

John Quincy Adams perhaps best described the situation which had given rise to this document when he said that it "had been extorted from the grinding necessity of a reluctant nation." When on September 17 the Constitution at last was approved, only thirty-nine delegates signed. Rhode Island had not sent any; and ten of the sixty-five who finally were appointed did not bother to come. Thirteen of those who had attended had gone home; three, Randolph, Mason and Gerry, refused to sign.

As it was, the Constitution was agreed to with little enthusiasm. Few of the delegates had any real hope for its success. They approved it because they were convinced that there was no alternative but anarchy. "What they [the Convention] actually did, stripped of all fiction and verbiage," says Professor Burgess, "was to assume constituent powers, ordain a constitution of government and of liberty, and demand the plebiscite thereon, over the heads of all existing legally organized powers. *Had Julius Caesar or Napoleon committed these acts, they would have been pronounced 'coups d'état'. ... It is probable that many of the members of the Convention itself did not fully comprehend just what they were doing.*"[4]

It is likely that all plans of whatever nature for world organization will stagnate. The nations will follow a do-nothing policy, responsive only to the aggressive actions of some of their members. While obeisance will continue to be made to democratic and universalist ideals, the power policies of the big states will develop along the most brutal and realistic lines.

The United States is compelled to weigh the fact that a

[4] Burgess, *Political Science and Constitutional Law*, Vol. I, p. 105.

perfect solution to the world's problems cannot be brought about at this time. It is impossible to visualize a total settlement of world issues in time to meet the emergency which demands it.

In addition to these utopian conceptions, we must be concerned with our capacity to survive the immediate crisis toward which all the world is moving. It suggests that the current problem is not only a universal question, but, on the score that charity begins at home, a specifically American one; and that the choice is not one of pure altruism against self-centered isolation, but a working compromise between the two.

For the United States, the situation is intimately concerned with the preservation of our power, and what is equally as important, our way of life.

Our policy must be contingent on these circumstances. It must involve a long-range, intermediate, and a short-range program, all of which must be operated at the same time. These contemplations must be mutually consistent both in logic and strategy; and must be concerned first of all with a realistic outlook on the problem of American security.

In reaching toward the eventual goal of a world community, American policy cannot fail to be affected by the fact that the growth of Russia is not a theory but a fact, and requires a reasoned offset to it in the shape of a comparable power gain by the United States.

The axiom to which we are driven is this: *the United States must renounce the antiquated principle of equality of all nations, great or small, since as a principle, it is both false and hypocritical.* The opposite principle of federated union is the only one which can possibly apply to the problems of this era.

In the principle of federation is embodied both a higher moral ethos and an abolition of the lawlessness which plagues states inhabiting the same region. The present sovereign isolation of the national states must be considered not as a right to be protected, but as a backward, anarchial, anachronistic and provincial stage of human development, which is to be condemned and if necessary, liquidated.

It is neither historically nor morally true that sovereign states are equal. They are equal only between themselves, under the higher sovereignty of the federation. While in this sense Rhode Island may be equal to New York, California or Texas, in no sense is Bulgaria equal to Russia, or Nicaragua to the United States.

Our view must be that republics and nation-states are quite different from federations, such as are represented by the Soviet Union and the United States, and that only such great federations can be legally or materially equal to each other in the world.

In the face of this perfectly realistic condition, the so-called abstract right of nations to independence and self-determination assumes fantastic dimensions. By definition, it poses the right to contribute to intrahemispheric anarchy, or to play dog in the manger and to sabotage the workings of whole continental areas. It suggests the right of the five hundred Danes and eighteen thousand Eskimos of Greenland, strategic key to the defense of the Americas, to render that defense impotent.

It implies the right of even the smallest areas, such as Brittany, Catalonia, or the Ruhr, to wreck the natural economies of which they are a part and to precipitate chaos wherever they choose to take a stubborn and intransigent position on any question. It indicates that the North was wrong in its attitude toward the Confederacy during the American Civil War, and that by compelling the South to remain within the Union, a grave injustice was perpetrated.

It suggests that a premium must be placed on non-co-operation and unsocial conduct, and that national chauvinisms possess a high degree of bargaining power.

Under federation, the loss of the much-hoarded rights of sovereignty is not fatal to the welfare of the small state or its citizens, but merely to the privileges and national conceits of certain groups such as the Prussian Junkers, who see their differences with their neighbors in terms of their own particular group prejudices and welfare.

This is not only impractical as a working arrangement, but is a dangerous psychological hangover from what is rapidly becoming an antique period.

The rights of sovereignty as they apply to individual states today are largely chimerical. Nations no longer are self-determining or retain exclusive jurisdiction over the welfare of their subjects, since this depends now on the actions of still other states.

From every point of view, it is far preferable that the words "independence" and "self-determination" refer not to the sovereign right of each national fragment to act as it pleases without reference to the welfare of others, but to control only its cultural and natural economy within the larger social order imposed by the federal union of which it is a part.

As far as the United States is concerned, the proposition reduced to its simplest terms is not whether the existence of independent national sovereignties is to be considered moral or immoral. It is rather this: either we can get along within the scope of our present frontiers and within the limitations of our existing military situation as an isolated body in a rapidly consolidating world, or we cannot.

Either we are totally self-sufficient and will remain so irrespective of the vast changes now taking place in the world, or we must re-examine our situation in relation to these things.

In short, the question must be related as much to our own survival as to any other set of considerations, and must be frankly faced in this light.

This takes the view that governments are not sacrosanct

and forever vested in their independent authority; and that the creation of new social conditions may render the old legitimacies worthless and morally indefensible.

Those who see the future in terms of the past merely because the past has always existed, are preparing the best possible way for World War III. They possess a total misunderstanding of the dynamic processes by which organized existence expresses itself. In large measure, they suffer the curious fate of the aged, the comfortable and the secure, in that they view the future with upside-down minds, tending to derogate the things which are possible as fantastic, and to view with confident optimism those procedures which already are stale and valueless under the new logic.

Chapter Ten

AMERICA'S DESTINY

IF WE wish to avert eventual defeat for this country, we must recognize that the U.S.S.R. and the United States must reorganize the world along federal principles. This is a responsibility we must share with the Soviet Union if the world is not to experience the most ruinous conflict it yet has seen.

The safeguards against this terrifying eventuality will not be created by high-sounding phrases, but by a practical understanding between the two major states which now dominate the world.

The fear of Russian hegemony should not cause the West to concentrate its energies in a negative attempt to prevent the Eurasian aggregate from spreading toward its natural limitations. This is an impossible task. The effort to stop the growth of Russia through such futile designs as alliances, leagues and synthetic world organizations, can result only in one possible outcome, war, and perhaps a final and terrible defeat.

Only an acceptance of the new historical development as representing a rational step toward the goal of human unity, can counter-balance the dreadful fear of these effects for the Western world.

This comprehension must cause the West to accept the lesson of the times, and to undertake a parallel integration of its own territories as indispensable to its future security, progress and well-being.

If America is to have any policy at all short of that projected by the war party, the expansion of the Russias must be regarded not as a menace to be counteracted, but as an example to be followed; and the isolation of America and other states must be considered not as a right to be protected but as a backward, provincial stage of civilization involving a selfish, anarchical and anachronistic social view which is to be condemned, and which by all right must be liquidated.

We have yet to make a proposition to the Russians based on a bold global-sized plan of settlement, which would embrace an acceptable conclusion as to the future of the Orient, as well as what remains of Europe. No one yet has proposed to them that the next steps to human unity be that of consolidating the world into its natural regional universes, thus reducing the present chaos into some semblance of order.

Russian ambitions may cause such a plan to fail. The Kremlin may see itself cast in the role of master of the world, and be reluctant to yield its opportunities. Nevertheless such speculations are altogether conjectural, for the effort has not been made. Were the Russians aware of our determination to bring the matter to an issue at the present peak moment of our strength, it is entirely possible that some basic conclusion could be arrived at.

If this approach proves unpromising, it will be necesary for us to move rapidly toward the creation of a three-power world, to forestall the inevitable emergence of a two-power global balance in which the United States will find itself by far the weaker party.

This involves one single important step toward which the entire history of this hemisphere has pointed from the beginning—the federation of the states of the West into a common union. Such an amalgamation of the West, as far as we are concerned, is the terminal conclusion of all plans for tomorrow's prosperity and peace, and is a necessary blueprint for any machinery which would weld this hemisphere into a common instrument of co-operative action.

If our hemisphere is to become strong, there must be no misunderstandings and no fundamental conflicts of interest between its parts. What we require is not the verbal expression of hemispheric solidarity, which depends upon conditions which could change tomorrow morning, but the actual solidarity itself. This can be effected only by union.

If it is too late to consolidate Europe into a single political unit, that continent must become either a field for the gradual extension of the Russias, or a sort of no man's land functioning painfully in a political and economic void. The keystone to the arch of western Europe is France. If conventional France were to disappear and a Communist society take its place, we should immediately have to establish a firm line in Asia, lend-leasing our men and machinery to the Orient in an effort to build it rapidly to a position of independent power.

Were Asia, on the other hand, to crumble and follow eastern Europe into the orbit of the U.S.S.R., America would have to establish itself in western Europe by force, also seizing hold of Africa and, if possible, Turkey and Arabia. Thus the two giants would face each other more or less evenly matched in a program which hardly could be designated as an attractive one.

It should be the heart of our policy never to allow China and India to fall under the control of a single Eurasian power. The only way to insure this is to set them up as strong industrial republics. From any view, it is of first importance to any policy open to us to encourage the rapid industrialization of the Orient and to assist the Asiatics in their enterprises with a view to creating an enduring body of interests between them and the West.

We can have no legitimate quarrel with these peoples unless we are entangled in the maneuvers of European imperial diplomacy. If we assist them, these turbulent millions would become a stable part of world society. They would have a stake in the common order which would give them an enduring interest in its preservation, a situation which hardly can be said to be true at present.

This policy, it must be conceded, would involve in addition to its obvious advantages, a most frightening set of dangers. It could bring into a larger arena of action the racial resentments, ambitions, hopes and dilemmas which activated imperial Japan. Only if the Western world were safely federalized would such a program be possible without bringing into existence new perils.

To a West broken up into thirty or more fragments, it is unthinkable.

II

The American federal system, like the Russian, is theoretically capable of embracing the entire globe. There is no legal or moral qualification which would bar this, though it is particularly in reference to the states of this hemisphere that our attention must be turned.

The historic course followed by the United States has been one of unqualified expansionism, differing from the classic imperialisms only in the fact that its end purpose was federal amalgamation and not the exploitation for profit of other humans.

We bought Louisiana, Alaska and Florida without bothering about consulting the wishes of the inhabitants of those territories. When Colombia refused to grant us permission to build a canal across her province of Panama, we stimulated a revolution in the Isthmus, and like the Russians in Azerbaijan, prevented the legal authorities from landing to put the revolters down. We took away Mexico's northern territories by force, and were turned back from a similar seizure of Canada by a military defeat. Even then the thirteen states continued to look nostalgically toward Canada as an unredeemed portion of their estate. In the original American Articles of Confederation it was stipulated that "Canada acceding to this Confederation, and joining in the measures of the United States, shall be admitted into and entitled to all the advantages of this union."

In the course of the long national policy of benevolent imperialism we acquired the then largely Latin Texas and California as free states, and similarly accepted Hawaii as a territory on the petition of her citizens.

In each case the revolt against the previously constituted authorities, and the subsequent request for admittance into the American Union, was led or stimulated by Americans.

As in all expansionism the methods employed were sometimes more zealous than nice; but the historic result was the achievement of new thresholds of prosperity, security and freedom, perhaps unequaled before in human experience.

All of this was a sign of the irrepressible energies which boiled in the veins of the young Republic. If today we have lost our capacity to grow, and to adjust ourselves to the new conditions of existence, then our civilization has become old and brittle. In the physical competitions of life it will prove itself inferior to the expanding dynamisms of the Soviets, who will offer the unnerved masses of mankind, caught in the vice of the nation-state, the Kremlin's own particular brand of union and equality.

Manipulation on the higher levels, and the handing out of baksheesh on the familiar W.P.B. basis, will not solve this problem. It cannot be answered by the usual hand-rubbing rectitude, but only if we utilize our massive material power as well as our moral strength on its behalf; and if an alignment with us poses to all of the peoples concerned, the inescapable tide of destiny.

Neither the people of our hemisphere, nor any others, will attempt to flow against the current of history, a fact which the British in their relationship with the nations of Europe and Asia are discovering.

It is futile to list the obstacles which undoubtedly exist to bringing the greater union about. We have only to realize that unless a co-operative Western Hemisphere is possible, a co-operative world is entirely out of the question.

These difficulties exist but are by no means insuperable. They are impediments similar to those which have attended all great historic processes.

None of the arguments offered against this solution are more meaningful than those proclaimed by the opponents of the American Constitution in 1789. If at the very meridian of our power our spiritual courage has so declined that these barriers seem immovable, then we of the Americas no longer can see our way to greatness. The future then is lost to us.

If it is true that the prevailing national and cultural differences automatically breed such antagonisms as to make the physical unity of the West a phantasm, then the Americas face a tragic future. If these differences are insurmountable, political division will not tend to decrease but to increase them. If by their nature they enjoin the absolute need for separation—if this is to be the measuring stick—then there can exist no inter-American fraternity except in the rhetoric of its statesmen.

If we cannot find the way, the words "good neighbor policy" will prove to be a glittering and useless phrase. We will find our true policies actually destroying the major friend-ships we require from our neighbors by making them the victim of both our handouts and our rivalry, rather than our comrade in the mutual affairs which concern us. In the end, we will discover ourselves quarreling with all of them over many questions, ranging from jealously guarded sovereignty rights to details of commercial advantage, and forced to compete with the Russians for their favor.

III

Under dispassionate analysis the differences between the peoples of this hemisphere* are not as extreme as might at first appear. The British, Canadians, Australians and New Zealanders possess a cultural outlook much like our own. Many of the Latin countries are melting pots like the United States. Costa Rica, Uruguay and the Argentine are almost purely European. Brazil and Chile are European for the most part.

In the Argentine, English names may be found among the leading families. Even in the present dictatorship are such typical Anglo-Saxon names as Rawson and Farrell. Perón had an English grandfather.

No matter to what degree racial acceptances may be a factor, however, we cannot allow them to be the major determinants in formulating our course. There is a special kind of madness connected with this so-called race question, which is the most dangerous of all possible issues in the world today. For the Caucasian especially, in a creation where he is overwhelmingly outnumbered, it is extremely hazardous to poison the well of civilization with the Nazi view on race.

The United States itself is now far from being an Anglo-Saxon community. The Pennsylvania Dutch have retained their own customs and language for generations without any untoward troubles ensuing. New Mexico is almost 45% Spanish-speaking. French Canada has spilled over into New England, creating strongly organized French-speaking sectors. In such cities as Woonsocket, Rhode Island, and Biddeford, Maine, the number of French-speaking folk is around 60%.

The United States contains fifteen or sixteen million people of Colored race. The German, Irish and Scandinavian contingent collectively is almost as numerous as the Anglo-Saxon.

* The Western Hemisphere is here considered to be that half of the planet of which the Americas constitute the dead center.

There are six million Italians, five million Poles, four and one-half million Jews, and still other millions from Hungary, Czechoslovakia, the Balkans and elsewhere. There are about 3,500,000 Spanish-speaking people who are for the most part Indians. Among the most vociferous of the American racial purists, ironically enough, is the descendant of a Spanish Basque immigrant, the present Senator from Mississippi, Theodore G. Bilbo.[1]

The inclusion of the Pacific islands or the Latin South need not fill us with apprehension lest there be a general exodus from these countries into our own. At present there is no quota system or restriction on immigrants from the free states of Latin America. People wishing to live in the United States may get their visas through the American consul without trouble, if they are normal, healthy, and without a criminal past.

The situation more likely would prove the reverse one. The territories of the Pacific and of Latin America are largely unpeopled, as well as rich in resources. These areas await only new manpower, energy and capital to come into an era of dazzling growth, much as did the United States when the West was opened.

Drawn by the magnetic attraction of opportunity the trend of immigration would be from the industrial to the pioneer countries. The millions of our boys returning from war, trained in new skills and techniques, would find new scope for their talents and know-how. They would not be catapulted back into clerking or ordinary labor, to become in their resentment the prey of Fascist or Communist agitators. The Latin and Pacific territories in turn would benefit from badly needed enterprise, know-how, character and wealth. These areas possess a deep hunger for new and capable immigrants.

The assumption that the different nationalisms which inhabit this hemisphere are incurably self-centered and cannot be

[1] Originally Bilbao.

moved from their attachment to old political habits and ideas, will not prove accurate where strong welfare considerations are concerned. If one may judge from the public announcements of their statesmen, both Australia and New Zealand realize that their economic and military security are now linked directly with the American mainland, with whom closer political bonds must be inevitable.

A Gallup poll in the spring of 1943 showed a considerable sentiment in Canada for a full political merger with the United States. On June 13, 1945, Major James H. Clark, Speaker of the Ontario Legislature, declared that if given opportunity, "forty to forty-five per cent of Canadians would vote for union with the United States."

Britain itself has given us the precedent of Mr. Churchill's offer to combine with France in one empire under a single parliament. The Draft Declaration of Union as communicated to the French government by His Majesty's Ambassador on June 16, 1940, proposed that "the two Governments declare France and Great Britain shall no longer be two but one Franco-British union," and that "every citizen of France enjoy immediately citizenship of Great Britain, every British subject [to] become a citizen of France."

Though the French Cabinet refused this offer by the narrow margin of one vote, it remains one of the most hopeful signs in what are otherwise sorry times, providing evidence of the willingness of men to settle their affairs by reason, and to attain at least during periods of crisis, a sensible conception of the future.

It is well to remark that Mexico, Brazil, Canada and Australia already are federations and not unitary states. It is hard to see how the existing federal institutions of these countries would be materially changed or weakened by merger into a union of more extensive dimensions. Each of the twenty states of the Brazilian union, for example, would continue to maintain its present autonomy over its local affairs, as well as its institutional forms.

An example which appears to refute the conception of a fanatical Latin American nationalism, exists in the recent move to amalgamate the states of El Salvador and Guatemala into a single republic. On June 16, 1945, the two countries moved to become one, in the express hope that still other Central American nations would join with them. The formal announcement from the Guatemalan government reads: "The Guatemalan-Salvador frontier no longer exists. Troops have been withdrawn and passports are not needed. We have become one people."

In principle, if these states are willing to lose their identity in a small federation, there is little reason why they should be less willing to do so in a larger and more effective one.

That love of country is not destroyed by the federative principle, was proved in the case of the Soviet Union during the invasion of the Ukraine. Even though the Ukraine once had been the seat of the most desperate revolutionary nationalism under the Tsar, its people stoutly resisted all efforts on the part of the Nazis to alienate them from the U.S.S.R. It is thus clear that, by conditioning, patriotism and love of country can be identified with social, moral or cultural objectives, rather than with the present isolationism and chauvinistic goals which guide the nations.

IV

The union we should seek to achieve should reach from Pole to Pole, and from Dover, England, to Perth, Australia. It should embrace all territories on which a human being can subsist in either the Atlantic or Caribbean oceans; and in the Pacific up to the very doors of Japan.

Possession of the far North is an absolute necessity both to our security and prosperity in the air age economy which is coming. Therefore we should act to insure our control of these regions without delay.

We should move similarly to incorporate the islands of the Caribbean as a permanent part of our system.

The independent states of this area, Cuba, Santo Domingo, and Haiti, already are wards of the United States. Their development is stultified by this equivocal status, by which they have become political and economic lackeys hanging on to the fringe of the American system, and not equal participants sharing both its obligations and benefits.

Other territories of vital importance to America, such as Trinidad, Jamaica, the Barbados and the Bahamas, are ruled by a Colonial Secretary in London, who in his own realm is an absolute monarch, capable of negating legislation, imposing censorship, or of any prejudicial action which might suit him. Both colonial policy, and the strictures imposed by the Sterling Bloc, act to exclude American trade. The industrial development of these rich islands is at a standstill.

The Caribbean has been described as the American Mediterranean. Despite its present sleepy unimportance it is the very lock to the front door of the Americas. If these islands are properly organized as an integral part of the American security scheme, their importance to the American economy will become comparable to that of Florida or Hawaii, though on a larger scale.

We should make the Caribbean solidly our own, by purchase, plebiscite, or such other means as are open to us. It could be formed into two great territories, ultimately to be admitted to the Union as free states. One would embrace Cuba and the Spanish-speaking islands; the other would be composed of Haiti, the Barbados and the other Negro communities, who in fairness are entitled to administer their own affairs.

Bermuda and the Bahamas could be subjoined to Florida or one of the other coastal states.

The territories owned by foreign powers in the Caribbean could be bought, as were Alaska, the Louisiana Territory and the Virgin Islands. They might be accepted in exchange for the vast amounts owed us under Lend-Lease; or in consideration of the additional loans these powers now seek to secure from us. In any event these islands may properly be regarded as American irredenta territory. Tomorrow, foreign ownership of the Caribbean will be as unthinkable as would be a renewal of Spanish possession of the Netherlands, or British control of the northern provinces of France.

If instead of adding these domains permanently to our estate as equal members of the American community we now withdraw from our posts in the Caribbean and the northern way stations of Iceland and Greenland, we shall be guilty of an act of injury against our own future.

If we return the islands of Indonesia and the South Pacific to the exploitation of European imperial states, who themselves are in danger of being gobbled up, we commit ourselves to equal folly, and to the certainty of another war in defense of these territories. They cannot be held by their present possessors who will only attempt to suppress their development along time-worn imperial lines. The best interests of the natives themselves will demand the incorporation of the islands in the great trading empire of the continental Americas, where their productive resources will be strengthened, their prosperity enhanced, and their rights as individuals respected.

In any settlement of world affairs, our ultimate design should be to assume full responsibility for these domains, merging them *in toto* with the Western Hemisphere, settling them with our people and developing them into a strong industrial base capable of being woven into a tight barricade of outposts covering all the approaches to the Americas. Only in this wise can America protect itself and strike a balance to compensate for the overwhelming population advantages of the Orient in future international competition.

A word of sympathy from us to the embattled Indonesians, which suggested a willingness on our part to embrace them in our union as equals and not as subject peoples, would bring an enthusiastic response. Indonesian independence has been quietly agitated by impassioned patriots from the Philippine Islands who regard themselves as one people with the Indonesians. A great Filipino-Indonesian empire under the political leadership of the emancipated Philippine Islands would lean toward America as its mentor and friend. Federated with the West, it would administer its own domestic affairs, and look forward to an era of true independence and prosperity.

Some token of these possibilities is shown in the formal petition sent President Truman by King John Sigrah, ruler of the strategic Caroline Islands, on February 7, 1946, seeking annexation of his territories by the United States. Similar requests, which have their historic precedent in the action by Hawaii, have come from the natives of the Marshall Islands and others.

Were the United States to admit Hawaii into the American Union as the forty-ninth state as has been proposed, or grant statehood to Puerto Rico, the Western rather than the local and racial character of our civilization would be demonstrated. A great fillip would be given American influence in the Pacific, and perhaps in Latin America, where Puerto Rico's admission would be regarded as a very real step in the direction of a bilingual civilization. It would condition both the Latins and the Americans of the English-speaking North to the idea of the admission of such states as Nicaragua and Panama, whose merger with the United States would depend largely on the amount of moral and economic pressure we were willing to exert.

If our purposes are to be confined to correcting the immediate deficiencies of our military and economic position, the expansion of our power need involve no more than an extension of the American Bill of Rights to other peoples. If on the other hand we are to attempt a comprehensive merger of the Western Hemisphere into a solidly organized fortress of prosperity, it may be desirable to encourage the formation of three federal structures, composed of (1) English-speaking North America, the British Isles, Australia and New Zealand; (2) Spanish- and Portuguese-speaking America; and (3) the Philippines and the Indonesian Archipelago. These would be united under a common constitution which defined the authority of the central government, presumably limiting it to such matters as defense, currency regulation, postal operations and interstate traffic.

Under this arrangement there would exist a dual citizenship within each of the great regions composing the total union. A precedent of course exists in the offer made by Mr. Churchill to France. The same conception is implicit in the triple citizenship now enjoyed by the citizen of Quebec. The Quebeçois is a citizen of his own autonomous Quebec, a citizen of Canada, and also a citizen of the British Empire.

V

In the first order of importance to the United States is the reordering of the British economy so that it assumes some rational relationship to the world around it. Until that time Britain's struggles to escape the power failure which threatens to swamp it on all sides, will be a standing menace to the United States. If Britain retains her Empire it will be at the expense of the United States which will find itself tangled in a world-wide maze of quarrels from which there is no retreat. If on the other hand the Empire collapses, Britain fails with it, immediately challenging America's position in the North Atlantic and perhaps elsewhere on the globe.

From this predicament it is apparent that Britain only can be rescued by an act of voluntary renunciation which divested her of her Empire and caused her to become a working partner in a federal union of equals.

To the United States the simple facts are these: Britain and her holdings are an integral part of the hemisphere in which we live. Britain herself cannot be defended without our intervention. Not only the mother island but Canada and the other Dominions must look to the United States for protection and for the necessary support for their economic systems, which cannot conceivably stand alone.

The British Isles have become so important to our economy that it no longer is possible for us to consider a divergent policy on their part as being an affair independent of our concern. Britain must be viewed as the most eastern extension of this hemisphere, and in certain respects, the key to its military defense. If she is in trouble, it is to our interest to come to her rescue; nor can she survive a major assault unless we do so.

If we are so to engage ourselves it is not the part of wisdom that we be compelled to rush to her assistance at the very last moment, as has occurred twice in a generation. It is necessary for us to seek a lasting arrangement which will prevent a recurrence of this risk. It must be made clear to Britain that we cannot go to war for her to perpetuate her Empire; and moreover that we cannot allow her to go to war for any cause which would act to place this hemisphere in jeopardy.

That Britain itself does not always see the primal relationship which fits her destinies to this security pattern, may be judged from a statement made by one of her foremost statesmen, Mr. Churchill, in-between her periods of military distress. Fifteen years after the conclusion of World War I, Mr. Churchill informed America that she should "have minded her own business and stayed out of the World War. If you hadn't entered the war," he averred, "the Allies would have made peace with Germany in the Spring of 1917. Had we made peace then, there would have been no collapse in Russia, followed by Communism; no breakdown in Italy, followed by Fascism; and Germany would not have signed the Versailles Treaty which has enthroned Nazism in Germany."

How short is the memory of man, and how poor the reasoning of even the noblest statesmen, when their thoughts are distorted by those phantasms born of political separatism! Can anyone imagine such a view expressed, for example, between the Territory of Hawaii and the balance of the United States after any period following the Japanese downfall; or that Maine thus could rebuke California? The very conception is an impossible one!

Instead of fitting into the Western community as an integral part, Britain's independent status as an isolated universe, and her closed Sterling economy, represent a source of disruption In the Latin South, London is moving heaven and earth to retain its privileged commercial position and to tie these countries to Europe rather than to the Yankee North. The suspicion exists, perhaps unjustified, that much of our present difficulties with South America are British-inspired in order to prevent the loss of badly needed markets.

It is grotesque for us to continue the pretense that Britain is still a great power, and that in our own interests it is necessary for us to tide her over a temporary embarrassment with loans and other favors. The fact is that Britain no longer can be one of the big military powers, and her whole system is on the verge of insolvency.

Today England is living in the past, in a world which does not exist any more. Her admirable tenacity and stamina no longer can prove useful in bridging the present situation, since it is the fundamental British economy which is dissolving.

It is folly to believe that this situation eventually will right itself, and to pretend that it will disappear like a bad dream. It only can grow worse, and involve both Britain and ourselves in a widening eddy of troubles. The effort to cure it by doctrinaire measures is hopeless. Where it would be possible to nationalize a sound and balanced economy like that of the United States without disaster, the attempt in Britain is compelled to heighten the existing dislocations.

What is at stake is not some antique national pageantry, which under examination is seen to amount to little and to be easily replaceable by a like structure under some other name. What is actually involved for the people of both Britain and the United States is something far more real and tangible. It is their security and well-being, as well as the free democratic way of life and the cultural institutions which go with it. What we have to determine is not whether this or that isolationist sovereignty is to apply, but whether the democratic cultural form is capable of survival, and under what conditions it may be most properly enhanced.

Once official Britain were rid of the obstinate Tory conceptions which color the views of even her Labour Ministers, the advantages of a merger with the West would be apparent. Linked to the Americas, England would be the front door to Europe, through which the trade of both continents would pour. The burden she now shoulders in the upkeep of air, naval and military establishments, would be spread over a vast community on whom the per capita drain would not be excessive. The enterprise and genius of her people would find unlimited opportunity for free function. The poverty, insecurity and tormenting apprehensions which threaten to corrupt the entire fabric of British existence would disappear as Britain thus moved out of the great historical trap in which she finds herself.

The severely rationed Britishers, who now must subsist on bare necessities, would find their situation dramatically re-

lieved. There would be no further need for rationing, no currency difficulties, or feverish seeking after disappearing markets. A great consuming hinterland for British products and
enterprise would exist automatically, exactly as it does now
for Pittsburgh and New York City.

The question of whether the Island gained or lost population would not be a matter of any more moment than it
would be to the American state of North Dakota. Britain's
prosperity as an integral part of the great union would depend
entirely on the advantages of her geographic position, the
nature and quality of her people, and the amount of import-
export business it was possible to do with the Continent of
Europe under the new conditions. She might conceivably
find the strength of her position diminishing as did industrial
Massachusetts when that state lost the weaving industry to the
South, or the agrarian dust-bowl areas of the United States
during the recent drought. Nevertheless, the situation of her
individual citizens would not be materially impaired, since
there would be opportunity for their redistribution and re-
absorption in other parts of the union.

Britain of course could turn as an alternative, toward federal union with Europe, which presumably would be a totalitarian unit dominated by the U.S.S.R. The day this occurs,
a Eurasian opponent of overwhelming size will be in prospect
for America, and a *casus belli* will have been issued in which
the question of war and peace will have taken on a critical
definition for our country.

It is only when the network of Empire in which Britain is
tangled, itself disintegrates and disappears, that she can join
her fortunes with ours and become a normal and peace-serv-
ing influence in the world. Until then she will remain a dangerous anachronism, whose desperate struggles to function
and exist will create a continuous menace to American security. This will be the more particularly true as the imperial

edifice falls into increasing bankruptcy, forcing frantic efforts on the part of British power diplomacy to shore it up.

If by determined pressures we can bring this situation to early decision, we will have managed to put an end to one of the most horrid of possible dilemmas and earn the enduring blessings of the British people.

Under union the present character of British institutions need be but little changed. Even the monarchial form of government, though a relic of the feudal period, and, on the whole, inappropriate to modern life, could be retained if Britain wished to do so. In the German federal state which existed under Wilhelm II, were incorporated both kingdoms and republics, which continued to keep their own peculiar characters.

VI

If Europe should come under one totalitarian rule, or Asia industrialize its teeming millions and unite against us, the question of our survival easily could depend on the status and sympathies of the Latin South.

Here we are in a quandary from which apparently we are unable to extricate ourselves. Where once the United States enjoyed unrivaled prestige and authority with the Latin governments, our influence has steadily waned. Politically as well as economically we are in grave danger of the competition of other world powers, who will not fail to offer Latin Americans the utmost in commercial and political inducements to attach our southern neighbors to themselves.

As the richest and most powerful nation in the world, which in crisis could be expected to follow a frank course devoted to the protection of our national interests, our policy toward Latin America has been surprisingly unrealistic, contradictory, and pointless.

It is out of tune with our own needs and even the principles we espouse. We pretend volubly that the smallest and most provincial of these states is our juridical equal; yet we treat with them as if they were political incompetents, and in each case pipe the tune and expect them to do our bidding. We play the part of *le grand seigneur* to people who are at the moment the recipients of our bounty. We tender these countries gifts, subventions and loans which are not repaid, yet these expenditures seemingly have no plan and no goal. We intervene actively in the internal affairs of the republics, though we are expressly forbidden to do so by the inter-American "law" which we ourselves have created. Though in several cases actually occupying some of these countries with our troops, we finally leave, having created nothing but the impression of querulous meddling.

By our loans, recognition, and Lend-Lease support we assist dictator regimes in Venezuela, Paraguay and other states, though we fulminate against the same regimes in the Argentine and Bolivia. "The United States," remarked a prominent Brazilian, "is supposed to be fighting to rid the world of dictators; yet in Brazil it finances one."

We castigate the Argentines for their known pro-Nazi proclivities, yet at the same time sponsor them for membership in the U.N.O. Then we engage ourselves in an undignified quarrel with the Argentine government as between equals, an exchange of accusations in which the Argentine dictator, Colonel Perón, is enabled to inveigh against us for our "insolent intervention" in the affairs of his country. Yet while we are shuttling between these minor crises which are creating a world of future ill will for us, we remain aloof from any help to the democratic underground, even of the Argentine, which itself has become bitterly anti-American.

Under our influence the Spanish democratic government-in-exile is prevented from functioning in Mexico, where we watch the growth of a vigorous anti-American feeling which has contaminated all parties and is sponsored equally by the Fascist Sinquaristas and Toledano's Communists.

Our relations with the Argentine reflect the deep dangers to which we are exposed by this program of equivocation toward fundamental issues.

In a recently issued and diplomatically unprecedented "Blue Book," the Argentine government is accused of "grave complicity" with Nazi Germany. Colonel Perón himself is described as an archconspirator. The German Nazis are declared to possess "today in Argentina the economic organization—industrial, commercial and agricultural—which they need to provide a base for the reconstruction of German aggressive power during the period when the Homeland is still occupied."

Thus the Argentine is described as a vital extension of a still live enemy program, and as such, a serious "danger to the Americas."

Adding further to this weird situation, the political rallies of the Perónist movement are characterized by torchbearing parades, violence, and wild anti-Semitic and anti-American slogans reminiscent of German political meetings during the heyday of the Nazi party. Opposing political organizations have been dissolved, newspapers suspended and civil liberties suppressed. There have been wholesale arrests and the establishment of concentration camps in which individual citizens have been tortured and brutally murdered.

The program of Perón and his colonels' clique looks forward frankly to making the Argentine the master of the Western Hemisphere, and toward the consolidation of Latin America under Argentine leadership.

This scheme is not as farfetched as at first it might appear.

There is to be a huge increase in the Argentine's population through a new flood of European immigrants, undoubtedly from countries already saturated with the Fascist ideal.

Perón now enjoys mass support from the Argentine workers themselves. His administration no longer is a government of clericals, army officers, hacienda owners and great industrialists, but of labor. In order to gain the support of the unions, Perón placed in effect typical totalitarian legislation, curbing the economic power of manufacturers and landowners, and favoring the workers. It was the latter who succeeded in placing him back in power after a nation-wide general strike which brought the economic life of the country to a standstill.

The bold actions of the Perón government, and its capacity to withstand the disapproval of the Northern giant, has attracted much attention among Latin States, where power, and the capacity to use it, are respected.

The Argentine already controls the police of Paraguay, and has moved to intimidate neighboring Uruguay by taking economic sanctions against it. The present Bolivian dictatorship is the result of a combined German-Argentine plan, and the two countries are working together in close harmony.

Perón also seeks among his immediate objectives a political alignment with Mexico, where anti-American sentiment is increasing. Though his relationship with Brazil is complicated by many drifts, he has been the recipient of the good will of the Brazilian military clique, the clericals, local manufacturers, and the Communists. The latter now accuse "predatory American interests of attempting to provoke a war between Brazil and the Argentine."

The Perónist government is not the usual dictatorial cabal, but an authoritarian movement of legitimate dimensions, headed by an ambitious, ruthless and convinced oligarchy who see the future playing into their hands. They believe the entire economy of Latin America to be on the verge of serious crisis. The picture they see is one in which the United States will stop its lavish buying. The artificially high prices now paid for such commodities as rubber, tin, copper and quartz will fall drastically. The sellers market which made South America prosperous will come to an abrupt end. The increasing flow of gifts, grants, subsidies, and premium prices will taper off, and, in the event of an industrial and unemployment crisis in the United States, will cease totally.

Such products as Brazilian and Peruvian cotton, and Argentine meat, will find themselves in competition with American products for the world market, and with world products for the American market.

The Argentine leaders astutely note that most of the Latin countries still possess a feudal-type economy, and depend on one or two products for their prosperity: Venezuela on oil, the Central American states on bananas, and Bolivia on tin. Though Brazil has been rapidly industrializing, coffee still constituted 45 per cent of her exports in 1938, while four agricultural and forest products, coffee, cotton, cacao and oil producing seeds and nuts, accounted for more than 70 per cent of her export trade.

In any world economic dislocation such as that which occurred in the late 1920's, Latin America is sure to suffer severely. In its pathway will follow an inevitable revolutionary ferment. Argentine and Bolivian Fascism are expressive of this fundamental nervousness and sense of unsettlement, which in one form or another is to be seen on every part of the Southern continent.

An additional speculation which moves the Argentine militarists is this: it is inevitable that the distorted economies represented by Latin American single-product countries must cause these states to be at each others throats, or to welcome political unity under a strong leadership. Bolivia wants access to the sea and seeks to recover the Pacific province of Araca. Brazil openly seeks an outlet on the Pacific. Peru and Ecuador continue to eye each other acrimoniously over border disputes. When the present deterring influence of the United States abates, it is freely predicted that the tensions between Brazil, Argentina, Paraguay and Chile must result in war.

The lack of true cohesion between the American republics was shown during the war. No one of them made any tangible contribution to the war effort with the exception of token forces sent by Brazil and Mexico. The latter actually placed a high import tax on the very aviation gasoline used in the planes sent to protect her territories.

The other states sold materials to us at inordinately high prices, and accepted large loans on which they promptly omitted payment despite the high level of their prosperity. Of sixteen Latin American countries, Guatemala was the only one having no dollar bonds in default.

Despite the agreements and arrangements which exist on the higher levels, there is to be seen in the lower echelons of American dealings with the Latin republics, certain budding misunderstandings and scarcely concealed retaliations against what is considered to be our predatory interest in their economy.

This is a condition which every American business man who deals in Latin America is acquainted with. In many of the countries, American business labors under most difficult conditions, and in some categories cannot operate at all. Even in Brazil, the country which has proved most friendly to the United States, strict laws prohibit the establishment of a company in certain important industries unless it is owned one hundred per cent by native-born Brazilians.

VII

It may be suspected that the same type of bloody outbreak which turned Spain into a shambles and invited the intervention of the great ideological champions of Europe, easily could explode at our own back door, inviting a totally new set of problems and difficulties. These in themselves could provide all the provocation needed for World War III, with the United States entering the lists on one side, and the U.S.S.R. on the other.

Here is a situation which presents ready opportunities for calculated mischief on the part of those willing to make capital out of the anxieties of this hemisphere.

The great question we must ask ourselves is this: what are the true influences now at work in Latin America? When a collapse in the present war prosperity forces revolutionary alterations in the existing feudal and dictatorial regimes, in which direction will the stream of change go? What will be the great magnet which will attract it? Will it be revolutionary Marxism? Syndicalism? Or will it be something comparable to the American Bill of Rights and the system of free enterprise on which our nation has been founded?

The latter can never exist unless we encourage it, unless we practice the democracy we preach, and unless we have sufficient vision to see our future not in some vague world design alone, but with our neighbors and those who have a common interest in the eventual fate of this hemisphere.

It is the trend of the times which has been the great ally of the Russians. We should make it our ally also. In the dictator countries we should frankly support the democratic undergrounds, making their program our own, and utilizing the full force of our economic and moral influence to bring about the Union we seek.

No part of this result however can be secured by pious talk, by declamation, finger-pointing or name-calling; but only by a full understanding of the moral obligations of power and an intelligent appraisal of the existing realities.

The United States is the hub and heart of the free enterprise system, and should be its inspiration and power source, the same as Russia is to revolutionary Marxism.

The moral law and the rights of men, as we visualize them, should outweigh the formal rights of individual despots and murderous oligarchies, whose actions place the whole hemisphere in jeopardy.

We cannot function in a vacuum of meretricious sanctity where our vital interests are concerned, and must be at least as interested in the system of human freedom we live by as in the so-called rights of some sovereign fragment to endanger the well-being of the entire hemispheric community by its antisocial actions. If such a state falls into the clutches of grim fanatics, or military hoodlums who have muscled their way into control of its governmental machinery, we must take corrective action at once. Otherwise we only prove, as was the case when Britain and France allowed Hitler to occupy the Rhineland, that we are unfit to wield power, and will earn the disrespect of all the Western nations by our weakness and floundering.

We ourselves will have to determine on our own initiative, what is required for the future welfare of ourselves and the hemispheric community and what is ethical and sound, and proceed from these conclusions. At present we are doing neither one nor the other, but vegetating in deadly inertia, rendering lip service to rhetorical ideals which have no more substance than the wind. Though we pretend we do this in the name of the higher ethic of humanity, we commit a monstrous act of violence against this very conception by abandoning humanity to the buffeting of powers willing to follow a more positive course.

Good sense tells us that the mere fact that Hitler achieved power by legal means did not make his movement less detestable or dangerous; and that the same circumstances apply to Perón. The latter will not be intimidated by the thoroughly pointless intervention we have made in Argentine affairs. Name calling expeditions of this sort can only react to Perón's advantage and be turned by him to the purposes of his own propaganda.

We could settle the Argentine question with a minimum of effort by sending a few airplane carriers to the mouth of the Rio Plata, where an expeditious end would be placed to both Perón and his pretensions.

Buenos Aires cannot be defended from the sea and with its fall all Argentina would at once collapse.

Our forces would be welcomed as liberators by the decent democratic elements of the Argentine who at present are intimidated and in full retreat. A free government sponsored by us could at once be placed in existence and meet the enthusiastic response of the people, who would be furnished a dignified and practical alternative toward which to turn in their battle to smash the gyves of feudalism which now hold them enchained.

Our government sent General Frank McCoy and his marines to supervise the elections in Nicaragua; we occupied Santa Domingo and Cuba, and invaded Mexico in a chase after the revolutionary leader, Francisco Villa. In this war, together with the English, we removed the Bey of Tunis whom we suspected of being pro-German. Together with the English and Russians we deposed the pro-German Shah of Iran and substituted his young son in his place, taking over responsibility for the administration of the country.

Yet in respect to the Perón Government which we officially describe as a menace to the well-being of the entire American community, our hand becomes palsied and our sense of power and responsibility completely vanishes. Why is it immoral to remove a Nazi dictator who constitutes an immediate peril to our well-being, and moral to depose an antiquated and obstinate old monarch of a far-away Asiatic state, also accused of Nazi sympathies?

The sense of the situation says that if the State Department's

published estimates of the Argentine situation is the correct
one, we should put an end to the Perónist presumptions. We
should not leave the Argentine before announcing the formation of a Latin federation intimately associated with us, not
this time by compact and treaty, but by a charter which will
apply the benefits of fundamental law to us both.

VIII

Once a common union had been brought into existence,
everyone without exception would benefit from the powerful
forces which would have been set in motion. To substitute
for the unregulated competition which otherwise must follow the end of the war between Latin America and ourselves
in meats, hides, and agricultural products, and Great Britain
and ourselves in the carrying trade and in manufactures, would
be an orderly and reciprocal effort. Instead of tragic conflict,
there would exist a balanced and sensible development which
would be a far cry from the one-product economies with
which the Latin South now is burdened.

In our hemisphere as well as in Europe, national boundaries
no longer bear any reasonable resemblance to economic
boundaries. This is the case with the South American west
coast as it is with that great future center of commerce and
trade, the conjoined Gulf of Mexico and Caribbean Sea. It
is true of the economy of Canada, where an endless struggle
exists "to hold together the tariff protected industries at the
center with the raw material producing and therefore low tariff
frontiers of the east and west—in brief, to maintain an east-
west Canadian economy when all the laws of geography and
economics work for a north-south inter-American economy."[2]

Once allowed to function as an integral apparatus, a political

[2] Bruce Hutchinson, *Fortune*, August, 1945.

union of the West, with the two American continents as its hard core, could supply virtually every agricultural, animal, mineral or other product required to support a flourishing modern economy.

Once the barriers created by the present antiquated national political systems were liquidated, new frontiers, new vistas and new opportunities would develop. Under a hemispheric union, which would represent the ultimate triumph of common sense, the magnificent machinery and vastly extended physical plant possessed by the United States and England would be used to raise the standard of living for all the Western peoples. Surplus manufacturing plants instead of being torn down, or exported to Europe and Asia for a song, could be used to develop all of the hemisphere's productive resources equally.

If this is truly to be the age of atomic power applied to the machinery of economic production, a golden age of human effort would result in which there would be an end to fear, want, and drudgery. New territories would be opened, new cities built, rivers drained, and industries created. Prosperous countrysides would arise where once were only pampas and tropical forests. We see the counterpart to this operation in the miraculous tempo of the Soviet East, and in the mushrooming growth of the cities of Central Asia and the Ural mountain regions.

Our ability to control a constant flow of raw materials of widely differing descriptions required by our factories, and to function in a market sufficiently large to absorb the whole product of a mass production economy, would enable us to operate if necessary as a self-contained universe. The idea that it is essential to sell goods abroad in order to exist is a relic of an age that is past. The export of organic wealth for the sake of a ledger profit is of value only to individual sellers, and in reality constitutes a profitless undertaking where the nation receives no tangible values in exchange.

The U.S.S.R. proved able to operate for a generation virtually independent of international trade. Its great diversity of resources and the widespread economy which enabled it to absorb the products of its own industry, made it independent of economic considerations which once were said to guide the existence of nations.

Instead of spending our billions abroad in a fruitless effort to buy our way into the good graces of the world, we should utilize these sums for the far greater opportunities presented in our own back yard. A small portion of these billions or of the moneys we have spent in importing rubber, tin, silk, tea, quinine and other products from the Old World, would build the Latin South and Indonesia into a true paradise of competence and prosperity.

Instead of seeking our oil by questionable deals with barbaric Arab kings in areas whose defense involves an almost insoluble problem in logistics, we could further develop the rich oil lands of Venezuela, and of other parts of Latin America. In the far North in the Mackenzie River country, extending for almost seven hundred miles to the northern peak of Alaska at Point Barrow, there exists what geologists believe to be one of the great oil-bearing belts of the world. This oil is less accessible and hence not as profitable from the dollar viewpoint as that in Arabia, but infinitely more profitable from the viewpoint of the national security.

Just as the Soviet Union has developed Siberia and filled it with people, so could we encourage large-scale industry throughout Latin America and Oceania, establishing foundries, shipyards and plants of every kind wherever raw material or strategic considerations made these desirable. By being a portion of our mutual estate, these activities in no wise could be looked on as jeopardizing either our immediate interests or our long-range future. If the bomb makes industrial decentralization mandatory, the equally valid reason of good economics exists for locating manufacturing plants near the supply sources of raw materials.

To North American and British centers of industrial output the raising of the standard of wealth of the whole hemisphere would enlarge rather than diminish markets, establishing a demand for the more complex and more expensive commodities in addition to simple cottons and hardware.

To the Latins such a program would mean not only full equality of opportunity, but a rapid development of their territories, bringing with it sanitation, roads, educational facilities, wealth and security.

Once the union were formed, even though it were not complete in the beginning, the social and economic benefits of this great act of political agglutination would be clear to everyone. All of the Western states eventually would be forced to follow suit. The greater Union would become a giant lodestone whose terrific magnetism could not be resisted. Its economic power, both as buyer and seller, as well as its gigantic cultural, military and financial resources, would give it the same force of destiny now enjoyed by the Russians on the continent of Eurasia.

IX

Now while the clock of destiny is striking is our great chance. It is all very well for us to talk of our moral superiority to the Russians, and of the virtues of our system as compared with the wickedness of theirs. This is mere vainglory; for the real worth of our protestations lies in our capacity to make the present juncture good, and to create a world fit for free men to live in, now while we can. If we are to miss our real opportunities in favor of a net of beautiful phrases which describe the glories of collaboration and unity but do not provide the framework for it, we shall find ourselves like Hannibal after the great victory at Cannae, imprisoned in the unhappiness of a lost occasion.

It is this moment which is the test of our right and ability to survive. If we can master it we shall be able to guarantee our future security by our own conscious action, independent of the buffeting of circumstance and the aggressive designs of others. At the same time we will have taken a long step forward, toward that ideal which should be the goal and one day must be the destiny of man: the application of universal law to the basic and overriding problems of universal man.

Set in Linotype Janson
Format by A. W. Rushmore
Manufactured by The Haddon Craftsmen
Published by HARPER & BROTHERS
New York and London